IN SEARCH OF SWIFT

DENIS JOHNSTON

in search of

Swift

DUBLIN

HODGES FIGGIS & CO. LTD.

1959

© Hodges Figgis & Co. Ltd. 1959

MADE AND PRINTED IN THE
REPUBLIC OF IRELAND BY
CAHILL AND CO., LTD., DUBLIN

CONTENTS

		Page
INTRODUCTION AND ACKNOWLEDGMENTS	ix

THE WITNESSES

| 1. | THE DEAN RIDES . . . . | 3 |
| 2. | ABOUT SOME OF THE BOOKS . . . . . . | 10 |

THE TESTIMONY

3.	MIGRATION TO IRELAND	27
	(a) As commonly accepted
4.	MIGRATION TO IRELAND	31
	(b) As it probably occurred
5.	THE TRAIL OF THE UNCLES	37
6.	PARENTS	44
7.	THE KING'S INNS	47
8.	SWIFT'S BIRTHPLACE	58
9.	THE WHITEHAVEN INCIDENT	66
10.	SCHOOLBOY AND UNDERGRADUATE	73

v

CONTENTS

Page

11. REFUGEE 78

12. WILLIAM TEMPLE AND DOROTHY OSBORNE . . . 84

13. THE JOHNSONS 90

14. STELLA'S PARENTAGE 97

15. TEN YEARS RECONSTRUCTED 110

16. AN OXFORD DEGREE 115

17. KILROOT 121

18. LARACOR 129

19. LONDON 138

20. THE SUPPOSED MARRIAGE 151

21. LATTER DAYS 174

THE AUTOPSY

22. THE DEAN'S DEATH 181

23. THE BATTLE OF THE GRAVES 188

24. TOWARDS A CONCLUSION 201

25. THE DILEMMA 214

APPENDIX 222

BIBLIOGRAPHY 225

INDEX 233

LIST OF ILLUSTRATIONS

A Page of the Autofrag . . . . . *facing page* 12

Jonathan's Memorial 32

Admission Entries, 1665-1666 48

A Page of Black Book Entries 50

Minutes of 17th November, 1663 51

Minutes of 6th June, 1665 52

Minutes of 25th January, 1666 53

Pilkington's Minute 56

Map of Dublin Towards the Close of the 17th Century
between pages 60 *and* 61

Abigail Swift's Memorial . . . . . *facing page* 68

The Posthumous Account 70

The Trinity Head 184

The True Death Mask 186

The Epitaph 188

Pedigree Showing the Relationship of the Principal Families
Mentioned in This Book . . . *between pages* 232 *and* 233

To

my Father

who in his turn

held the office of

Bencher and Treasurer

of the Honorable Society

of the

King's Inns

this book is gratefully

dedicated.

INTRODUCTION AND ACKNOWLEDGMENTS

THIS addition to the existing shelf load of volumes about the stormy Dean of St. Patrick's may possibly be unwelcome in some circles. New and eccentric opinions on matters of scholarship are things that can be readily advanced without evoking any particular feeling of irritation amongst those already in possession of a special field. But I have noticed that the man who is rash enough to suggest that established text-books are wrong, not so much in their views as in their facts, must be prepared for a rough time.

However, for nearly twenty years I have been an unwilling target for a succession of adverse comments on a short paper that I read to the Old Dublin Society in 1941, and that subsequently appeared in the Journal of that body.[1] And as this annoyance is a continuing one, and shows no signs of coming to an end, a man who happens to have been serious in what he said is driven eventually to make matters either worse or better by repeating his point in louder and better documented tones. As a general rule no one will ever come to one's rescue in such matters except oneself.

The circumstances under which I first became involved in this trouble are described fully in the preface to a volume of my plays entitled *The Golden Cuckoo*,[2] and need not be restated here. It is sufficient to say that ever since my attention was first drawn to the Black Book of King's Inns by my father—who at the time was a successor of Sir John Temple as Treasurer of that ancient corporation, and who was also the heir of what was left of the office of Master of the Rolls—the subject of Swift has been a matter of absorbing curiosity to me—a curiosity that has now developed into a wider interest in the prevailing methods of biography itself, and the fascinating processes by which history comes to be written.

Like most tyros in the realm of research, I began with a deep respect for the printed word, especially when it has been repeated several times over by more than one reporter, and I was quite unaware of the fact that, in such matters, two and two do not necessarily make four. Nor had I

---

[1] " The Mysterious Origin of Dean Swift." *Dublin Historical Record*. vol. III. no. 4. June-August, 1941.
[2] Published by Jonathan Cape, London : 1954.

yet discovered another peculiarity of pseudo-history, that the further one gets away from the origins of an imaginary story, the more circumstantial and detailed the accounts usually become, and not vice versa as one might suppose. Examples of this phenomenon will appear several times over in the course of my analysis of what we have been told about Swift. But what I hope will intrigue the reader as much as it has intrigued me is not the mere revelation of some scandal about his origins. As a character, the Dean is probably much more exciting in his guise of a fabulous monster than as an intelligible human being, behaving as anybody else might act in a difficult situation. What I find far more interesting is an examination of the literary process under which a colossal pastiche of absurdities can be brought into existence, without protest, in the course of a couple of hundred years. For if this can happen in the case of a public figure who has no present political or religious significance, it is very sobering to consider what monstrous perversions of fact may equally well have taken place in the case of characters who happen to have both.

We have recently been shown how our prevailing picture of Richard III[3] is actually a caricature based upon Tudor propaganda and a Shakespearean melodrama. Some of my readers may also have cause to doubt the factual background of several of the events that form the essential basis of our religion, while still being a little puzzled by the overwhelming weight of evidence in their favour. So, perhaps as an exercise in the application of practical methods to a checking-up on history, we may find it helpful to begin with a problem which has neither dynastic nor theological overtones, and which it is still comparatively easy for anybody to investigate with a knowledge of English, and a return ticket between London and Dublin. Whatever we learn from this preliminary exploration may, perhaps, be applied later on to other and more fundamental matters, if we so wish.

The roots of this particular jungle are still close enough in time to enable us to observe the tangle in the course of its growth, as each biographer in turn grafts his story on to an earlier epiphyte. So this book is a piece of literary detection where most of the clues are still available in their pristine condition and can be re-examined by anybody. All that one needs is to know where to look for them ; and in providing some of this information I hope that I can be of some practical use to a younger generation of students of Swift. I am not such a fool as to imagine that

---

[3]*Richard III.* Paul Murray Kendall, New York, 1955.

anybody else, who has already committed himself to paper on the subject of the Dean, will listen to me with any degree of pleasure while I am engaged on impeaching his data.

Through the generosity of the Guggenheim Foundation, I recently obtained the leisure to prepare the equipment for such an investigation, and the results are here presented, not as any pompous and definitive pronouncement on the subject of the Dean, but as a guide book and a series of warning posts for the benefit of others who may decide in the future to pass through this heavily mined area. If, in the matter of names and figures, I am discovered from time to time to be as prone to inaccuracy as any of my predecessors, I can only apologise, and say that this inadequacy on my part only adds weight to my contention that incorrectness in copying out such things is a characteristic of everybody who has so far written about Swift—a man whose epitaph has never yet been printed fully and with complete accuracy, in spite of the fact that it has been in full view for over two hundred years. The *tu quoque* riposte only admits the original premise, and I am willing to accept it quite humbly on that basis.

Although in the end I do offer a solution of the enigma that happens to fit in with the actual facts of Swift's life, as well as with recognisable patterns of conduct, this diagnosis is not tendered with any idea of forcing an answer of my own upon the reader, or of proving any particular thesis. My primary purpose in writing this book is the more modest one of pointing out some of the many misstatements, and indeed lies, in the existing record and, incidentally, of advancing the proposition that young men who read undocumented papers to small, learned societies are not necessarily ignorant, nor should they be dismissed by a rough-and-ready use of the word " misrepresentations," until it is quite certain that they have no knowledge of what they are talking about.

With this in mind, I have indicated the available sources of information with an insistence that may at times prove tedious to those who are more interested in a good story than in the formalities of scholarship. But, were I to skimp this task, however incompatible it may be with facile reading, I would only lay myself open once again to the grave charge of " theorising about Swift's relations with the Ladies on insufficient evidence "—to quote one eminent editor. So I must ask my readers to bear with me patiently while I dwell at length on some of the clues, and cross-examine fully the more suspect of the witnesses.

In addition to the Guggenheim Foundation, I am greatly indebted to the Benchers of King's Inns and to the Librarian of Trinity College, Dublin, for their ready permission to reproduce photographs of some essential original documents that are in their possession. I have also been greatly facilitated by the courtesy of the authorities at the British Museum, and at the Victoria and Albert Museum, and at the Houghton Library of Harvard University, who have allowed me to inspect and take copies of MS. material in all of these places. To the late Mr. T. U. Sadleir of the former Office of Arms in Dublin Castle, and to my friend Dr. T. G. Wilson, I would also like to express my indebtedness for the benefit of their wide knowledge of several specialised aspects of the question. Next, I am indebted to Mr. Ben Reid and Mr. Joseph Bottkol of Mount Holyoke College, who have both been kind enough to study the completed manuscript and to assist me with their suggestions.

Finally, may I add that it gives me particular pleasure to have had my MS. published by a knowledgeable and adventurous firm in the very city to which both book and subject and writer properly belong.

SOUTH HADLEY, MASSACHUSETTS, 1958.

D. J.

THE WITNESSES

THE DEAN RIDES

On a late spring day in the year 1723, the Dean of St. Patrick's in the City of Dublin mounted his horse and rode out of town, down the narrow winding roads that led towards the west. Through Palmerston and Lucan he trotted, a black intimidating thundercloud under a lowering sky— turning left from the main Galway turnpike before reaching Leixlip, and coming at last to the pleasant little town of Celbridge. Here he dismounted and beat on the door of Marley Abbey.

Inside this house, a distraught woman of about thirty-five heard and recognized his knock. Handsome in her day, she was now looking older than her years, and her face was beginning to show signs of dissipation. She rose to receive him as he came up the stairs. He confronted her in terrible silence, and drew from his pocket a letter which, without a word, he flung down on her table.

Then, turning abruptly, he left the room, remounted his horse, and rode back again towards Dublin. With a wild cry, she picked the letter up and discovered what it was. Then, with a gesture of frantic despair, she ran to her desk and searched for a document which she proceeded to tear up. This done, she sat down, and started to write another paper—coughing and weeping as she worked.

She had not much time to spare, for within a month she was dead, and on June 4th the gravedigger of St. Andrew's earned two pounds for breaking ground within the Church to receive the body of Miss Esther Vanhomrigh.

Another enigmatic glimpse. A few years earlier—on some date in 1716, Dr. Patrick Delany, then a fellow of Trinity College, was calling on Dr. King, Archbishop of Dublin. He had hoped to discuss with this prelate a strange gloom and agitation that was troubling his friend, the Dean of St. Patrick's.

At the door of the Archbishop's library he met Swift coming out, his face distorted with emotion. The Dean rushed past him without a word, and when Delany confronted King inside the room, he found the latter in tears.

"My Lord, what is the matter with the Dean?" asked Delany.

But all that the Prelate would say was this:

"You have just seen the most unhappy man on earth, but on the subject of his wretchedness you must never ask a question."

Some readers may—at this stage—know very little about Swift, except that he wrote *Gulliver's Travels*, and is said to have had a very enigmatic relationship with a little girl called Stella—a relationship that other writers still quarrel about. But the above two literary snapshots—the factual basis of which there is no reason to doubt—may intrigue the reader, and inspire him with a desire to know something more about this extraordinary man, and the reasons, if any, behind this strange remark of the Archbishop.

Any curiosity about the circumstances surrounding both episodes will be satisfied later on. What I want to point out before going any further, is the multi-dimensional nature of both tales. Each story has itself got a story—and this is an aspect of biography that must be kept in mind. When Orrery and Hawkesworth[1] recount the first incident in their books, it is a letter of Swift that is thrown back at Vanessa in this peremptory fashion. But when Thomas Sheridan,[2] a few years later, gives his version of the same encounter, it is a letter of her own that is returned. On the other hand, Dr. Lyon[3] disbelieves that there was any letter at all, while Scott[4] avers that there were actually two—both of them replies to an enquiry of Vanessa.

Furthermore, we may very properly ask, from what source did the story originally come? There were only two people present at the time, so one of them must presumably have repeated the details to a third party. Not even a servant, listening at the door, could have overheard the flinging down of a letter without a word. So which of these two would be the most likely to repeat such a tale—the man who had nothing to say, or the woman who was so deeply upset and humiliated? These variants and peculiarities now form an essential part of the whole episode, and add to its interest rather than the reverse.

Next, turning to the incident in Dublin Castle, there is here nothing

[1]*Remarks*, p. 75. Hawkesworth, vol. 1, p. 38.

[2]Sheridan, p. 325.

[3]MS. note in Hawkesworth, V. & A.

[4]Scott, vol. 1, pp. 252-253. Scott does not allege that two letters were brought to Celbridge by Swift, but that Stella had already answered Vanessa in a letter of her own.

surprising about the fact that the story is in circulation. On the other hand, it is rather odd that neither of the two principals made any printed reference to the occurrence, although Dr. Delany was the author of two publications about the Dean, and the Archbishop was a literary man of even greater distinction. Nor did Deane Swift refer to it—our own Dean's cousin and biographer. The first person to print an account of the event is Sir Walter Scott, as late as 1814.[5] Scott says that he was told the story by a friend of Mrs. Delany, and Bertram Newman[6] adds, quite credibly, that this friend was Lady Louisa Stuart. But Maxwell Gold[7] concludes from the wording of Scott's first draft (which he has studied at Harvard) that Delany himself told Scott's informant, although, as we have seen, Delany leaves it out of his own writings.

It will be seen that there is more to be considered in connection with both anecdotes than can be conveyed by a simple repetition of the words of whichever authority we choose to select. Unless we have the story of the story as well as its substance, any conclusions we draw from it may depend as much upon our selection of a source as upon the actual facts themselves.

This leads us to another aspect of Biography that must also be mentioned now. In the prevailing temper of the English Departments, it is the general practice today to frown upon any attempt to associate the personality or life of an author with his work. I have even heard it argued that a graduate student engaged on the preparation of a thesis ought not to get into touch with the subject of his researches when living and accessible, because it is felt that any information that a writer will give about himself and his intentions is irrelevant, and is likely to be of more harm than good to a serious student of literature.

This, of course, is a reaction from the absurd lengths to which an earlier generation of commentators has gone in trying to make us believe that practically all great works of fiction are expressions of some aspect of the author's personal history. To some extent, Biography may perhaps be said to be getting repaid what it deserves; but the danger of the situation lies in the fact that some celebrated pieces of literature *are* partly autobiographical—*Finnegans Wake* is a case in point—and it is difficult to appreciate the real significance of these books unless one is in a position

[5]Scott, vol. 1, pp. 239-240.

[6]Newman, p. 256.

[7]Gold, pp. 97-98.

to recognise subjective quirks and irrelevancies, and so save oneself the time and labour of exploring the many blind alleys that they often so temptingly offer.

The case of Swift is not quite the same as that of Joyce. If a modern critic tells us to enjoy *The Journal to Stella* for its own sake, without any vulgar enquiries as to whether the writer was or was not a psychopathic case who drove two women into the grave, we may legitimately demur by applying the same argument to a cheque. Should we appreciate it only for its colour and for the beauty of its engraving, and treat any information that the drawer is a well-known criminal as a matter into which it is in rather bad taste to enquire ? Maybe one should, but one doesn't.

So also, when Psychology has been called in to the aid of criticism, as it now frequently is, and particularly so in the case of Swift—we may fairly point out that the strictly semantic rule is not being observed by the critics themselves. However much the Psychologist may protest that he is operating clinically, he cannot contemplate the Dean or his work without accepting certain biographical assumptions as a basis for his data. And if the data themselves are founded on false information, where are we then ?

The trouble with the Dean is that any serious examination of the source material is bound to disclose the fact that it is a mass of contradictions, misdescriptions and deliberate mendacity. The best explanation for this state of affairs—as I hope to show—is that it is largely deliberate. But there are other reasons, too. To begin with, we are here dealing with information that has been provided by an unusually high proportion of clergymen, and most lay scholars with experience in the various fields of research will agree with me, I am sure, when I say that clerical sources are almost invariably the most unreliable of all. It may be that the danger of experimental disproof keeps the automobile salesman and the scientist nearer to the truth than those who are peddling less tangible wares, or it may be that the traditions of spiritual argument get its followers into very bad habits. The lamentable fact remains that one generally has to be more careful of the word of a literary parson than of anybody else who puts pen to paper.

Then there are hazards to which I am especially vulnerable myself—those that spring from confusion of meaning, simple mistake, and the mysterious difficulty already mentioned of copying down correctly any name or date connected with Swift. What is worse, the fanciful has a way of coming to life, as in the case of Isaac Bickerstaff, who began as an imaginary astrologer, invented by the Dean to annoy an Almanack maker, and who now appears to have a place in the *Dictionary of National Biography* as the author of several plays.[8] I have, myself, a letter from a lady in Kensington who says :

" My Mother-in-law is a direct descendant of Dean Swift and also of the Gullivers, his own relations, about whom he wrote, and I do not doubt that she could give you information on this subject which is not generally known and might be of interest."

Most of Swift's work was published anonymously, and there are many forged imitations, such as a third volume of *Gulliver's Travels* published in London in 1727.

Then there are the confusing names of his cousin and early biographer, Deane Swift,[9] and of one of his publishers, L. Gilliver. And there is the chaos caused by the practice of dating the new year from late in March instead of from January 1st, a state of affairs that requires the use of tricky symbols such as 1712/13 whenever it is necessary to be precise about any date in January, February or the earlier part of March. This is a precaution that is easily forgotten.[10]

It will also appear from these pages that a good deal of professional biography proceeds without much reference to original sources at all. A careful analysis is made of most of what has been written on the subject to date, the documents quoted are assumed to have been correctly and fully copied, a democratic vote is taken on matters of opinion, a bibliography is prepared that is longer than ever before, a few graceful compliments are paid to the present proprietors, and a new vote is thus added to the majority column which, of course, is merely a repetition of the previous vote, and no additional authority whatsoever. There are, of

---

[8]Vol. V. pp. 2-3.

[9]Deane Swift was a grandson of Uncle Godwin Swift by Hannah Deane, Godwin's third wife. He was also the husband of Mary Harrison, a granddaughter of Uncle Adam Swift, and the daughter of Mrs. Whiteway.

[10]In this book all such dates are written according to the modern usage. There is a further point that arises through the legal correction of the British calendar in 1752. The actual anniversary of Swift's birth is not any longer called the 30th November—St. Andrew's Day—but is the day now known as the 10th December, while to find the anniversary of his death it is necessary to add, not ten, but eleven days to the 19th October, since this event occurred between 1700 and 1752.

course, many honourable exceptions, but on the whole, this sort of thing happens more frequently than one imagines, and it is at the back of some of the suspicion that contemporary critics feel towards the biographical method.

Nevertheless, in spite of these hazards—or maybe because of them—the Swift enigma presents us today with a challenge that has all the fascination of a good detective story, and can be approached in much the same spirit. The clues are actual papers that can be found and examined in libraries and Record Offices, in vestries and in muniment boxes, many of which are doubtless still waiting to be turned out.

For instance, in the course of a broadcast in 1945, I mentioned a statement of Sir Shane Leslie[11] that since the destruction of the Record Office in Dublin there are no known documents in Ireland bearing Stella's signature. On the following day I was rung up by a Dublin Solicitor, one of whose secretaries had heard the talk. It had called to mind something that she remembered having seen upstairs, and after a brief search, a lease was brought to light bearing the signatures of both Swift and Stella and witnessed by Dingley. Was this of any interest? On being informed that it had very great interest indeed, the solicitor gave the document to Dr. Wyse Jackson, then Rector of Nenagh, who very properly presented it to the Library of Trinity College.

We must apply our powers of observation not to the mud on the deceased's boots, but to the handwriting of his father in the Black Book of King's Inns, to the marginal notes and corrections written by Dr. Lyon in a volume in the Victoria and Albert Museum, and to the deletions and second thoughts that make the original MS. of Swift's *Autobiographical Fragment* far more informative than any printed copy could be, and to the pictures of the Dean's two death masks. We will have to account not only for the positive parts of the record, but also for the significant gaps that appear in it, whether by accident or design, like the great black clouds that obscure sections of the Milky Way, always remembering that the printed word acquires no added sanctity with the years, but remains what it always was—something written down with a purpose, whether good or bad. Many of the witnesses will turn out to be mendacious, but although we cannot now quiz them under an arc lamp, there are other ways in which we can catch them out, if we set about it in the right way.

---

[11]Leslie, *The Script of Swift*, p. 10.

For here we have got a real-life riddle to which there must be some solution. Why did this popular ladies' man, whose "amativeness and philo-progenitiveness" were "excessive," never marry? Or if he did marry, why did he keep it a secret? More pertinent still, why did his supposed wife—a woman of considerable character—allow him to keep secret such an important fact concerning himself and her reputation?

He was apparently a prudish model of discretion with no discretion at all—a monster of ingratitude who carried loyalty to his friends to absurd lengths—one of the most conscientious Deans that St. Patrick's has ever had, who wrote some verse that even today is seldom discussed except amongst the delinquent young—a patriot who loathed his country—and a benefactor who indited an attack upon the whole human race, that is now popularly regarded as a children's book.

We will see that most of the fog is the deliberate work of Swift himself. And how delighted he must be—wherever he is—to observe that after two hundred years, the fog is still billowing around him.

2

ABOUT SOME OF THE BOOKS

ALTHOUGH the books about Jonathan Swift are innumerable, and continue to flow from the presses of many countries, biographies that introduce any real source material or fresh facts about his life are not as numerous as might be supposed. A bibliography of the principal writings that have informed—and sometimes confused—the present writer is given below, but the only ones that need be discussed now are those few vehicles that are actually going to take us somewhere on our present excursion. There is, of course, a very massive Bibliography that was published in The Hague by Dr. Teerink in 1937, to which the reader is referred for a fuller record down to that date.

The Autofrag

The most important document of all is Swift's own *Autobiographical Fragment* which was written in or about the year 1728—probably shortly after Stella's death—the original holograph of which is now in the Library of Trinity College, Dublin. An interesting page of this is here reproduced by permission of the Librarian, so that the reader can see for himself some of the things that we will have to consider.

This document has certain peculiarities that strike the eye at once. First of all, it is written in the third person, as if JS, aware of the fact that future biographers would be interested in his background and early life, was eager to give them what appeared to be some outside party's objective outline of what was to be said on the subject, and so save them from the labour of any independent research, or even of thinking up phraseology of their own. How extremely successful he has been in this, may be judged from the number of subsequent works that not only accept without question everything that is written in that paper, but even make use of its precise—or very nearly its precise—forms of expression, without, as a rule, making any reference to the fountain of supply. For what, after all, could be more convenient and authentic than a man's own account of himself—always assuming that his intention is to inform us, and not the reverse? [1]

The opening sentence, " The Family of the Swifts was ancient in Yorkshire," or words to that effect, is the clue that usually announces a new paraphrase or recitation of the *Autofrag*. One of the earliest of the biographers, W. H. Dilworth, writing in 1758, provides us with a very good example of this happy acceptance of the Dean's own words and phrases that must have been exactly what JS hoped for. This does not necessarily mean that all the information in the *Autofrag* is wrong or unacceptable. It simply means that the earlier portion of a book such as Dilworth's is not really by Dilworth, but by Swift.

Although the *Autofrag* never mentions Stella, it was written at a time when the question of what might be said about their relationship was in the forefront of Swift's mind. Whatever may have been his motives in writing it, most of the packaged information on which it is possible to check turns out to be an odd mixture of truth, careless mistake, and deliberate mendacity. Swift was always vague about facts and figures, but apart from some errors of this kind, it is significant to note that the *Autofrag* also contains what must either be two intentional lies about his age, or alternatively, one lie, together with the second of the only two pieces of information that we actually have on the subject.

Mrs. Whiteway had this document in her possession after the death of JS, and she gave it to her son-in-law, Deane Swift, the biographer, who published an inaccurate copy of it in the Appendix of his *Essay*, after having lodged the original in the College Library in 1753.

On p. ii. of the Appendix to his *Essay*, published in 1755, Deane Swift stated—presumably on the authority of his mother-in-law—that the *Autofrag* was written " six or eight and twenty years ago," which places it about the time of Stella's death.

About 1738, Charles Cobbe, then Bishop of Kildare and Dean of Christ Church Cathedral, having heard of this piece of writing, asked JS for permission to make a copy. At once Swift's concern about his biographical record seems to have become active again. He amended some parts of the copy that Cobbe made, and turned a Minor Canon of his

---

[1] Richard Ashe King, on p. 19 of his book *Swift in Ireland*, says of him : "——a more scrupulously truthful man never lived——."

Cathedral, the Rev. John Lyon, on to the job of searching certain public records in order to ascertain what information was to be found there about himself and his parents. Lyon's marginal note to Hawkesworth's statement[2] that JS " pointed out the house in which he was born " adds :—" and had y Register Book of St. Werburgh's Church searched for an account of his Baptism but y entry of that and of many more was omitted through y carelessness of y Vestry Clerk at that time." Forster[3] goes rather further than this, and says in general terms that Lyon was then " engaged in biographical researches connected with his (Swift's) family," and that there are amendments to this Cobbe copy in Lyon's hand as well as in that of JS.

Forster's note on the whole transaction is a masterpiece of confused information that requires several readings before its meaning can be extracted. It appears that " a few years " before 1875, the Bishop's descendant, referred to by Forster as Thomas Cobbe of Newbridge, Donabate,[4] lent this Cobbe copy to Forster, who purported to publish it in his *Life of Swift*, after comparing it with the Trinity holograph, which he did not consider to be the more important document of the two. The copy that Forster himself made of this document is supposed now to be in the Victoria and Albert Museum, although it does not appear to be catalogued amongst Forster's papers. Nor have I been able, so far, to locate where it actually is[5].

It is clear, however, that neither Deane Swift nor Forster has reproduced the original correctly. Even in the absence of the Cobbe copy one can see—without accusing them of deliberate bowdlerisation—that Deane Swift has not made an accurate transcription of the Trinity holograph, much less referred adequately to the really interesting part of this important relic—the deletions, some of which can be seen in the photograph, and will be commented on at a later stage.

The *Autofrag* deals only with the family history and early life of the

[2]Hawkesworth, V. & A. vol. I, p. 6.

[3]Forster, p. 4.

[4]Forster possibly means Charles Cobbe, who was then and for many years previously the owner of Newbridge.

[5]A recent member of the family occupying Newbridge—T. L. Cobbe—in response to my enquiry, wrote to me in 1938 to say : " I do not know of any MS. here of the kind to which you refer." Nevertheless it is still probably in Donabate, as it is unknown to the authorities at the Victoria and Albert.

happening so suddenly before he
could make a sufficient
establishment for his family;
and his son (not then born) hath
often been heard to say that he
felt the consequences of that
marriage not only through the
whole course of his education
but during the greatest part
of his life.

He was born in Dublin on St.
Andrews day, and when he was
a year old, an event happened to
him that seems very unusual;
for his nurse who was a
woman of Whitehaven,
~~having absolute~~ being under an
absolute necessity of seeing
one of her relations. who was
then extremely sick and from
whom she expected a Legacy,
and being at the same time
extremely fond of the infant
she stole him on ship board
unknown to his mother and
Uncles. and carryed him with
her

Dean down to the year 1700, when JS obtained the Vicarage of Laracor and his public life began. According to Forster's book, the Cobbe copy continues with an additional five paragraphs of dates and miscellaneous information, roughly thrown together, and mainly concerned with Swift's attendance at meetings of the Chapter of St. Patrick's. But even these come to an end in 1714, which confirms the impression that the principal interest of the author was not autobiographical in the wider sense of telling the leading facts of his life, but was to fill a certain vacuum in the early information—which vacuum, if not eliminated by JS, might in the end become the subject of more careful scrutiny by somebody else.

As an example of Swift's vagueness over facts and figures, we have his statement that his grandfather " left ten Sons and three or four Daughters, most of which lived to be Men and Women." This is contradicted by his Uncle Godwin's Funeral Entry, certified by his Uncle William on the 20th April, 1698, in connection with Godwin's death—a copy of which is in the Genealogical Office, Dublin Castle. This discloses six sons and four daughters. It also makes it clear that Uncle Thomas was the third and not the second son, and that JS's own supposed father was the fifth, and not the " seventh or eighth." Godwin Swift was a member of Gray's Inn, and not of the Inner Temple, as stated. And there is no evidence whatever that Uncle Dryden Swift ever visited Ireland, much less " lived and dyed " there. JS states that none of his Uncles left male issue, except his Uncle Godwin, when in fact both William and Adam did so, one of whom left a son who was still alive when JS wrote the *Autofrag*, and was buried in St. Bride's in 1758.[6]

He alleges that he himself was " for about two years " in Sir William Temple's household before returning to Ireland, when actually he was there for little more than one. And he appears to forget that when he first went to live with this magnate, Sir William was not at Moor Park but at Sheen. This patent error causes an odd effect, when, a few pages later, he describes Sir William's return to Moor Park, where, according to the earlier paragraph, he was already living.

None of these errors is likely to be deliberate, and most of them could be attributed to the fact that JS was not in the slightest interested in accurate data about the Swift family or its affairs, and seldom took any trouble to check it. But before passing on from the subject of the *Autofrag*,

---

[6]St. Bride's books. This is Uncle Adam's son, Adam, buried on the 12th July, 1758.

it is important to refer to some misstatements in it that must be intentional —in particular, to those about his age.

It may have been noticed in the photograph reproduced above, that the reference to the day of his birth merely gives this as " St. Andrew's day " (the 30th November) and makes no mention of the year. The Lists of Members of Trinity College, published by the University Press under the title, *Alumni Dublinenses*, which lists presumably cite a very early record of Swift's existence, describe him as entering College on the 24th April, 1682, "aetat 14." This means, of course, that the St. Andrew's Day referred to must be that of 1667.[7]

On the other hand, in the last paragraph of the Trinity holograph he gives his age as thirty in February, 1700, which means that the year of his birth was 1669.[8]

Finally, in an earlier passage, he describes himself as giving advice to King William III about the Triennial Bill, while still under the age of twenty-one. As the controversy over this Bill took place in 1693, it follows that, if the statement is true, the year of his birth could not have been earlier than 1672. And as it is extremely unlikely that he could have been passed off on Dublin University as aged 14, when he was actually only nine, this last statement is clearly a lie—and a deliberate one—since an original " three and twenty " in the Trinity holograph has been amended to " twenty-one," showing that it is no casual mistake.

Without labouring the matter any further, it is sufficient to say at this stage that Swift is not only very inaccurate in this document, but does not hesitate to lie deliberately whenever it suits him. Consequently the *Autofrag* is not a reliable foundation for any account of the Dean's background, although it is generally accepted as such. It can, however, be regarded as a valuable account of what JS wished to have said about himself—which is not quite the same thing.

On the other hand, Mrs. Laetitia Pilkington, who comes next on the list, is usually dismissed as a gossip of the worst description, yet it is

---

[7]The existing Senior Lecturer's Book in Trinity is not the original Register. But is merely a copy made at a much later date.

[8]If this is an intentional lie on Swift's part it is a very odd one, since it errs in the wrong direction. He was trying to show the absurdity of Lord Berkeley's excuse that he was " too young " for the Deanery of Derry. If he was actually thirty-two, his argument would have been even better.

hard to see what purpose she could have in lying about the Dean, however much she may have lied about herself.

Mrs. Pilkington's Memoirs

Laetitia Pilkington was a relation by marriage of the Dean, being a
grand-niece of Elinor Meade, the fourth and last wife of Uncle Godwin
Swift.

The first two volumes of her *Memoirs* appeared in 1748, three years
after Swift's death, and a third volume was published six years later. Her
references to the Dean are, of course, incidental to the story of her own
life, and may, on the whole, be described as anecdotal. Although they
may sometimes exaggerate her own importance as a friend and confidante
of Swift in his declining years, there is little in what she recollects of
their conversations that is incredible, and when she tells us stories of his
earlier life there is no reason to suppose that, even if they are untrue, she
has invented them herself. The important thing is that—whether correct
or not—they were probably told to Mrs. Pilkington by the Dean.

What most supports her credit as a reporter of the talk of the Deanery
is the fact that on the subject of JS's secret life she is far from being a
gossip. In fact, as a source of useful information about the Dean and his
circle, Mrs. Pilkington is generally underrated.

She makes no mention of Vanessa, except for one brief reference to
the poem referred to below. Nor does she ever refer to Stella until her
third Volume, and then only in a most perfunctory way, expressing her
belief in the marriage, and telling us that the mere mention of Stella's
name would draw tears from the Dean.[9] In a footnote to the same page she
also dismisses the rumour that Swift and Stella were brother and sister.
So far as Swift is concerned, her so-called gossip is actually of quite a
conservative nature.

> I doubt not but the World will expect to hear from me ſome of the
> Dean's Amours, as he has not quite eſcaped Cenſure, on account of
> his Gallantries ; but here I am not able to oblige my Reader, he being
> too far advanced in Years, when I firſt had the Honour of being known
> to him, for Amuſements of that kind. I make no doubt but he has
> often been the Object of Love, and his *Cadenus* and *Vaneſſa* ſeem to
> aſſure us that he was the Favourite of one Lady ; but to ſpeak my

[9]Pilkington, vol. III, pp. 56-57.

Sentiments, I really believe it was a Paſſion he was wholly unacquainted with, and which he would have thought it beneath the Dignity of his Wiſdom to entertain.[10]

This can hardly be described as the outpouring of a scandal-monger, eager to invent tittle-tattle about a celebrity for the benefit of her book.

The Earl of Orrery

Orrery's *Remarks* appeared in 1751, between the opening and the final volume of Mrs. Pilkington's opus. They are in the form of a series of letters to his son, Hamilton, then at Oxford, and it is intriguing to speculate on how much of their ponderous periods on the subject of Swift was ever read by the titled undergraduate to whom they were supposedly addressed. Orrery is usually sneered at as a writer whose birth and wealth was the only reason for his publication, and he is generally supposed to have allowed a personal animus against the Dean to have infused his account of his life.

Bishop Berkeley wrote of Orrery, " He would be a man of genius if he knew how to set about it." Monck Berkeley[11] writes of " treachery that blackens every page," and then proceeds to put it, rather over-dramatically, in this way :—

> . . . when the venerable pile was mouldering in the duſt, the right honourable biographer erected on the ruins a *temple* to *Perfidy* ; and though he had not even the courage of the aſs to inſult the dying lion, yet, monſter-like, he preyed upon the carcaſe.

Although Orrery's book is highly inaccurate, it hardly justifies such rhetoric. Nevertheless there may be some truth in Monck Berkeley's story that Orrery once wrote a letter to the Dean which several years later he found unopened in the Dean's study endorsed with a note : " This will keep cold." He says that he heard this from the Rev. Mr. Berkeley, Prebendary of Canterbury, a son of the Philosopher, and also from an Archbishop of Tuam.

There are in the Library of Harvard University two valuable copies of Orrery's book, one of which has many marginal notes and interleaved pages containing further material and corrections, some written in Orrery's hand, and the rest written by a Secretary under his direction as he states.

[10]Pilkington, vol. I, p. 107.
[11]*Literary Relics*, pp. xvi-xvii.

The other copy contains a number of additional pages with holograph copies of reviews of the first edition, and of letters to Orrery on various subjects, and of his replies. These annotations amplify our knowledge as to the sources of Orrery's information, and are referred to, and partly printed by, Maxwell Gold in his book, *Swift's Marriage to Stella*.[12]

But however reckless Orrery may have been over some of his facts, and whatever irritation he may have felt about the Dean, his occasional sneer is nothing when compared to the venom that breaks forth in the 19th Century. Actually, Orrery combines quite a becoming regard for the Dean as a great literary figure with a pleasant scepticism about some of the biographical details that he has heard from JS and his cronies—a scepticism that is fully justified, and might well have been carried a little further. It is amusing to hear him lament with Dr. Delany over the amount of time wasted by the Great Departed over the writing of *Gulliver's Travels*. But he appears neither to be deliberately mendacious, nor dishonest in the expression of his own views. Where he has infuriated some of his contemporaries—notably Deane Swift—is in a vein of social *snobisme* with which he dismisses many of JS's family flourishes. Apart from some personal knowledge of the ageing Swift, his information is all hearsay, and most of the personal details that he includes actually came from Mrs. Whiteway.

Dr. Patrick Delany's " Observations "

A reply to Orrery by an old friend of the Dean appeared in 1754, and forms an interesting corrective—though not necessarily an accurate retort —to some of his Lordship's remarks. It also provides us with a lot of useful sidelights not touched upon by Orrery, as, for example, in certain references to Stella. In his book, Delany reflects the prevailing view of Swift's immediate circle, and he must be read with attention on this account.[13]

Deane Swift's Essay

Next in line comes an important and likeable, though badly-written,

---

[12]Gold, pp. 8 and 21-25.

[13]Dr. Delany, Fellow of Trinity and later Dean of Down, was a sincere and well-meaning man, with but little talent as a writer. He was destined to live all his life under the shadow of greater celebrities than himself, including a much more distinguished wife. He left behind him a number of minor theological works, including an Essay expressing his disapproval of Polygamy.

book from the only other member of the Swift family to display any literary talent—Deane Swift, already referred to. This appeared in 1755, and contains a great deal of family information of doubtful accuracy. However it has, at least, the interest of not having been taken from the *Autofrag*. As an authority, Deane Swift suffers from a firm determination to protect his distinguished relative from any allegation, true or false, that might cast a slur on the family—particularly those of Orrery, whom he treats with heavy sarcasm. He is also much too anxious to underline the kindness of his grandfather, and, indeed, of the connection in general, towards the orphan boy. But he has the virtue of being perfectly honest even in his exaggerations, and is not uncandid whenever the facts turn out to be against him. Dr. Delany replied to him also, in the same year.

Another member of the family, Mr. J. G. Swifte McNeill, was an anti-Parnellite member of the Irish Party in the House of Commons during the Home Rule agitation, and has written a book of reminiscences, the literary value of which is not great. The only other public figure that the family has produced since the 17th Century was a Police Magistrate in the City of Dublin. A recent head of the connection—Major Swifte of Swiftsheath, Co. Kilkenny—had a distinguished military record, and was Military Attaché in Persia during the First War, but was not a writer.

Hawkesworth and Lyon

Next comes a full-scale biography written by John Hawkesworth as an introduction to the 1755 edition of Swift's *Works*. As Hawkesworth never knew JS personally, what is of more interest to us now is the fact that Dr. John Lyon filled the margins of a copy that is now in the Victoria and Albert Museum with his comments and corrections. Lyon, as already stated, was a Minor Canon of St. Patrick's, and is generally regarded as having been the guardian of Swift's person during his senility, although there is no documentary confirmation of this fact. Consequently his recollection of Swift, and his views on the accuracy of Hawkesworth's account, are of the greatest value, coming from a friendly source, although —again—from a disciple who only knew JS in his latter days.

These notes of Lyon cover almost every phase of JS's life story, and although sections of them have been frequently referred to by various writers, and were partially included by Nichols in a 1779 supplement to Hawkesworth, they have never been edited and printed in their entirety, so far as I am aware. I have tried to copy them into my own copy of

Hawkesworth, but in the way of all such Swiftiana, it will be a miracle if I have managed to do so correctly.

The same copy of Hawkesworth in the V. & A. also contains some useful notes by Edmund Malone, made about the beginning of the 19th Century.

The Gentleman's Magazine

The next original material principally concerns Stella and her family. It is to be found in a much-abused article, signed C.M.P.G.N.S.T.N.S., —shortened hereafter to C.M.P.—that appeared in the November issue of the *Gentleman's Magazine* for 1757. It will be discussed at some length when we come to consider the Johnsons. What these elaborate initials stand for is a question that has never been solved.

Johnson and Sheridan

Dr. Samuel Johnson, in his *Lives of the Poets*, adds little that we have not already heard, except to give voice for the first time to the fact that JS sometimes alleged that he was not an Irishman at all, but was born in Leicestershire.[14] Thomas Sheridan in 1784 gives the last account of JS from anybody who had actually met him—although in this case the biographer was only a child at the time of Swift's death. However, he is also in a position to give us the recollections and opinions of his father, one of the Dean's most intimate associates, and he is the last significant source of direct information that comes from any of those who actually took part in the events of Swift's life. His account is to be found as a preface to Nichols' edition of Swift's *Works*, published in 1808.

Monck Berkeley, etc.

After Sheridan, we pass into the phase of anecdote and hearsay, that begins with Monck Berkeley's *Literary Relics*, published in 1789, and includes the anonymous *Swiftiana* (1804) that is sometimes attributed to Richard Phillips and sometimes to Claude Henry Wilson.

Monck Berkeley sometimes drops into the strain of acute indignation

---

[14]Dr. Johnson excuses the thinness of some parts of his Essay by saying that he has already given all his information on JS to Hawkesworth.

that becomes more and more of a familiar note as we go on. He knew Richard Brennan, Swift's servant, as an aged and impoverished bell-ringer in the Cathedral, and no doubt was told some of Brennan's fanciful recollections. Typical of these was a yarn spread by this old man to the effect that Stella had had a child by Swift, a young boy hanging around the Cathedral whom everybody—including Brennan—knew well, until he died soon after Stella. Monck Berkeley himself writes in an entertaining style, but slips easily into absurdity, as when he suggests that the reason for keeping the marriage a secret was because it might cause some pain to Vanessa.

In looking back over the information that can be attributed to these primary authorities, it may be noticed that there are some very odd deficiencies in the record to date, principally in connection with Stella and Vanessa. Of Stella, herself, we know practically nothing except from secondary sources. We have a few of her poems, and a couple of un-interesting letters on business matters. But of her correspondence with Swift we know nothing whatever, save what little may be inferred from his letters to her. For her background, we must go to C.M.P. and Dr. Delany. For her character and conversation we must rely almost entirely on JS. It is assumed by all their friends that they are man and wife—except, significantly enough, by Mrs. Dingley and Dr. Lyon—although why this relationship should have been kept a secret is something that is never adequately explained.

To begin with, Vanessa is almost entirely ignored, or else dismissed as a misguided woman whose pursuit of JS with her unwanted attentions was something that had best be forgotten. *Cadenus and Vanessa* had been published, but their actual correspondence had been supposedly destroyed by her Executor, Dr. Berkeley, who somewhat inconsistently assured everybody that it contained nothing whatever of a questionable nature that might reflect upon the Dean, in spite of the fact that he would not allow it to be read. However, when some extracts from these letters found their way into print in Hawkesworth's additional volumes, and could be judged independently, it must have become apparent that Berkeley had neither destroyed the correspondence nor told the truth about its contents.

The actual history of these letters—some of which are obviously missing from amongst the survivors that are now in the British Museum—is as intriguing a mystery as anything connected with JS. To begin with they were presumably in Berkeley's possession—although Scott tells us that the other Executor, Marshall, made copies. A. Martin Freeman, in the introduction to his book, *Vanessa and her Correspondence with Jonathan Swift*,[15] says that Berkeley's " study, containing Vanhomrigh documents, was broken into during his absence in England." This, however, creates quite a misleading impression of cloak-and-dagger work. The incident merely consisted in the breaking open of a cupboard by Prior at Berkeley's own request.

Scott says that he obtained his transcripts of the " suppressed correspondence " for his edition from a Rev. Mr. Berwick of Esker, near Lucan (which is not far from Celbridge). An unpublished letter in the British Museum[16] from D. Hailes to Robert (later Sir Robert) Peel, dated 2nd April, 1816, probably refers to a later stage in the underground career of the originals, which by that date had been bound together in a volume :

> Mr. Hailes presents his compts. to Mr. Peel and takes the liberty of begging him to forward the Volume sent herewith to the Lord Lieutenant by his next Courier. It is a literary curiosity which came by post to Mr. H. from Lord Whitworth being a correspondence between Dean Swift and the celebrated Vanessa.

An envelope dated 1892 and addressed to Miss Leslie of Glaslough is now mounted amongst the pages. But probably all that this signifies is that Miss Leslie perused the volume somewhere and left a marker in it. But where she saw it, we do not know. All that can be said of the letters during the later period of their career is that they came to light at an auction at Sotheby's of Alfred Morrison's effects in May, 1919, and were then purchased for the British Museum. On the cover of this volume in which they were bound was at one time an escutcheon, which has now been erased and is indecipherable.

These are the letters that were edited and published by Martin Freeman in 1921, so enabling a mass of errors in Scott's edition (later repeated by Elrington Ball) to be corrected.

Jeffrey, Thackeray and Macaulay

After the appearance of Monck Berkeley's *Essay*, followed by Scott's publication of the Correspondence, a new note comes into the comment

---

[15]Freeman, p. 40.
[16]Add. MSS. 40254, f. 10.

on JS. The last of the Biographers who were in touch with Swift's circle, and who had usually explained his odd conduct towards both the women by assuming that he was a married man, have now gone, and an intense distaste and hostility is the line of most of their early 19th Century successors. Jeffrey, Thackeray and Macaulay are quite open in their hatred for Swift, and the few apologists promptly reverse their line regarding the supposed secret marriage. If he had written such letters to Vanessa, at a time when he was secretly married to another woman, nobody could possibly regard them as blameless. And so, the marriage is a myth, or alternatively, a question not worthy of scholarly attention.

Leslie Stephen and Churton Collins provide us with a good example of this last attitude, which has the double advantage of striking an impressive note, while at the same time making further laborious research unnecessary. It is still one of the most popular answers today.

Barrett, Monck Mason and Wilde

We have, however, at the outset of the new century three useful contributions to our knowledge of the subject. In 1808, Dr. John Barrett, Vice-Provost of Trinity, published a work on the earlier part of the Dean's life, which contains the results of the author's careful examination of the Trinity Books. In 1820, Monck Mason published his monumental account of St. Patrick's Cathedral, which, though hardly easy reading, contains a lot of honest information, and a lengthy note on the most celebrated Dean. Then, in 1849, Sir William Wilde produced his *Closing Years of Dean Swift's Life*, which includes the first coherent analysis of the Dean's supposed madness from a medical point of view.

Scott, Forster and Craik

Of the 19th Century " Lives," Scott is readable but slipshod, while Sir Henry Craik has left us a fat volume which would be the best of the more ponderous authorities were it not for the Author's unquestioning respect for the printed word that has gone before him. In 1875 John Forster died —actually before the publication of Craik's book—leaving only the first volume of what was clearly intended to be the definitive Life of the Dean. In this work, Forster has gone to enormous trouble to collect, collate and reproduce everything that he can find about Swift. The result is a work that is a mine of useful details of the Dean's public life, so far as it goes. But in other respects it is disastrously unreliable, owing to the writer's bad temper over the more intractable parts of his material, and his habit of trying to resolve matters of doubt by means of categorical statements that have little tangible evidence to support them.

Later Writers

Then in 1884 we have the tutor and Uncle-by-marriage of Bernard Shaw, the Rev. Mr. Carroll, Vicar of St. Bride's, attempting to prove that Swift was born in Bride Street in his Parish, by means of statements about the contents of his Parish books which are not substantiated by an inspection of the copies that he gave to Trinity College. He is followed by a number of twentieth century writers who on the whole make excellent reading, but whose works as a rule are based on the false assumption that the data require little or no further examination.

Of these, Churton Collins', Sir Shane Leslie's and Carl Van Doren's are probably the best written. Hone and Rossi and Middleton Murry have introduced the argot of modern psychology into the story, with some success, while M. Emil Pons of the University of Strasbourg has made a brilliant contribution in French.

Mention should also be made of two good short books on particular aspects of the matter; Maxwell Gold's Harvard Thesis on *Swift's Marriage to Stella*, and Herbert Davis's book on *Stella*. The fact that the present writer must reluctantly disagree with both of these authors on some of their major points does not detract from his indebtedness to both of these works.

Where we must really demur is when confronted with the two slim volumes by the present Dean of Cashel, Dr. Wyse Jackson, who bowdlerises some of his subject's text in order to conform to his own—or possibly his Publishers'—views on propriety and good taste. For example, Swift did not write :

> Under the oak in stormy weather
> John George and Jane were wed together,

as reported by Dr. Jackson, on p. 39 of *Swift and his Circle*.[17] If it is

---

[17]This satirical marriage certificate actually reads :
 Under an oak, in stormy weather,
 I join'd this rogue and whore together;
 And none but he who rules the thunder
 Can put this whore and rogue asunder.
See *The Poems of Jonathan Swift*, edited by Harold Williams, vol. III, p. 1146.

necessary to make Swift a better ornament to the Church of Ireland by rewriting his verse for him, it would be wiser not to quote him at all.

Lastly, F. Elrington Ball's notes to his excellent edition of the *Correspondence*, though not strictly in the category of a biography, contain a wealth of useful biographical information that has been most painstakingly gathered together, and that, as a rule, is impeccable.[18]

What then is the story that is told by this library of eminence?

---

[18]According to the late T. U. Sadleir of the former Office of Arms, to whose professional researches in that office I am deeply indebted, Elrington Ball was a reliable scholar of immense erudition, who had, nevertheless, some surprising gaps in his knowledge, due to the eccentric views of his father in the matter of education.

THE TESTIMONY

3

MIGRATION TO IRELAND

(a) As Commonly Accepted

Family Background

" The Family of the Swifts was ancient in Yorkshire." So runs the *Autofrag*, moving on from this much-repeated formula to a reference to a person described as Cavaliero Swift, who is said to have attained the height of a peerage, as Baron Carlingford, during the reign of Charles I.

In this connection, the Earl of Orrery[1] rather tartly remarks that " although his anceſtors were perſons of very decent, and reputable characters, he himſelf has been the herald to blazon the dignity of their coat." It should be mentioned, however, that JS himself is quite modest in the social claims that he makes for his father's family. As will be seen, it is on behalf of his mother that he really extends himself, and when he comes to invent stories about an English birthplace, it is his mother's county that he selects and not his father's.[2]

His grandfather, the Rev. Thomas Swift, was Vicar of Goodrich in Herefordshire, and the husband of Elizabeth Dryden, a grand-aunt of the Poet Dryden—a writer whose comment on Swift's earlier verse was : " Cousin Swift, you will never be a poet."

This story of Dryden's comment is hinted at on p. 123 of Deane Swift's *Essay*, but its best known form originates in Joseph Warton's *Essay on Pope*.

The Vicar of Goodrich appears to have been a very unfortunate character. Although his mother was a rich heiress called Philpot, we are told by Swift that she was a capricious and ill-natured woman who " absolutely disinherited " her only son for robbing an orchard when he was still a mere boy. As a result of this unnatural act, he never had more than £100 a year—the miserable income of his Parish. Then came the

---

[1]*Remarks*, p. 5.

[2]An interleaved note by Orrery in one of the Harvard copies of his book states that he so honoured the birthplace of his mother that he had a map of Leicester constantly hung in his bedroom—an unusual way of paying respect to the memory of one's mother.

Great Rebellion, in the course of which the Reverend Thomas underwent further sufferings on account of his unswerving loyalty to the cause of the ill-fated Charles I—sufferings that were " more than [those of] any [other] person of his condition in England," according to the *Autofrag*. His £100 a year property was plundered by the Roundheads, some say thirty-five, and others say over fifty times, and the large rambling house, built by himself, was set on fire five times. Indeed, as Sir Walter Scott tells us, the very clothes of the infant in the cradle were snatched away by the licentious puritans, who left the Vicar without even a loaf to feed to his numerous family.

Betham reports the marriage of the Vicar of Goodrich and Mary Philpot as of the 5th October, 1592. Deane Swift thinks that it was in 1594. Mary Philpot (spelled Philpott by William Swift) survived till 5th March, 1628, when she died at the age of fifty-eight (Betham).

Scott[3] is drawing his information from Deane Swift's notes to Section VIII of the Appendix to his *Essay*, where a detailed account of many such outrages is set forth on the authority of *Mercurius Rusticus* and Walker's *Sufferings of the Clergy*—two atrocity pamphlets of the familiar type, that ruin their own credibility by absurd overstatement. For Scott to add that the Vicar was " almost ruined " by such treatment seems to put it mildly. Deane Swift discloses that the Vicarage actually survived all this burning and plundering, and that he eventually inherited it himself. All that the Vicar permanently lost was a plurality called Bridstow, which was never recovered.

However, in spite of these repeated barbarities, he managed to present the King's local Governor with a waistcoat quilted with several hundred pounds in gold, which brought seasonable relief to his Majesty immediately after the disastrous Battle of Naseby. And, we are told by Hawkesworth, Lord Clarendon generously considered that the King received no contribution more acceptable and timely than this one throughout the entire war.

In 1646 the Vicar was put out of his living by the rascally Parliamentary Committee of Hereford, and also suffered a long term of imprisonment in Raglan Castle. How he managed to survive all this trouble for another twelve years of his life may be partially explained by the fact that the rival first installed in his Vicarage was his brother-in-law, the Reverend Jonathan Dryden, and also by the fact that the Commonwealth later

[3]Scott, vol. I, p. 6.

revoked the sequestration of his temporal estate at Goodrich, and permitted the old man to be honourably buried in 1658 under the altar of his Parish Church—two years before the Restoration.

Uncle Godwin

The Vicar left a large family, of which the eldest son, Godwin, was married—so the *Autofrag* tells us—to a relation of the " old Marchioneſs of Ormond." Finding himself destitute through the sufferings of his father, this elderly orphan—now about thirty-four—resolved to repair the family fortunes by migrating to Ireland. So he " generouſly reſigned the Profits of his Tythes, and little Eſtate, into the hands of his Mother, which he made her a Preſent of during her life to support herſelf," and set off for the sister island, where, thanks to the reports of his father's loyalty and to his own eminent abilities as a Barrister, and also presumably to his relationship by marriage to the Ormonds, he was appointed Attorney General for the Palatine County of Tipperary. This, in spite of the fact that, according to JS, he was " an illpleader, but perhaps a little too dextrous in the subtil parts of the Law."

Deane Swift[4] is the source of this quotation about his grandfather having resigned a life interest in Goodrich to the Vicar's widow. It is another amusing example of the desire to have it every way. For the gesture to have been a generous one, the Vicar can hardly have been permanently plundered.

JS's comment on his uncle Godwin is also illuminating. He originally wrote : " an illpleader, but dextrous in the subtil parts of the Law," in order to account for the appointment of this illpleader as Attorney General for Tipperary. But later his hatred for his uncle overpowered biographical considerations, and he interlined the words, " perhaps a little too."

Jonathan the Elder

We are next told that several of Godwin's brothers—" Men of Abilities, at leaſt equal, if not ſuperior to their Profeſſions "[5], encouraged by the reports of his success, followed him to Dublin where they, too, entered the law, and of these, the second last was a young man of " integrity, with a tolerable good understanding "[6] called Jonathan, who first devoted

---

[4] *Essay*, p. 16.
[5] *Loc. cit.*
[6] *Autofrag.*

himself to "some employments and agencyes" before becoming an
Attorney. As an indication of his success in this latter calling we may
include the fact that he was barely a year in practice before he received a
permanent appointment from the Benchers of King's Inns as Steward of
that respectable Corporation, in which capacity he kept the Minutes and
ran the business affairs of this Irish Inn of Court until the time of his
premature death.

Abigail Erick

In the summer of 1664, this Jonathan married a Leicestershire lady
called Abigail Erick. The date and place of his wedding are unknown as,
for some reason, it was celebrated in private, by Special Licence, issued
by the Prerogative Court of the Archbishop of Armagh—an expensive
and unusual method of getting married, and one frequently adopted by
those who, for one reason or another, did not want the date of the marriage
to be ascertainable. Miss Erick had apparently a very distinguished lineage
—being descended from Erick the Forester, a warrior who raised an Army
to oppose William the Conqueror, but being defeated by that monarch,
was then very generously appointed commander of the Conqueror's
forces. In the sunset of this remarkable, but otherwise undocumented
career, Erick retired to his mansion in Leicestershire, where, as "very
private Gentlemen," his descendants dissipated the family fortunes for
five and a half centuries, until the birth of Abigail. The story is that of
JS, and with the exception of Mr. Elrington Ball, nearly everybody seems
to be quite happy about it down to the present day.

It will therefore not be surprising to learn that she brought to her
husband "little or no fortune" on the occasion of their marriage, and
it is lucky that his employments and agencies—whatever they were—
were profitable enough to enable him to settle an annuity of £20 per
annum upon his bride, which annuity, we are told, was secured in English
funds. It was what JS describes as a marriage "on both sides very indiscreet," and this gesture on the part of the young bridegroom with, then,
no permanent employment must have been a very providential and
foresighted act, because, after she had borne him a daughter in 1666, he
left her a widow "about two years after his marriage" and seven
months before the birth of his son.[7]

No mention is made by Orrery of this Annuity.

---

[7] Both the statements are in the *Autofrag*. The information about the Annuity comes,
not from the *Autofrag* but from Deane Swift.

4

MIGRATION TO IRELAND

(b) As It Probably Occurred

THE sufferings of the Vicar of Goodrich may, perhaps, be attributed to causes beyond a mere loyalty to the throne. As his great-grandson, Deane Swift, points out,[1] his determined opposition to the Commonwealth was more in keeping with the behaviour of a soldier in the field than with that of a parish clergyman, and JS, himself, describes with some relish how this gentle shepherd, " having a head mechanically turned," devised a type of iron hazard with multiple spikes, which, when scattered under the waters of a ford, could decimate the unfortunate horses of a troop of Puritan cavalry.[2]

Furthermore the Commonwealth, no less than the Crown, expected Ministers of the established Church, in return for their tithes, to conform to the prevailing ecclesiastical arrangements of the day, and sometimes turned them out of their livings if they refused to do so. The fact that this Vicar was restored to the major part of his temporalities before the Restoration, and in spite of his determinedly episcopal views, is an indication, either that the Government was extremely liberal in its treatment of " Malignants," or that the Vicar was more ready in the end to conform than is generally supposed.

After describing at some length the great sacrifices incurred by his grandfather in his defence of Episcopalianism, JS goes on to tell us in the *Autofrag*, that his sons were " settled in Ireland (driven thither by their sufferings and by the death of their father)." Following this lead, the regular biographical line has always been that the first of the family to make the crossing to Dublin was Uncle Godwin, and that, inspired by his success, the other brothers followed in his wake.

---

[1] *Essay*, pp. xxiv-xxv.

[2] Actually, this hazard was not an invention of the Vicar, but was a well-known device in the Middle Ages known as the Caltrop. It is still used as heraldic badge by the Drummonds.

We will also recollect having being told that this uncle was related through his first wife to " the old Marchioness of Ormond," which influential connection, together with his unswerving attachment to the Royal cause, was at the back of his advancement after the Restoration. The fact that it is difficult to make out who Swift means by this expression, " the old Marchioness," may be intentional on his part, as he started to write " Duchess " in the *Autofrag*, and then deliberately altered the word to " Marchioness." At any rate, none of the earlier writers prior to Hawkesworth refer to this distinguished connection—not even Deane Swift—nor do they provide any evidence to support it. As usual, it is the later biographers who are happy to restate it categorically, and even to develop it further, as Forster does when he informs us in 1875 that this old Marchioness and Godwin's first wife were " cousins."

The wife referred to was Elizabeth Wheeler of London. The Harleian Society Publications and the London Registers of Marriage Licences mention many people of that surname, but none of them are identifiable with the Elizabeth in question. It is significant, too, that Elrington Ball has nothing whatever to say on the matter.

The only Ormond wife to whom Swift could be referring is the wife of the first Duke, formerly Elizabeth Preston, the only child of Sir Richard Preston, a younger son of a family residing at Whitehall, near Edinburgh, who came to England in the train of James I and was created Baron Dingwall in 1609. According to Wood's *Peerage of Scotland*, Preston married Lady Elizabeth Butler, the sole heiress of Thomas, 10th Earl of Ormond, and became involved in a legal dispute with the 11th Earl, who took the estate and title under the will of Thomas, and was imprisoned by James I for refusing to hand it over to Dingwall. The tangle was finally resolved by James, the 12th Earl, marrying the younger Elizabeth, Dingwall's daughter.

From this it will be seen that Elizabeth Preston could have had no cousins german on her mother's side, and it is not very likely that she was related to the Wheelers of London through her father—a Scottish peer from Edinburgh. Nevertheless, between the date when Charles I made the 12th Earl into a Marquis, and 1661 when Charles II elevated him to a Dukedom, his wife was " Marchioness of Ormond," though why Swift should refer to her by an inferior title is not at all clear, unless he wished to fog the issue as to whom he was writing about. This, he has most successfully done.

To his Grace the Ld Chancell[o]r the [...]
Right hono[ble] the Judges and other the hono[ble] Benchers
of the hono[ble] Society of the Kings Inns Dublin
The humble Pet[itio]n of Jonathan Swift

Humbly Sheweth

That the Stewardshipp of this hono[ble] Society is now become void
by the Death of Thomas Nash the late Steward thereof

That yo[r] Pet[itione]r his father and theire whole ffamily have beene
alwayes very Loyall and faithfull to his Sacred Ma[jestie] and his Royall
father and have beene very greate Sufferers upon that Accompt

That yo[r] Pet[itione]r for this five or seaven yeares last past hath beene
much Conversant about the said Inns and is very well acquainted
w[i]th the duty and Imployment belonging unto the Steward thereof his
haveing Assisted the said Thomas Nash in Entring up the Ord[er]s of the
hon[ble] and in the Things and Ordering other things belonging to the
said Imployment

That yo[r] Pet[itione]r doubts not but if yo[u] hon[rs] will bee pleased to Conferr
the said Imployment or Steward uppon yo[r] Pet[itione]r, that hee shall discharge
hen all faithfull and impartiall therein

[He] therefore humbly prayes that yo[r]
hon[rs] will bee pleased to Conferre the said
Steward upp[on] him

And hee shall pray &c

JONATHAN'S MEMORIAL

As for Godwin's English background, the Gray's Inn Admission Entries show that he was a member of that Inn in London from the 12th November, 1650, about eight years prior to the death of his father. He was married twice in that City, produced three children there, and was apparently doing so well under the abominable Commonwealth that he did not depart for Dublin until three years after the Restoration. It is true, however, that having gone to Ireland, he was appointed Attorney General for Ormond's Palatinate in Tipperary. But it is equally important to add that he did not succeed in holding this appointment for very long,[3] and that he was out of it again as early as June, 1668.

Ball, whose researches are always painstaking and usually reliable, doubts the traditional order of the coming of the Swifts to Ireland, and refers[4] to a view that the first migrants were the younger brothers, William and Jonathan, who are said to have arrived shortly after the Restoration. Actually, the evidence goes to show that, even before this Uncle William made the crossing, the shadowy Jonathan was already hanging around Dublin Law Courts, a fatherless youth of eighteen or nineteen, picking up whatever employment he could find. His undated Memorial to the Benchers of King's Inns that was ruled upon by their Lordships on the 27th January, 1666, is here reproduced, by permission of the Benchers. and can speak for itself.

Forster[5] states that this Memorial was presented to the Benchers " on the 14th of the previous November." This statement is merely based on a gloss on a copy of the Memorial printed by Scott[6]. There is no such date in the Black Book, and the copyist's inference is simply based upon the fact that the 14th November is the date of the previous minuted meeting.

It will be seen that, applying for the job of Steward of the Inns, he stated :

> That yr Petr for these fix or feven years laft paft hath been much Conversant about the faid Inns and is very well acquainted with the Duty and Imploymt belonging unto the Steward thereof he having Affifted the faid Thomas ·Wale in Entring up the Ords of yr hons and in the Setling and Ordering other things belonging to the faid Imploymt.

---

[3]*Correspondence*, vol. I, p. 372 n.
[4]Ibid., p. 9 n.
[5]Forster, p. 18.
[6]Scott, vol. I, p. 9.

It is unlikely that he would lie very extravagantly in a matter that must have been common knowledge to those around the Inns, or indeed, that he would have any occasion to lie at all about the length of his sojourn in the neighbourhood. And if what he says is true, it means that he was probably in Dublin from some date in 1658—the year of his father's death—or at the latest, from well before the Restoration.

Sir Walter Scott makes the same point,[7] but is generally ignored. It does seem within the bounds of probability that, when the Vicar of Goodrich died on the 2nd May, 1658, his teenage son, Jonathan, then left home to look for work abroad. It is not so probable that he kept going back and forward " to England from time to time "—as Forster volunteers —while still " wavering between such chances of a livelihood as either country presented "—surely a very expensive method of job-hunting for a penniless youth in the 17th Century.

Forster, of course, is puzzled as to how this young man later met and married a Leicestershire woman, so he fills out the gaps in his narrative with statements based on surmise, but not so described[8]. Hawkesworth,[9] when confronted with the same problem, tells us that Jonathan married her before he came to Ireland—a matter which the Prerogative Licence proves to be equally fanciful.

Without at present going into any further analysis of all that the Black Book reveals about Jonathan Swift the elder, it is here sufficient to quote what he, himself, says that he was doing from about 1659 till the end of 1665.

There is no evidence that the Vicar's second and third sons, Dryden (or Dreyden, as his brother William spells his name) and Thomas, ever came to Ireland. Dryden was a member of Gray's Inn from 22nd April, 1651, and was never admitted at King's Inns, nor has he left any other

[7]Scott, vol. I, p. 8 n.

[8]Another example of Forster's practice of citing authorities that do not exist, is to be found in his footnote to his p. 20. In this he tells us : " The facts stated in the text are derived from the original documents printed in Duhigg's *History of the King's Inns, Dublin*." It is hard to believe that he was not aware, when making this statement, that the document that he was particularly concerned with is not reproduced by Duhigg at all, but is merely abstracted. Duhigg offers, as an excuse for this omission, " the languid dullness " of the original. On the other hand, a supposed full copy was made by Hartstonge for Sir Walter Scott, who prints it in Vol. I of his edition of Swift's *Works*. The peculiarities of spelling that may be seen in the original do not appear in Hartstonge's copy, and these may be used as a simple guide to distinguish those of the later biographers who have looked at the Black Book, from those who have merely looked at Scott, or at Scott's copyists. I do not think that any of them pass the test.

[9]Hawkesworth, vol. I, p. 4 of the *Life*.

trace in the Irish records that I have been able to find. Thomas was an undergraduate at Oxford from 1653 to 1656, had a son born in Oxford-shire in 1665, and was Rector of St. Edmund's, Lombard Street, London, from 1666.[10]

The fourth son, William, was still in London as late as the summer of 1660, for on the 17th August in that year, when aged about twenty-three, and described as " of Gray's Inn", he obtained a licence there for his marriage to Susannah Hall. The first trace of his presence in Dublin is his admission as an Irish Attorney, which took place in November, 1661.

Owing to the omission of a comma by Deane Swift,[11] Scott[12] makes the mistake of calling the second brother Dryden William, so adding some support to the general belief that Dryden came to Dublin. Uncle William's wife Susannah was buried in St. Michan's, Dublin, in 1674, and within a few months, he married again. He was never, in fact, a full practising member of Gray's Inn, but presumably got his legal training there. There is some evidence to suggest that before the end, William, and not Godwin, was the wealthiest of the brothers. His son William was the only one of the next generation of Swifts to go to Trinity with the exalted classification of a Fellow Commoner.

What emerges from the above is the fact that the tradition mentioned by Elrington Ball is much nearer to the truth than what JS says. Uncle Godwin did not lead the procession of the brothers to Ireland, nor was he a distressed dependant of his suffering father. Gray's Inn advanced him another step in his profession as late as the 9th July, 1660,[13] and he had two sons and one daughter, all of whom were born in England in and after 1658. He then married a second wife, Katherine Webster, the daughter of a London Merchant, from which it may be assumed that he cannot have come to Ireland much before his admission to King's Inns in May, 1663.[14]

---

[10]*Correspondence*, vol. I, p. 369 n.

[11]*Essay*, p. 16.

[12]Scott, vol. I, p. 10.

[13]Gray's Inn Pension Book.

[14]Swiftsheath in Co. Kilkenny, the seat of the present head of the family, has a date on the front of the main building that is taken to indicate that it was built during the Commonwealth period. But even if this was the date of the house (which seems improbable), the family has no documents of title that prove that it was built by the Swifts. It was Godwin II of Dunbrew who first went to Swiftsheath, between 1708 and 1711. See *Alumni Dublinenses* for the birthplaces of his sons Godwin III (Cork) and William (Kilkenny).

Uncle Adam, the youngest of the brothers, was also an Attorney; and the first evidence of his presence in Dublin comes as late as 1670, or in the early part of 1671.

He was born about 1643 and, while living in Richmond and aged about twenty-four, he obtained a licence for his marriage to his first wife, Martha Hopper, in August, 1665.[15] In later life he moved to south County Down, and was Member in the Irish Parliament for the Borough of Newry.[16]

So whatever may have been the motives behind the migration of the Swift brothers to Ireland, they were not " driven there by their sufferings" under the Commonwealth,[17] or even by the death of their father, with the probable exception of Jonathan—the first to go, and the youngest at the time of going, and incidentally, the only unsuccessful Swift. Like most migrants, they went abroad largely in reverse order of importance—the ones with the least at stake being the pioneers. First, Jonathan, probably towards the end of 1658. Then William in 1661. Then the more prosperous Godwin, probably early in 1663. And then a gap, until about 1670, when the good news finally brought over Adam. Our next step is to examine what traces they left behind in Dublin.

---

[15]*Canterbury Marriage Allegations.*

[16]An Abraham Swift of St. Catherine's Parish, who sometimes intrudes his name into the books, and is even included in the family tree by Elrington Ball, is not a relation, and has nothing to do with the story.

[17]In the light of their loud claims upon the gratitude of the Crown, it is amusing to note that Godwin Swift chose for his third wife, Hannah Deane, a daughter of one of the Regicides. It is from this connection that Deane Swift, the biographer, gets his confusing name. Uncle William tries to cover up this embarrassing association by referring in his brother's Funeral Entry to Godwin's father-in-law as " Major " Richard Deane, when in fact he was the celebrated Puritan Admiral who was a party to the execution of Charles I. When writing the *Autofrag* in 1728 JS, on the other hand, makes no effort to conceal the real identity of this relation—a fact that adds colour to the suggestion that he then had little interest in whitewashing the Swift family. When we come to consider the Temples, we will find this same entanglement with both sides in the Civil War occurring in an even more striking way.

5

THE TRAIL OF THE UNCLES

MUCH time can be spent, if one is so disposed, in the absorbing occupation of piecing together the clues to be culled from the various public records, into a Dublin Directory for the latter part of the 17th century. For the benefit of anybody who is so inclined, a description of many of the principal pointers, and of what they disclose, will now be given. Those readers who prefer to get on with the story and to accept the summarised conclusions without getting themselves involved with such minutiae, may do so without loss of face, by skipping the rest of this purely informative chapter.

To put it briefly, what the surviving records show is this : that in spite of the lapse of time, and the destruction of many valuable records, it is still possible to trace with reasonable clarity the changing residences of every member of the Swift family in Dublin from the early sixteen sixties, with one exception. The exception is Jonathan the elder, who never appears to have been a householder with an ascertainable residence of his own. The same is true of his widow.

A list of the available Public Records

As the Irish Records, when placed in proper custody, have frequently been burnt or blown up in bulk, we paradoxically find today that those that have at some stage been improperly retained by private individuals are often the only ones to have survived. This particularly applies to the Parish Registers, of which some 17th Century Dublin books of six Parishes, and of St. Patrick's Cathedral (in the latter case, for baptisms and burials only) are still to be found.

Unfortunately, this list does not include any of the four principal parishes that interest us most—St. Michan's, the parish of King's Inns ; St. Werburgh's, the parish of Hoey's Court ; St. Bride's, the parish of the later years of Uncles William and Adam ; and St. Andrew's, the parish of the Vanhomrighs and others who will interest us later. Fortunately, this loss has been repaired to some extent by the useful

publications of the Irish Parish Register Society and the Irish Memorials
Association, which cover (*inter alia*) St. Michan's[1] from 1636, St. Bride's
and St. Andrew's from 1632 and from 1672 respectively (but in both
cases for marriages only), St. John's from 1619, and finally St. Catherine's
and St. James's both from 1636.

Some extracts from the vanished St. Bride's Vestry Books were
published during 1895 and 1896 in a periodical called *The Irish Builder*.
The compiler was fully aware of our interest in the Swifts, and presumably
gave us whatever he could find on the subject. So we can console ourselves with the reflection that his somewhat meagre references were the
only ones to be found. More important are copies of some of the St.
Bride's Registers and Vestry Books that were deposited in the library of
Trinity College by the late Rev. W. G. Carroll, the last Incumbent of
this Parish before its absorption by St. Werburgh's. The original books
are said to have been destroyed with the Record Office in 1922, but these
copies cover the period that interests us, with some annotations and
comments by Mr. Carroll himself. They are particularly useful in correcting
the impression that the Incumbent attempted to create in his book on the
Parish,[2] that there was evidence in his parochial records to show that
Godwin Swift was a resident of a house in Bull Alley or Bride Street at
the time of the birth of JS. This, of course, was with the object of claiming
the birthplace for his Parish. An examination of these books and of Mr.
Carroll's own notes in them, not only fails to lend any support to any
such supposition, but shows that the Incumbent was not even certain
about it himself, notwithstanding the confident statements that he makes
in his book.[3]

---

[1]St. Michan's was the only city parish north of the Liffey until almost the end of
the 17th Century, when an Act of William III created the parishes of St. Paul and
St. Mary as from the 20th November, 1697. King's Inns had at one time its own Chapel
in Mass Lane, a cul-de-sac on the site of the present Chancery Place. (See Gustavus
Hamilton's *King's Inns*). But no documents relating to this have apparently survived.

[2]*Succession of Clergy in the Parishes of S. Bride, etc.* Dublin, 1884.

[3]The baptismal records of the Parish for November and December, 1667, are included
in the Trinity transcript and do not mention any Swifts at all. The earliest reference to
the family is on page 145, and records the burial of : " Counsellor Swift's man out of
Bull Alley, 1681, Oct. 8." Opposite this entry Mr. Carroll has pasted a slip with the
comment : " This is the earliest mention of the Swifts in the Books . . . The Uncle
Godwin is probably the one named in this Entry." This faulty supposition is all that
he has to go on, and it will be shown to be much more probably a reference to Uncle
William. In any event, the entry comes almost fourteen years after the birth of JS, and
signifies nothing as regards the sixties.

Our greatest loss, however, is in the case of St. Werburgh's which had a private fire of its own in 1754, when all the records prior to 1704 are said to have been destroyed. Our only present knowledge of the contents of these books comes from some extracts made by Dr. John Stearne, at one time Rector of the Parish, and also Swift's immediate predecessor in the Deanery, which are now also to be seen in Trinity College Library. These extracts, which cover many of the Dublin Parishes, were made by Dr. Stearne for some purpose of his own that is difficult to ascertain now. They are far from exhaustive and seem to have been selected on no very clear principle. At the date of their compilation (the late 1680's) Stearne had no special reason to be interested in the Swifts. Nevertheless he mentions William three times, Godwin only once, and Jonathan the elder and his family not at all, although the baptism of Swift's sister Jane occurs during the period covered, and was in the St. Michan Register. St. Michan's interests him most of all. He is careless and very cursory about St. Werburgh's and St. Audoen's, and he appears to be more concerned with baptisms and deaths than with weddings.[4]

Apart from the information to be extracted from the parish records, there is a copy of a Poll Tax Roll of 1658 or 1659 (wrongly described as a " Census Return ") in the Royal Irish Academy, and some plain copies of the Hearth Money Rolls for 1663 and 1666 in the reconstituted Record Office.[5]

There is a *List of Proprietors of Six Hearths and Upwards* reprinted in the Deputy Keeper's Report, no. 57, from an MS. volume stated to have been purchased in a Dublin bookshop.[6]

The Quit Rent Office has a copy of a *Rental of Landgable Values and City Dues* dated circ. 1665, which is also printed in the Deputy Keeper's Report, no. 57, p. 526. In his Report no. 55, p. 117, there is a transcript

---

[4]It will be remembered that Lyon's additions to Hawkesworth confirm the fact that there was no entry of JS's baptism in the books of St. Werburgh, although Lyon merely attributes this to the carelessness of the Clerk.

The Rev. S. C. Hughes has published two small books giving the history of the two churches of St. Werburgh and St. John. These contain—*inter alia*—a good deal of miscellaneous information that must have originally come from various parish books. Where it is still possible to check this, Mr. Hughes' books are sometimes found to be unreliable.

[5]A note on the 1663 Roll queries the date, but there is nothing about it to suggest that this is incorrect. The original was blown up in the old Record Office.

[6]This is marked 1664, but it must be 1665 at the earliest, as it shows St. Andrew's as a reconstituted parish, separated from St. Werburgh's, which did not occur until 1665.

of a list of Protestants who took an Oath under the Act of 13 Car. II. in order to become free subjects of Ireland. And in Trinity College Library there is a short, and obviously very incomplete list of Protestant Refugees, giving the names of some of those who escaped to England during the Jacobite crisis before the Battle of the Boyne.

The useful *Alumni Dublinenses*, 1593-1846, published by Burtchaell and T. U. Sadleir, shows the entries into Trinity College, with details of each Freshman's birth and education. Finally, there is a quantity of ancestral information about the Swifts in the Genealogical Office, Dublin Castle, principally collected by Betham from unspecified sources. Much of this last has since found its way into the pages of Burke's *Landed Gentry of Ireland*, and is frequently wrong, and usually unverified.

The Testimony of the Rolls

Now follows a summary of what can be gleaned about the family from these documents. The Poll Tax Roll of 1658 discloses no Swifts at all in Dublin. The Hearth Money Return for 1663 shows one " Mr. Swift " only, who occupies a house somewhere in the Parish of St. Michan. This is probably William, and the fact that there is only one, bears out our belief that Godwin did not appear on the scene until this very year, at the time of his admission to the Inns.

Now comes the first scrap of news from the Parish Registers, namely the burial in St. Michan's of Godwin Swift's daughter, Elizabeth, on the 16th May, 1664. Next month, the younger brother, Jonathan, makes one of his rare excursions into view, when the Special Licence dated the 25th June is issued by the Prerogative Court for his marriage with Abigail Erick.

Next year the *List of Proprietors of Six Hearths and Upwards* is much more illuminating, for it mentions by name William Swift as having three hearths in " the Inns " (which is probably the same holding as that which appears the same year in the *Rental of Landgable Values* as " Hamon Lane or Loughboy "),[7] and it also refers to Godwin Swift as possessing four hearths in Church Street (which runs across Pill Lane). This also appears as a Swift holding in the Landgable list. All of these are, of course,

---

[7] " Loughboy " is now Bow Street, and it may be worth mentioning that " Hamon Lane " was evidently called after Hammond, the maiden name of Lady Temple, the wife of the Master of the Rolls.

in the Parish of St. Michan. There are no further Swifts mentioned in the Landgable List, except a Philip Swift away to the east in Lazar's Hill, St. Andrew's Parish. But he is no connection, and probably belongs to a Holyhead family of this name that has confused some of the historians.

One of Betham's earliest references to Godwin—although there is no date—describes him as " of Ormond Quay."

The 1666 Hearth Money Return has only survived in part—the section dealing with St. Bride's, which appears in the issue of *The Irish Builder* for the 15th November, 1895. But its interest, though negative, is great, as it shows that at this date no member of the family had as yet penetrated to that part of the City, notwithstanding Rev. Mr. Carroll's hopes to the contrary.

Uncle William's Trail

On the 27th July, 1669, Uncle William took the Oath under the Act of 13 Charles II and became a fully-fledged Irish subject of His Majesty. Throughout the 70's we note, in the St. Michan Registers, the burial of his daughter Ann (1670), of his first son William (1677) (another son was later baptised in this same name), and of his first and second wives, Susannah Hall (1674) and Dorothy Bromeston (or Burnstone) (1676). Around the time of his third marriage, about 1679 or 1680, he appears to have moved to St. Bride's Parish—probably to Bull Alley[8], and became connected thereafter with this Church, as well as with St. Nicholas Within, in which another of his daughters and his third wife, Frances King, were buried, in 1680 and 1684 respectively.[9]

With the outbreak of the Williamite Wars, he fled to England accompanied by his fourth wife and four children, and apparently returned to live in Bride Street, in the same parish, from which both he and his son Billy Swift were eventually buried in St. Bride's (1706 and 1711

---

[8]Malton's Preface to his *Picturesque and Descriptive View of the City of Dublin* refers to a house and garden near the Patrick Street end of Bull Alley "formerly Counſellor Swift's." p. 6n.

[9]" Counsellor Swift's man was buried in St. Bride's out of Bull Alley." 1681, Oct. 8. No significance should be attached to the description " Counsellor " when applied by a Parish Clerk to one who is merely an Attorney. On one occasion Adam Swift is even referred to in the St. John's books as " Serjeant Swift," and several other " Counsellors " in the early part of the 18th Century Registers are not even members of King's Inns. For the burials of his daughter Frances and " Mrs. Swift from Bull Alley" in St. Nicholas Within, see vol. XI, Irish Memorials Association, no. 6.

respectively). According to Elrington Ball, it was from this house that the Dean's sister, Jane, was married in 1699 to Joseph Fenton, the currier.

Concerning Uncle Godwin

We are not so certain about Uncle Godwin's doings. Sometime about 1665 or 1666 he appears to have left St. Michan's Parish and moved across the river to live in St. Werburgh's—presumably in Hoey's Court. By taking himself and his family out of one of the best documented parishes into one of the worst, he does us a great disservice. But no doubt his real reason had something to do with the proximity of the Law Courts, then in Christ Church Place. Henceforth his affairs are wrapped in some obscurity, but as this prominent citizen, between 1665 and his death nearly thirty years later, married twice and presented the town with fourteen offspring,[10] it is fair to say that the household which he moved from St. Michan's can hardly have gone to any other City Parish except St. Werburgh's. In any other Parish some surviving records would have provided us with indications of so prolific a family life. And actually, whenever he or his family do step out of St. Werburgh's we are at once reminded of their presence in Dublin. Thus, we find the licence for his marriage to Hannah Deane directed to Crumlin in 1673, and the marriage of his son Thomas to Mary Pooley taking place in St. Michan's in 1679. The rest is silence, except that Rev. Mr. Hughes[11] gives us :

> 1695. December 7. Counsellor Godwin Swift of Hoey's Court buried in St. Werburgh's.

From these facts, as well as from the fact that he was nowhere else in Dublin, we may perhaps accept the generally reported story that he was

---

[10]Godwin II. (1671) and Robert (d.s.p.) by Katherine Webster. Deane I. (1673), Hannah Maria (1676), Joseph (1677), Elizabeth (1679) and Dryden (1680) by Hannah Deane. Meade I. (1682), Thomas (1683), William (1684), Michael (1685), Christopher (date unknown), Edward (date unknown) and John (1691) by Elinor Meade. The above dates can be put together from Betham, Monck Mason, *Alumni Dublinenses* and Burke's *Landed Gentry of Ireland*.

[11]On the other hand, as Mr. Hughes is wrong in claiming both Hannah Deane's and Thomas's marriages for St. Werburgh's, he may be wrong about Godwin's burial too.

There is no evidence that Godwin fled to England at the time of the Revolution, as did his two brothers. He may, as alleged, have been in his dotage by this time, but it should be noted that, according to Burke, he had another son as late as 1691.

living in St. Werburgh's Parish in the house subsequently known as 7 Hoey's Court, which is generally regarded as the Dean's birthplace.

Uncle Adam's Record

The only other uncle in Ireland was Adam, who was apparently living in St. John's Parish from about 1670. Several of his children were baptised or buried there during the 70's. After his first wife had gone the premature way of most Swift wives, he married again, at least once, if not twice. At Easter, 1687, he paid Parish Cess as " Serjeant Swift of Fishamble Street Ward "—probably for a house stated by the Rev. Mr. Hughes to have been in Smock Alley. Meanwhile, like his brother Godwin, he kept a pew in St. Michan's, probably for professional reasons, and he fled to England with his wife and four children[12] to escape from James II. While there, in Chester, the daughter who became Martha Whiteway was born. After returning to St. John's and then moving to Bull Alley in the 90's, he moved north to Greencastle in County Down, where he died on the 8th April, 1704, after having sat in the Irish Parliament as Member for Newry.

---

[12]The entries in the Parish Registers are somewhat confusing in the case of Adam's children, as there was apparently an Edward Swift in St. Peter's Parish who had a wife, Ann, who is sometimes confused with Adam's two daughters, Ann who died in 1675, and Nan, who lived to marry James Perry of Perrymount, Co. Down. It seems most probable that Adam only married twice, and that his second wife was Margery Cottrell. His last child was his son, Adam, baptised in St. Bride's in 1676, and who was buried in the same Parish in 1758.

According to Elrington Ball, Uncle Adam died on the 8th April, 1704, and his will was proved on the 26th May in the same year (Betham). Bull Alley is mentioned as his residence in an entry in the St. Bride's books, dated June, 1698. The house was probably that previously occupied by Uncle William.

6

PARENTS

WHAT of the exception—Jonathan? Might not he, like his brother Godwin, have been the occupant of a well-stocked residence in this undocumented Parish of St. Werburgh—perhaps even in Hoey's Court, as Forster would have us believe?

This is possible, but it is not at all likely, as we do happen to have one or two clues as to his whereabouts, all of which point to St. Michan's as being his home ground. On the 1st May, 1666, his daughter was baptised there, and it was the Parish of the King's Inns, where both his predecessor and his successor in the office of Steward were buried.

The most probable reason for the universal silence in all the municipal records on the subject of a home for Jonathan is that, after his appointment as Steward, he and his family were accommodated in the Inns, and that prior to this event, he lived in lodgings, or on the bounty of one or other of his brothers. This difficulty in tracing him also makes it unlikely that he was ever in any substantial practice as an Attorney—a conclusion that throws some doubts on the story of his death, as told by Mrs. Pilkington, and given below.

As regards his age, his brother William assures us that he was the fifth son coming between William and Adam. As the London and Canterbury *Marriage Allegations*[1] respectively show that William was about twenty-three at the time of his marriage to Susannah Hall in 1660, and that Adam was about twenty-five at the time of his marriage to Martha Hopper in 1668, the year of Jonathan's birth must have been between 1638 and 1642—say 1640—a date that matches up very neatly with a belief that his Hegira to Ireland came shortly after the death of his father in 1658, and at the age of eighteen.

This, together with the fact that he was married in private in 1664, and that his daughter was baptised in St. Michan's in 1666, is the sum total

---

[1]Published in vol. 23 of the Harleian Society Publications.

of our knowledge of him, apart from the testimony of his handwriting in the Black Book of King's Inns, which will be referred to presently.

Abigail Erick

The Leicestershire background of his bride has been looked into by the Rev. W. G. Dimock Fletcher, and the results have been published in the Transactions of the *Leicestershire Architectural and Archeological Society*,[2] under the title *On Dean Swift's Mother*. As the English parish records have not been subject to the same hazards that have afflicted the Irish ones, it is surprising that this information was not discovered at an earlier date, particularly as there were many Ericks, Herricks and Heyricks in this county, and the family was by no means an obscure one.

Nothing more comes to light about Erick the Forester, but it does appear that a Thomas Herrick, whose name is sometimes spelled Erick, and who is described as a butcher of Wigston Magna, about four miles from Leicester, had five children, as follows :—

> William, born 1628,
> Abigail, born 1630 and baptised on the 16th May,
> Anne, born 1632,
> Thomas, born 1634, and
> Robert, born 1637.

That this is the Abigail of whom we are in search is shown by the fact that the above younger Thomas became Vicar of Frisby in Shropshire, and was the father of a daughter who married the Rev. John Kendall, Vicar of Thornton, near Leicester, with whom JS corresponded in 1692, subscribing his letter : " I am, good cousin, your very friend and servant."[3]

Although this butcher was in humble employment, his family must have been a bright and intelligent one. Thomas was ordained, and the daughter Anne had sufficient property to leave a will in which Abigail is mentioned.[4] As for Swift's mother, everybody who describes her personally

---

[2]Vol. VI, p. 162.

[3]In a note to vol. I, p. 4, Elrington Ball says : " In one place Nichols says she (Kendall's wife) was sister, and in another place niece of Swift's mother, but there is no doubt that the former was the relationship." The only doubt arises from the fact that when Elrington Ball writes " the former," he almost certainly means " the latter."

[4]*Miscellania Genealogica et Heraldica*, vol. I, Second Series.

is at one in praising her charm, her liveliness and her sense of humour. Deane Swift[5] says :

> —she declared in her latter Days (for indeed fhe was a Woman of an eafy contented Spirit) that fhe was rich and happy, and abounded with every Thing.

Lyon, in one of his notes to Hawkesworth, tells an amusing story of a gentle hoax she played on Mrs. Brent, while staying in that lady's house during one of her visits to Dublin. Here she led her landlady to believe that she was expecting a lover to call. But the lover turned out to be her son, Jonathan.

The point to be observed about her is not, of course, any absurd social pretensions to an ancient lineage in the Midlands, but the fact that her branch of the Herricks was of good yeoman stock that was rising in the world. And—this is important—that she must have been about ten years older than the invisible scrivener who became her husband.

Was love the basis of this marriage ? And what was this Leicestershire butcher's daughter doing in Dublin at the age of thirty-four ? For it is too much to suggest, as Hawkesworth does, that she went there to get married, after having been betrothed for about six years to a younger son of a Herefordshire Vicar, who had been out of the country since the age of eighteen. It is even more difficult to imagine that this penniless clerk conducted his courtship by travelling to and fro between the two countries, while looking for suitable employment, as some would have us believe.

It will also be noticed that we have as yet no tangible information as to the date of his death, except two indirect statements in the *Autofrag*— one of which is related to the date of his marriage and the other to the birth of his son. As his marriage was celebrated in private, and we only know the date of the Special Licence, and as his son does not give us the year of his own birth when telling us that his father died seven months previously, we will observe with some surprise that although the *Autofrag* pretends on two occasions to tell us when he died, it actually gives us no information whatever on the subject.

This is all very curious, and calls for some further persistence. So let us turn next to the King's Inns, where this man was employed, and see whether there is anything there that throws any further light on his strongly obfuscated career.

---

[5] *Essay*, p. 25.

7

THE KING'S INNS

NOWADAYS the important duties of the Under-Treasurer of this Corporation and College of Lawyers are carried out by a member of the Society, appointed for that purpose, who is also a member of the Bar. During the early part of the 17th Century, however, they were performed by a Steward, who held office during good behaviour at a salary of £5 per annum, though no doubt with other perquisites. Sometimes he combined this position with that of Cook, and very often his wife was Laundress at half a crown a week. There was also a staff of lower servants, including a Butler who, in 1663, and for "a long time" previously, had been a man called Thomas Wale. The Lodge MSS.—of which there is a copy in the reconstructed Record Office—makes it clear that the Steward was a person standing not very high in the social scale. Indeed he was so much of a servant, that when the Steward Crowe "went to other employment" in this year, the Butler, Thomas Wale, applied to the Masters of the Bench for the job, and succeeded in getting it.

One of the matters that may have weighed with Their Honours in making this appointment was Thomas Wale's Petition, a copy of which is still to be seen in the Minute Book of the Inns, written in a finely-flowing hand with obvious care but with an uncertain grasp of spelling. The Minutes of the Benchers' Meeting at which the prayer of this application was granted are written in the same hand, and probably at the same time, when the petition was copied into the book. They are here reproduced in a photograph, as in all probability we are now looking upon the earliest example of the work of Jonathan Swift the elder in the Black Book of King's Inns—as it is called.

It will be remembered that in his later Memorial, a photograph of which has already been shown, Jonathan Swift stated that he had been engaged in entering up the orders of the Benchers for several years prior to his own application for the Stewardship.[1] We may assume, therefore,

---

[1] The Petition of Izabel Wale, presented on the 6th February, 1666, confirms this statement of Jonathan, and says : "That your Petitioner's said husband did in his lifetime employ Mr. Jonathan Swift for the assisting him in making up his accounts and entering orders and other entries."

that an appreciable quantity of the handwriting in the Black Book must
be his. Now here before us we have the first entry that seems at all likely
to fall into that category.

But before turning our attention to matters of calligraphy or attempting
to draw any conclusions therefrom, it would be well to say something
about the Book itself.

The Black Book

The Black Book of King's Inns is a fascinating volume, which by some
miracle has managed to survive all of Ireland's upheavals to date. But as
it is tempting fate to assume that this good fortune will continue
indefinitely, it is hoped that it will shortly be edited and published in full,
if possible with photostats, before it meets with a similar fate to that
which befell most of the Parish Registers.

Occasional references have been made to it in the two histories of the
Society,[2] but so far only a few brief extracts have been printed or
paraphrased.

This neglect may be due to the fact that it is a strictly functional volume,
consisting of source material in its rawest form, providing hard reading
for all except seekers after the plainest of facts, or for those with a taste
for detective work. Its arrangement has not been dictated by any artistic
considerations and, like a single cupboard in which different things are
stored on various shelves, it records diverse facts and figures, of widely
different categories, out of chronological order, that would nowadays be
found in three or four separate ledgers.

It is a Minute Book for the Benchers' Meetings. It also contains transcripts of some of the Petitions on which Their Lordships were humbly
besought to move. It is a record of Admissions to the Society, and—
through the Society—to both branches of the legal profession, and of the
fees paid therefor. It is also an Accounts Ledger for the Inn as a whole.

Compiled over the years by a many-handed Vishnu of scribes, each
writer has tended to select a new set of pages for his entries, and to run
on therein, until death, lack of material, or his departure to other employment puts an end to his work. Or else he runs up against a set of pages
that are already occupied, and is forced to jump to another place further on.

---

[2] *The History of the King's Inns*, published in 1806 by Bartholomew Thomas Duhigg,
is a ponderous mixture of useful research and of bad-tempered personal opinions.
Gustavus Hamilton's *Account of the Honourable Society of King's Inns, Dublin*, published
in 1915, is a more readable sketch, but is hardly more than a lengthy pamphlet.

Trinity terme 1665 — June 6—

Memorand that on the 6—th of June James Shorly
gent: was Admitted into the Society of this house
and hath paid for his Admission ye Some of

$\left.\right\}$ l. d
13:04

—th
—1665

Memorand that Henry Martin Junior gent. was
Admitted into the Society of this house and
hath paid for his Admission the Some of

$\left.\right\}$ l. d
00:13:04

—20

Memorand that on ye twelveth of June 1665
John Campell gent: was Admitted into the
Society of this house & hath paid for his
Admission ye Some of — — — — — —

$\left.\right\}$ l. d
00:13:04

02:00:00

Memorand that on the 26th Day of
January 1665 Jonathan Swift gent
was Admitted into the Society of this
house & hath paid for his Admission

$\left.\right\}$ 00:13:04

Memorand further that _____
_____ Booth gent was admitted
into the Society & _____ & hath
paid for his Admission the Some of

$\left.\right\}$ 00:13:04

Memorand that on the first Day of
_____ 1665 _____ gent was
Admitted the Society of this house
hath paid for his Admission the Some of

$\left.\right\}$ 00:13:04

Memorand that on the fourteenth Day of
_____ Thomas Richardson Jun Esq gent
admitted into the Society of this house and
hath paid for his Admission the Some of

$\left.\right\}$ 02:13:04

Memorand that on the first Day of Aprill
1666 John Davies Esq was admitted into the Society
of this house and hath paid for the Some of —

$\left.\right\}$ 02:13:04

ADMISSION ENTRIES, 1665–1666

For this reason, the entries during the period that is relevant to our present enquiry come in blocks, and have to be sorted out before any chronological picture emerges—Admission Lists from p. 153 to p. 166; Minutes, Petitions and Orders from p. 183 to p. 211; and Accounts from p. 212 to p. 220. It must also be remembered that these entries are not always contemporaneous with the events with which they deal, and are frequently copies of other documents and memoranda, the originals of which may or may not have been kept separately on a file until the time was ripe to enter them up in bulk. This particularly applies to the Admission Lists, which often combine a consistency in handwriting and ink with a wide divergence in dates.

Consider for example the Petition of Thomas Wale, about the billeting of soldiers in the Inn (undated, but appearing on p. 201 of the book) which has on the same page a copy of Ormond's later Order in the matter, dated the 20th May, 1664, together with the Mayor of Dublin's reply, dated almost a year later. They are all entered up probably at the same time and certainly in the same hand, when the whole incident is over, and a record is required. It will be noticed, too, that the signatures are not in the actual handwriting of Ormond and the Mayor, but are merely copies.

This artless lack of form has certain advantages for the researcher today, once he can bring himself to straighten out the actual order of writing. The book is filled with genuine attestations, actual handwriting, corrections, blots and second thoughts that can be far more revealing than any printed page that has been edited into a presentable shape. But it also has certain dangers that lurk for the unwary, a good example of which—combined with our old bugbear, the start-of-the-year confusion— is to be found in a mistake in the reading of page 162 by both Duhigg and Hamilton (and enshrined in the canon by Forster)[3] which has resulted

---

[3]Page 162 of the book begins with three admissions for the Trinity Term of 1665. Then a line is drawn, and four Hilary Term admissions follow (including that of Jonathan Swift), each with a different date, but probably all entered up at the same time. After these comes a single admission for the Easter Term following. It will be noticed that, in accordance with the practice of the time, the date of the year changes after the Hilary Term, and not before it. All the Hilary Term and Easter Term admissions on this page are in what we would now call the year 1666, and Forster's mistake in attributing Swift's admission to the previous year was pointed out to him in a letter dated the 31st December, 1875, from John B. O'Hanlon, then Under-Treasurer of the Inns, which is to be found in the Forster Collection. As Forster did not live to correct any subsequent edition of his book, this error remains in print, and has since been repeated by everybody who has taken Forster's statement as an authority.

in the idea that Swift the elder was admitted as an Attorney almost a year before he was made Steward of the Inns.

The supposition that he was already an Attorney of a year's standing did not play any part, as is generally imagined, in his selection for this office. On the contrary, he was made an Attorney the day after his appointment as part of the same transaction, and possibly to add something to his status and qualifications as Steward, which up to that time had been far from apparent.

Another matter that will turn out to be of some importance appears from an examination of the dates of the entries, and can be checked by a glance at contemporary calendars. The dated proceedings are almost invariably confined to four short periods in each year—the four Legal Terms ; Hilary, Easter, Trinity and Michaelmas—during which periods the Judges were sitting in Dublin, the Benchers held their meetings, new members were admitted to the Inns, and communal dining took place, as it does to the present day. It was principally in connection with these dinners that the Steward was responsible for the collection of the cost of Commons from the members of the Inn, and was required to give an account of his receipts each term to his employers, the Benchers.

As in England, these four terms were then surprisingly short. In the latter part of the 17th century the Irish Hilary Term usually began on the 20th January—actually on Monday the 21st in 1667—and ran for just over three weeks till the 12th February. The Michaelmas Term was longer—running from approximately the 23rd October until the 28th November. The dates of the other two terms depended upon the incidence of Easter and of Trinity Sunday, but the terms themselves were also only from three to three and a half weeks in length.

These terms, of course, have nothing to do with the three Circuits, or Assizes : Spring, Summer and Winter, when the legal profession circulated through various parts of the country in company with the itinerant Judges. These peregrinations took place each year at times decided upon by the Bench, and the Spring Assizes, for example, normally went out in March. But so far as any business at King's Inns was concerned, all activities took place within the span of the four Legal Terms—a fact that accounts for the intervals in the dates in the Black Book that regularly occur each year.

201

To His Grace James Duke of Ormond,
Lord Lieut. Genll. and Generall Governor of Ireland.

The humble peticon of Thomas Walsh, Steward of
the Kings Inne and to the Judges &c.

Humbly Sheweth That on the 5th of March last, by Lieut. Hartleys Order, Six Musquetiers
were put into the Kitchin of the Kings Inne in yr. petrs. absence, who before they would quitt the
said place demanded and constrained yr. petr. to pay three and twenty shillings for
their free-quarters, whereas the late Mayor his Sheriffes deny any such assesment, In that
that Mr. Brookes one of the new Lord Sheriffes hath assessed yr. petr. after the
rate of £22 p. annu. abateing yr. Guards pence; Now forasmuch as it was never
knowne that Souldiers were quartered within the verge of the Kings Inne before this affaire put
upon yr. petr. being but a servant to the honble. the Judges & Society of the Kings Inne.

Yr. petr. therefore most humbly prayes yr. Grace, that the priviledge of the said
Inne formerly may be respected and yr. petr. freed from such forced payments
for the future.

And he shall pray &c.

Dublin Castle 20th May 1664.

Referred to the Mayor of the City of Dublin to informe himselfe & how
the matter stands, and to certifye us thereof with his opinion what he
shall conceave fitt to be done therein.

ORMOND

May it please yr. Grace,

In obedience to yr. Graces within Order of the 20th of
May 1664 upon the peticon of Thomas Walsh Steward of the
Kings Inns I have Examined the Sheriffes both for the
last, and their present yeare, and cannot find that they, or any
of them have Quartered any Souldiers within the verge of
the Kings Inns, And I doe know that this City hath allwayes
had so great a respect for the reverend Judges, and the rest
of that Society, that they have never given Order that any
Taxx should be laide within the said Inns. All which I
humbly Certifye unto yr. Grace this 12th day of May 1665.

Willm Smyth Mayor Dublin.

A PAGE OF BLACK BOOK ENTRIES

At a Councell houlden att the Kings Armes Dublin the 17th day of November 1663

Present The Lord Chancelor
ye Barron of Santry
Lo: Chief Barron
Mr of ye Rooles
Mr Justice Storkton
Mr Justice Booth

Sr Jerom: Alexander   Mr Barron Peney

Ordered that Mr Justice Storkton and Mr Justice Booth take the Accompt of the Lord Chief Justice the present Treasurer./

Ordered that Thomas Wale uppon his Peticon bee admitted Steward of this house:/

Ordered that noe ffamilies shall remaine in any Chambers within the soriety and if any bee that they remoue before the next tearme./

Ordered that an accompt bee brought in of all the Chambers belonging to this soriety and in whose possession they are and which of them are in the disposeall of the house and that the said Chief Barron haue the preference to the Romes Late belonging to Mr: Barron Dongan./

Ordered that Sr George Wentworth bee admitted into this soriety./

Ordered that a note bee given to the bench of all such Counrellrs officers and Atturneyes as are not admitted of this soriety./

The Identification of the Entries

Thomas Crowe's Minutes and Admission Entries, which run from 1658 until the summer of 1663, show him to have been a man of some education and ability. They are clearly in his handwriting, as they cease precisely at the time when we know that he " went to other employment."[4]

If Swift the elder was around the Inns from late in 1658, it was in a very humble capacity, and whatever writing he may have done for Crowe, was not in the Black Book. Whether the Minutes of Wale's appointment are in the same handwriting as that which follows, from the meeting of the 28th November, 1663, to that of the 16th November, 1666, is a matter of opinion. The first entry is so carefully written in an effort to create a good impression that the real character of the scribe is hard to assess. But there can be little doubt that on and between the two dates mentioned, with one exception, we are looking at Minutes in the actual calligraphy of Jonathan the elder, engaged in " Entring up the Ords of yr hons and in the Setling and Ordering other things belonging to the said Imploymt."

The hand could not be Wale's, for it continues after his death. Wale probably kept the accounts, because the handwriting in which these are written vanishes shortly before he died. Indeed it is interesting to note that the only occasion on which young Swift was allowed to write up these disbursements was when Wale was probably on his deathbed. On all other occasions the Steward looked after the money, while the younger man looked after the Benchers, and did the bulk of the clerical work, including most of the Admission Lists.

It is probable that this Butler-Steward—unlike his predecessor Crowe—had neither the education nor the inclination to do his own clerical work, and employed this English clergyman's out-of-work younger son, already engaged on odd jobs around the Inn, to do it for him. How the younger man did it, is a matter that may be deduced from the entries themselves.

The Handwriting

Conclusions drawn from handwriting must, of course, be matters of opinion, and every expert in the field of calligraphy will not agree with

---

[4]Another Thomas Crowe, possibly his son, was appointed to the lowly post of Porter in November, 1683.

the findings suggested here. So some more of the relevant pages are here reproduced in order to enable the reader to form his own view.

At first sight it might seem that a wide variety of hands has been at work, and some differences both in capitalisation and spelling will support this impression. But on closer examination it will be noticed that all of these differences can be found occurring from time to time in the course of one document, which discounts their significance as evidence that there are several writers at work. There is a general, basic style that runs right through the entries between the dates mentioned, whether or not the writer is being careless, or is on his mettle, whether he is watching his spelling, or galloping through his work in order to get it done. And above all—whether he is drunk or sober. These recognisable characteristics, I suggest, are to be found in all the Minutes between November, 1663, and November, 1666, with the sole exception of those of what is stated to be a second meeting on the 14th November, 1665, which are admittedly by somebody else.

On the whole, the handwriting is literate enough, and the spelling noticeably improves as time goes by. But it has a pretentious flourish about it, and is often extremely careless. On at least one occasion (6th June, 1665) the writer is either drunk, or suffering from an acute hangover. Indeed, this is confirmed by the fact that on the previous page he has attempted to write some similar minutes for a supposed meeting on the previous day. He then finds that he is unable to continue, or that it is all wrong; so he crosses it out. In the Autumn that follows this inferior secretarial work, the familiar hand disappears altogether for a time, and somebody else has to do the job in his absence. It was during a more successful period in the previous summer of 1664, that this mercurial character—then possessing only " certain employments and agencies", to quote his son's encomium—obtained his expensive Marriage Licence, and is supposed to have settled on his bride the annuity of £20, secured in English Funds.

About a year and a half later, his immediate superior, Thomas Wale, sickened and died. He was buried in St. Michan's on the 18th January, 1666, and exactly a week later, when the earth can hardly have settled on his grave, young Swift had already drafted a Petition of his own, and had succeeded to his position as Steward of the Inns. A day later he was admitted as an Attorney, but if he ever practised as such—which is very doubtful—it was hardly for a year. In mid-November, 1666, the familiar

At the Kings Inns Dublin 6ᵗʰ...

Present {
The Lord Cheife Barron
Sⁱʳ Jerome Alexander
Mʳ Justice Booth
Mʳ Justice Stockton
Mʳ Barron Povey
Mʳ Sollicitor Forwarth

Ordered That Staples & Padlocks be fastned upon the doors of the Treasury of yᵉ Kings Bench in the possesion of Mʳ Theo: Kennedy, and the Treasury of the Exchequer in the possesion of Phillip Hawnsley Esqʳ.

MINUTES OF 6TH JUNE, 1665

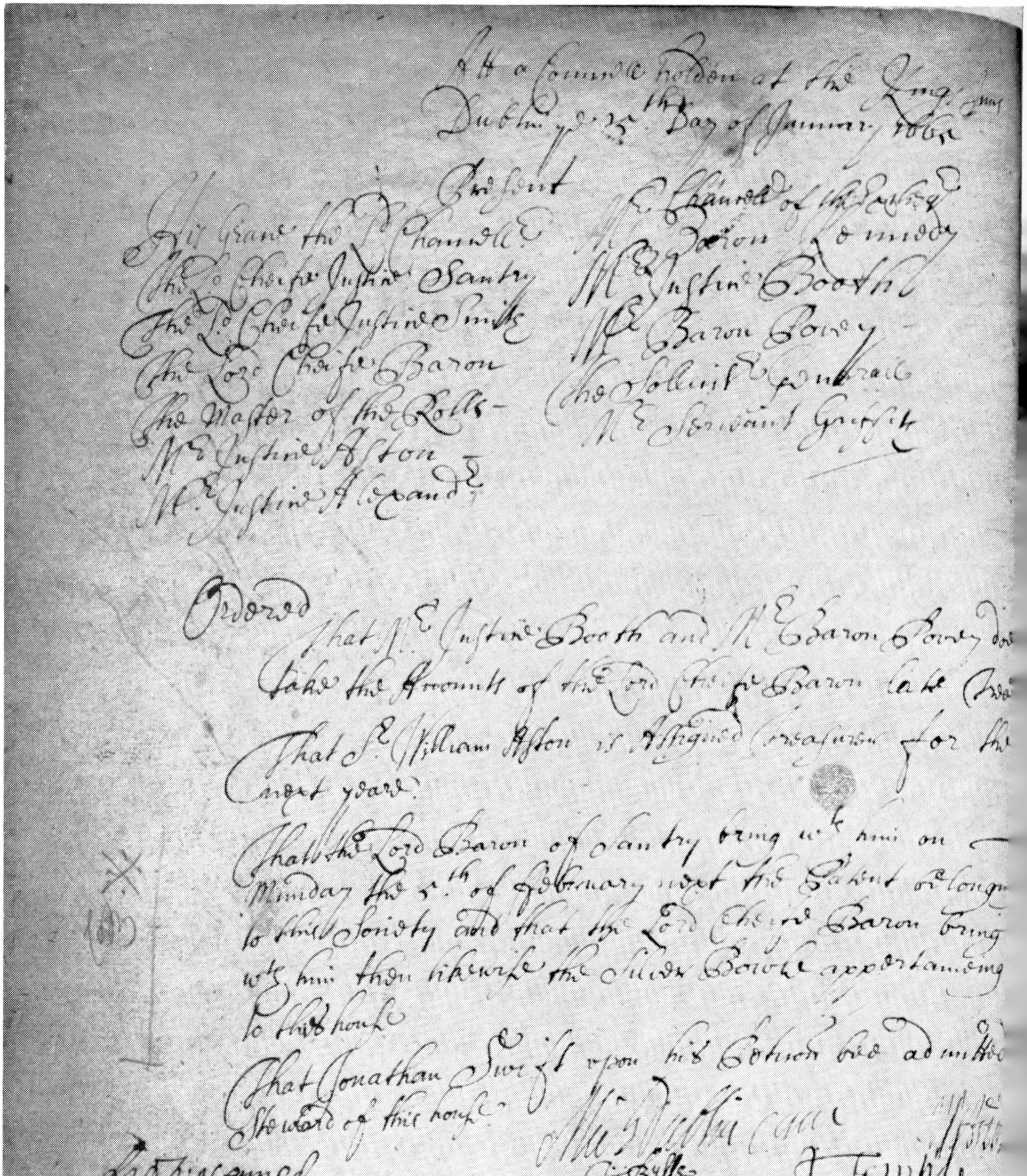

At a Councill holden at the King's
Dublin ye 25th Day of January 1666

Present

His Grace the Ld Chancellor Mr Chancellor of the Excheqr
The Ld Cheife Justice Santry Mr Baron Lo...edy
The Ld Cheife Justice Smith Mr Justice Booth
The Lord Cheife Baron Mr Baron Povey
The Master of the Rolls The Sollicitor Generall
Mr Justice Aston Mr Serieant Griffith
Mr Justice Alexander

Ordered

That Mr Justice Booth and Mr Baron Povey doe
take the Accounts of the Lord Cheife Baron late dead

That Sr William Aston is Assigned Treasurer for the
next yeare

That the Lord Baron of Santry bring wth him on
Munday the 5th of February next the Patent or longe
to this Society and that the Lord Cheife Baron bring
wth him then likewise the Silver Bowle appertaining
to this house

That Jonathan Swift upon his Couch bed admitted
Steward of this house

Not Kenned

MINUTES OF 25TH JANUARY, 1666

hand writes the Benchers' Minutes for the last time. Then there is silence during the entire Hilary Term of 1667, and when the book comes to life again with a flurry of activity in the following April, new hands are at work on both the Minutes and the Admission Lists, and we can tell from the subject matter that Jonathan Swift the elder is definitely dead.

It is here that the value of an unedited holograph record of this kind becomes apparent as a means of checking the accuracy of information with which we have been supplied. In the *Autofrag*, JS's own statement about his father runs as follows :—

> . . . dyed young, about two years after his marriage. He had some employments and agencyes, his death was much lamented on account of his reputation for integrity with a tolerable good understanding.

We will remember that elsewhere in the *Autofrag*, he has told us that this death occurred seven months[5] before his own birth which—thanks to the Trinity College Admissions—we have now fixed as taking place on the St. Andrew's day of 1667. Both statements about this death are now shown by the Black Book to be wrong. Assuming that the marriage was celebrated about the time of the Special Licence, the Steward, according to one report, should have died in the summer of 1666 ; but his Minutes of November in that year show that he did nothing of the sort. On the other hand, the fact that he was actually dead in mid-April, 1667, makes it clear that he died more than seven months before his son's birth. How many months before, is another question, which we cannot answer as yet. So let us, for a moment, look elsewhere.

It is curious that, in describing his father, JS should have made no mention of his principal job as Steward of the Inns, or, if this office was not sufficiently respectable, of the fact that he was an Attorney. Nor does he make any mention of his mother's annuity of £20, which Deane Swift[6] says the father " purchafed for her in *England*, immediately after his Marriage : and which, I think, was her whole independent Fortune." On the contrary, with a feigned objectivity that is supposed to be reported rather than quoted, JS writes in the *Autofrag* :—

This marriage was on both sides very indiscreet, for his wife brought

---

[5] A note inserted into the Fisher MS. in the Genealogical Office opposite the name of Jonathan the elder follows this in stating that he died in April, 1667.

[6] *Essay*, p. 24.

her husband little or no fortune, and his death, happening so suddenly
before he could make a sufficient establishment for his family ; And
his son (not then born) hath often been heard to say that he felt the
consequences of that marriage not only through the whole course of
his education, but during the greatest part of his life.

At the time when he wrote the *Autofrag* he seems to have been disposed to give us as little information as possible about his father. Yet
in later life he made no secret of what he was, and the account that he
gave to Mrs. Pilkington is to be found in her *Memoirs*[7]—the only detailed
account, incidentally, that we have of the circumstances of Jonathan's
death, although most of the subsequent writers ignore it. She says :—

> The Account I have frequently heard the Dean give of himfelf, was,
> that . . . his Father was a Lawyer, and returning from the Circuit,
> he unfortunately brought home the Itch with him, which he got
> by lying in fome foul Bed on the Road. Somebody advifed him
> to ufe Mercury to cure it, which Prefcription coft him his Life in
> a very few Days after his Return. The Dean was a pofthumous Son
> to this Gentleman, but, as he faid, came time enough to fave his
> Mother's Credit.

Orrery has evidently read Mrs. Pilkington, because he makes a marginal
note in almost the same concluding words in one of the Harvard copies
of his book. In a letter from Deane Swift to Nichols, quoted by Forster,[8]
the former states : " Her husband having died a very young man about
the time of the Spring Assizes in the year 1667, she was invited . . . etc."

The Circuit referred to by Mrs. Pilkington could be either the Winter
Assizes of 1666, or the Spring Assizes of 1667, but if we take it that her
statement and that of Deane Swift are not in conflict, we may assume
that the Spring Assizes are the ones referred to, and that, consequently,
the Steward must have died late in March, 1667. This now gives us a
third alternative time for this elusive event, but still no actual date—a
plethora of indeterminate information that should make us all the more
intrigued by the fact that—unlike his colleagues, Wale and Pilkington—
there is no record of his burial at all.

---

[7] *Memoirs*, vol. I, pp. 67-68. Attornies do not, in fact, go on Circuit.

[8] Forster, p. 24. Forster summarily dismisses Deane Swift's account, and also Spence's
Biographical Sketch, as " worthless," but gives no reasons for this characteristic
generalisation.

However, we are not by any means finished with the Black Book. After the death of the Steward—whenever it may have been—there is, for a time, considerable confusion amongst the entries. It seems that a number of important decisions of the Benchers and other business matters concerning the Inns had remained unrecorded since November, 1666. There had been some trouble with Lord Santry, one of the previous Treasurers, over some articles of plate belonging to the Society which he had taken possession of during his term of office, and would not return. There were some difficulties relating to the final accounts of the last two Stewards—Wale's as well as Swift's. New members had joined the Bar, and were now practising without any record of their admission. And there was also the important matter of the appointment of a new Steward—Stephen Pilkington.[9]

Particulars of all these matters were now written into the pages of the Black Book by new hands, sometimes in bulk. The fact that they were entered in order of urgency, rather than chronologically, strongly supports this suggestion of *ex post facto* inscription. First comes a Minute of a meeting dated the 25th April dealing with Santry's delinquency.[10] Next comes a petition from the widow Swift, followed by a ruling thereon dated the 15th April. Then there are petitions from Pilkington and from the widow Wale, followed by another minute, again dated the 15th April.

Finally, buried seventeen pages further on amongst the Accounts, in a position that shows it to be a 1667 document in spite of its ambiguous date,[11] we find a Minute concerning the admission of a barrister called John Wilson that is so puzzling that it is necessary to reproduce it here

---

[9] This Pilkington is not a relation of Laetitia, so far as is known.

[10] To the Minutes of the 25th April there is added an endorsement in Pilkington's own hand, dated the next day, and recording Santry's response to the order of the Benchers. It was obviously of importance that this should be placed on record, and the endorsement also shows, by the handwriting, that none of the minutes at this period were actually written by Pilkington.

[11] A date in the Black Book at this period, appearing as January, 1667, would presumably mean 1668. However, these Minutes are on a page that immediately follows some accounts for the Hilary Term, 1667, and are followed on the next pages by disbursements and accounts for the Trinity Term of 1667. These last accounts would have immediately followed the Hilary ones had the Minute not been written on the intervening page before the later Accounts were compiled. This makes it reasonably clear that, as suggested below, the date of the Minute was originally the 3rd June, 1667, and that this is the date on which the entry was actually made.

in another photograph. It appears to be dated 13 Junÿ (*sic*) 1667, and is signed by Pilkington in person, as Steward. If this means January—as it seems—the inference that Pilkington had been appointed as early as this month, leads us to a startling conclusion. What is even more peculiar is the fact that the 13th January, 1667, was an impossible date for the admission of a barrister for two very good reasons. Firstly, it was a Sunday ; secondly, it was in the legal vacation, and before the opening of the Hilary Term.

However, a closer examination of the page will reveal the fact that the date was originally written as 3 Junii (hence the presence of the double dot), and was later amended in a different ink by adding " 1 " to the figure and a downstroke to the ii, thus turning it into a y.[12] This puzzling alteration can best be explained by linking it up with the absence of any clerical work whatever at the Inns during the Hilary Term of 1667. The appearance of the Minute in such a place could well be the result of a complaint by Wilson that no record had been made in the books of the Inns of his admission to practice. Pilkington was instructed to record the meeting of the Hilary Term at which this admission had taken place. He had not himself been Steward at the time ; nevertheless he did this " by order of the Society "—signing his own name in lieu of the usual Benchers' signatures ; and he dated the entry with the date on which it was actually written—3rd June, 1667—to account for his own signature as Steward. But this, of course, did not regularise Wilson's earlier appearances in Court ; so somebody later changed the " June " to " January," and the " 3 " to " 13," in an attempt to date the thing back to the actual occasion of Wilson's admission. The fact that " 13 " should probably have been " 23 "—the second day of the Hilary Term, and a very likely date for the admission of a new barrister—is just part of the general confusion arising from the fact that there was no Steward at the Inns during the Hilary Term to minute the resolutions of the Benchers, or to collect the dues and cost of commons from the members of the Inns.

From this state of chaos we may reasonably conclude that Deane Swift's March date for the death of the Steward is also too late. Jonathan had no protracted illness—" dying suddenly "—" in a very few days

---

[12]There are several more unimportant amendments to the text of the Minute in the same darker ink.

13ᵈ Junij 1667.

Present

Lord Chancellor & Mr Justice Booth
Lord Justice Smith Mr Baron Potts
Mr of the Rolls Mr Sollicitor Genᵉ &
[Serjeant] Aston Knt
[Serjeant] Jerome Alexander
Mr Justice Stockton

Ordered

That [and] John Wilson Esqʳ Barrester at Law
be & is admitted of this Society, he first taking
the Oath of Supremacy in Chancery [and] &
afterwards entring into Comons & conforming
to yᵉ Rules & orders of the Society.

Entred the day & year above written
by order of the said Society
stephen pilkington
Steward

PILKINGTON'S MINUTE

after his return "—" his death happening so suddenly "—are some of
the references that are made to it. So there are no grounds for supposing
that his absence from the Inns in January/February was merely due to
a lengthy sickness from which he died in March or April.

Here, then, is the sum total of our information to date. Swift's father
probably died before the 23rd January, 1667, but if there was ever any
record of his death or burial it has somehow been lost, destroyed or
suppressed. He was, in short, a mystery . . . mysterious in his coming
to Ireland—in his employments there—in his qualifications and abilities
—in his private marriage and marriage settlement—and finally in his end.
Everything about him is enveloped in much the same fog. Only one thing
is certain—that what little we have been told about him from family
sources is not in accordance with the facts.

8

SWIFT'S BIRTHPLACE

BEFORE passing on to the earliest events of Swift's life, we must deal with the question of his birthplace, if only to show how, here too, a molehill of doubt has been turned into a mountain of argument, while the real issue lies almost unnoticed. Over the salient facts of the Dean's pre-history, many of which ought to be called in question, there has actually been very little dispute amongst the early authorities. It is true that Deane Swift has waxed indignant over Orrery's slighting references to the undistinguished record of the family, and is probably irked by his Lordship's myopia on the subject of Erick the Forester. But on the fundamentals—however absurd—there is, at least, the general agreement of silence. The canon of the *Autofrag* is never called in question.

Now, however, a grave difference of opinion is going to appear amongst the Victorian writers over the identification of the birthplace and its owner—a matter on which it is quite possible that the original obituary notice was perfectly right. The relevant parts of this notice, which is in *Faulkner's Dublin Journal* for Tuesday, 22nd October, 1745, run as follows :—

> . . . born in the Parish of St. Werburgh's, Dublin, the 30th. of November, 1667, at his Uncle, Counsellor Godwin Swift's house, in Hoey's Alley, which in those times was the general residence of the chief lawyers.

The real source of doubt lies not in any competition between Hoey's Court or Bull Alley, as the Rev. Mr. Carroll would have us believe, or as to whether the house was Godwin's or Abigail's. It arises through the particulars attached to Swift's name in the Trinity books.

> Eodem die (1682 Vicefsimo quarto die Aprilis) Jonathan Swift Pensionarius filius Jonathan Swift Natus annos Quartuordecim Natus

in Comitatu Dublinensis Educatus sub ferulâ Mri. Ridar Tutor St. Geo : Ashe.

He was a Pensioner of parentage on which there seems to have been some confusion in the original entry. He was over fourteen years of age in April, 1682. He was educated by Mr. Ridar—that is to say, at Kilkenny College. His Tutor in Trinity was to be St. George Ashe, later Bishop of Clogher. And he was born in the County of Dublin.

Now, Hoey's Court is not in the County of Dublin, but in the City. And although a mistake might have been made in the entry by the addition of the words " in comitatu", it seems an odd sort of mistake to make. Such errors usually consist in the omission of necessary words, not in the addition of unnecessary ones.[1]

The Rev. Mr. Carroll, having argued that Hoey's Alley means Bull Alley and not Hoey's Court, next goes on to insist that, as JS is described by Trinity as having been born in the County, he cannot have been born in St. Werburgh's. Nor, we may add, could he have been born in Bull Alley. For St. Bride's Parish, although outside the ambit of the original City walls, was also a City Parish, and is listed as such in the Poll Tax Rolls.

However, the point on which we can be certain is that JS, himself, usually pointed out his Uncle's old house, 7 Hoey's Court, as the place of his birth, and wanted it to be accepted as such, although he was not averse, whenever it suited him, to telling quite a different story. In the circumstances, it is not surprising, only four years after his death, to find Mrs. Pilkington reporting a certain amount of controversy in the matter.[2]

It has been a Matter of Difpute amongſt the Learned, whether *England* or *Ireland* had the Honour of giving to the World this admirable Perſon. . . . And tho' in reality 'tis of no great Importance where a Man is born ; yet as the *Iriſh* are the eternal Ridicule of the *Engliſh* for their Ignorance, I am proud *Hibernia* had the Happineſs of producing this brilliant Wit, to redeem the Credit of the Country. . . .

The Account I have frequently heard the Dean give of himſelf, was, that he was born in *Hoy's - Alley*, in *Warburgh's* Pariſh, *Dublin*. . . .

It will be noticed that she mentions no date for his birth, an omission

---

[1]The original Register of which the Senior Lecturer's book is a copy cannot be found in the Muniment Room. Peculiarities in these entries may, therefore, be mistakes of the copyist, and are perhaps not in the original.

[2]*Memoirs*, vol. I, p. 67.

that is repaired by Orrery[3] two years later, in words that may or may not
have been taken simply from the Obituary Notice :—

> . . . many of his friends imagined him a native of *England*. . . .
> He was born in *Dublin, November* the thirtieth in the year ſixteen
> hundred and ſixty ſeven. . . . But perhaps, he tacitly hoped to inſpire
> different nations with a contention for his birth : at leaſt in his angry
> moods, when he was peviſh, and provoked at the ingratitude of
> *Ireland*, he was frequently heard to ſay, " I am not of this vile country,
> I am an Engliſhman ". Such an aſſertion, although meant figuratively,
> was often received literally : and the report was ſtill farther aſſiſted
> by Mr. POPE, who in one of his letters has this expreſſion, " Tho'
> one or two of our friends are gone, ſince you ſaw your *native country*,
> there remain a few". But Dr. SWIFT, in his cooler hours, never
> denied his country : on the contrary, he frequently mentioned, and
> pointed out the houſe where he was born.

Furthermore in a holograph note on one of the interleaved pages in
the Harvard copy of his book (opp. p. 6) Orrery has noted 'Hoey's
Alley' opposite the account of his birth, and added that whenever JS
was in a good mood, through being saluted respectfully in the street,
he would point out the precise house to Orrery himself.

On this sober and convincing confirmation of Mrs. Pilkington's recollection, Dr. Delany[4] makes the following comment :—

> Your account of SWIFT'S birth, parentage and education, is ſo juſt,
> that, I believe, nothing is to be added to it.

There is as yet, no confirmation of the Obituary as to whose house it
was, and it is left to Deane Swift in 1755 to elaborate his grandfather's
share in the transaction, while neither mentioning nor denying that the
events took place in Hoey's Court.[5]

> MR. SWIFT dying about two Years after his Marriage, before he
> could make a ſufficient Eſtabliſhment for his Family, left his Widow
> in very narrow Circumſtances. But, her Huſband's eldeſt Brother,
> Counſellor GODWIN SWIFT, received her into his Family with

---

[3] *Remarks*, p. 4.
[4] *Observations*, p. 48.
[5] *Essay*, p. 23.

great Affection; where, about feven Months after the Deceafe of her Hufband, fhe became the Mother of her fecond child, the famous DR. JONATHAN SWIFT, who was born upon the 30th. Day of November, 1667.

. . . [6]Sometimes he would declare, that he was not born in *Ireland* at all; and feem to lament his Condition, that he fhould be looked upon as a Native of that Country; and would infift, that he was ftolen from *England* when a Child, and brought over to *Ireland* in a Band-box. . . .

. . . [7]Soon after Dr. SWIFT had been ftolen from *England*, and brought over to *Ireland* in a Band-box, he was fent at fix Years of Age to the School of *Kilkenny*. . . .

Hawkesworth[8] in the same year tells an almost identical story of Godwin's hospitality, but it is left to Lyon to add the date and the address in two marginal notes. Hawkesworth also adds:

It has been generally believed that *Swift* was born in *England*.

And he then goes on to correct this impression.

This story of an English birthplace seems to have been confined largely to oral gossip, and the only place where it found its way into print was in Spence's *Anecdotes*.[9] Here, JS is reported to have told his friend Pope that he was born in Leicester, and that his father had been the Incumbent of a Parish in Herefordshire. Pope related these details to Spence, who published them. A sceptical footnote from an Editor is added later. The story is then repeated by the great Dr. Johnson, in his *Lives of the Poets*, who adds very characteristically:—

During his life the place of his birth was undetermined. He was contented to be called an Irishman by the Irish; but would occasionally call himself an Englishman. The question may, without much regret, be left in the obscurity in which he delighted to involve it.

Sheridan and Scott repeat the original Irish account, but the latter goes a step further, and identifies for the first time the actual house in Hoey's Court by a number, its position, and by its then Occupant—a Mrs.

[6]*Essay*, p. 27.
[7]Ibid., p. 31.
[8]Hawkesworth, pp. 4-6.
[9]*Anecdotes*, vol. II, p. 273.

Jackson. By 1820 the possibility of an English birthplace was fading away into the past, and we find Monck Mason[10] attributing it, not to Swift's deliberate misrepresentations, but simply to a misunderstanding of the Whitehaven incident in the Dean's childhood, which will be referred to in the next chapter,

> —a mistake to which his own expressions did, without his so intending it, in some degree contribute.

In 1849, Sir William Wilde, in his *Closing Years of Dean Swift's Life*, gives us an elaborate description of the Alley, and identifies the house once again—although neither his nor Scott's description tallies with the No. 7 as shown in the Ordnance Survey map of 1839. A study of Wilson's Dublin Directories does not make this discrepancy any clearer.

It will be seen that up to this date, apart from Spence's hearsay, which everybody chooses to disregard, there has been no real controversy amongst the biographers over the three main points, namely, the date of his birth—the house in which it took place—and the fact that this house was Uncle Godwin's. Not everybody tells the whole story, but nobody's account is inconsistent with anybody else's, except the Trinity books, to which nobody refers. And although JS himself seems to have coquetted with Leicester, everybody agrees that in his less anti-Irish moments, he always returned to his same old story. Whether true or not, the canon might have remained fixed in this form, had not Mr. Forster entered the scene in 1875 with a lively determination to stop at nothing in the task of discrediting Deane Swift, whose book he describes as having[11]

> a minute particularity which will be always found to characterise his alleged facts in the exact ratio of their unlikelihood, or (if likely) of the impossibility of their being known to him.

In other words, Deane Swift is to not have it either way. If his account is particularised, his story is unlikely, while if it is likely, the author could not possibly have known about it. This writer is not to Mr. Forster's taste.

So, beginning with a misstatement of his own to the effect that the

---

[10]Monck Mason, p. 230.
[11]Forster, p. 24 n.

site of the house in Hoey's Court, at the date of his writing, was " taken into the Castle grounds",[12] he then sweeps aside the whole account of the reception of the sorrowing widow into Uncle Godwin's household, by stating that the Hoey's Court premises belonged to Abigail, and not to Godwin, who presumably lived elsewhere. Deane Swift's story " would not be worth adverting to. . . . . if it had not imposed on Nichols and others, and if it were not an illustration of the entire untrustworthiness of all Mr. Deane Swift's family flourishes." He concludes with that intimidating formula : " no careful enquirer has adopted it."

This formula, " No careful enquirer has adopted it ", is of course calculated to put an abrupt end to further argument, and is a type of literary terrorism that is not unknown today. In the present case it might also be described in other terms, because up to the date of Forster's remarks, so far from anybody having contradicted Deane Swift on this particular subject, no enquirer, careful or otherwise, had ever questioned his story—a fact that must have been within Forster's knowledge. However, such is the effect of his reputation, that the subject of Swift's birthplace is never again quite the same carefree international dispute. It becomes an intra-mural one. For close behind Forster follows Sir Henry Craik, who at the same time is being fed from below with supplementary misinformation by the Rev. W. G. Carroll, Vicar of St. Bride's.

This Mr. Carroll is the clergyman who—as we have seen—was anxious to claim for his otherwise undistinguished Parish (amalgamated with St. Werburgh's at the end of his incumbency) the honour of possessing the Dean's birthplace. In advance of the book which he was then in the process of writing, he provided Craik[13] with a new address for Godwin Swift in Bride Street or Bull Alley, which Sir Henry happily adopted, with a further gloss of his own.

So now we read in Craik that Godwin's house was " close by in Chancery Lane or Bride Street". It should be noted that Craik does not thereby abandon Hoey's Court as Swift's birthplace, much as the Vicar

[12]A public pathway called Castle Steps lay between the outer wall of Dublin Castle and Hoey's Court, which fact a glance at a map would have revealed. In this error Forster is followed by Craik.

[13]See Craik's Preface (p. xiv) for proof of his source. Carroll's book, *Succession of Clergy in St. Bride's &c., Dublin*, was published in 1884, two years after Craik. We have already gone into the value of his arguments. Craik's additions are on p. 9.

of St. Bride's would like him to. It is Godwin who is shifted elsewhere, and in this unsubstantial project of Mr. Carroll, the new path is followed even by such meticulous biographers as Carl Van Doren, Hone and Rossi, and Emil Pons. The next step, of course, is to combine Deane Swift's statement that his distinguished cousin was born in his grandfather's unidentified home, with Craik's statement that this home was in Bride Street or Chancery Lane, and we have at once two entirely new birthplaces, and Mr. Carroll's dream has come true.

The rest is confusion and repetition, and not always even correct repetition, as in the case of Lecky, who gives the birthday as the 30th March, and one of the best of the recent biographers, Mr. Bertram Newman, who distinguishes himself in his opening sentence by saying :

" Jonathan Swift was born at 6 (*sic*) Hoey's Court."

Actually, all that emerges today from this heap of confusion is the fact that the Obituary Notice accurately reports the general belief of the best-informed people of the period, which information, ultimately, is solely that of Swift himself. 7 Hoey's Court was the birthplace in which the Dean—after some doubts about the matter—wished us to believe. So also, the 30th November, 1667, receives his final vote as his official birthday. There is no evidence on either point apart from his own word, except the evidence of the Trinity books which, if correct, contradicts him about the birthplace, and indicates that he was born neither in the Parish of St. Werburgh's nor in that of St. Bride's, but somewhere in the County.

The fact that such information was given to Trinity either by Swift himself at the age of fourteen, or by some other party (probably Uncle Godwin) on his behalf, long before its truth or falsity could be regarded as having any significance, argues strongly for the fact that it was probably not a lie, in so far as it is not merely a mistake of the copyist.

The fact that the Dean had the Parish records searched—and in particular, those of St. Werburgh's—may mean, of course, that he never really knew for certain where he was born—an ignorance in which he would be entirely at one with ourselves. But if a conclusion must be reached by the present writer, it is as follows :—Swift's concern over the Parish Registers was not about place, but about date. After all, the fact that he was baptised in a particular Church proves little about his birthplace. Shaw was baptised in St. Bride's, but he was not born in that Parish.

But the fact that Swift was baptised in a certain year may be of very great significance. On the balance of probability, Swift probably knew where he was born, and the necessary information on this point was given to Trinity at a time when others were still around—including Uncle Godwin, who remembered the answer as well as Swift did. It was not in the City. It was some place elsewhere—in some house that the Dean would prefer us not to know about. But at a later stage of his life, when time had dimmed the likelihood of contradiction, and his friends and admirers wished to know all about him, he said that it was in the most creditable place—his uncle's house in Hoey's Court.

9

THE WHITEHAVEN INCIDENT

THERE is substantial agreement about the next phase of Swift's peculiar history. It seems that his nurse, being a woman—name unknown—of Whitehaven in Cumberland, had occasion to return there not long after Swift's birth. Mrs. Pilkington, who is presumably reporting the story as told to her by the Dean in later life, begins :[1]

> He was given to an *Irish* woman to nurſe, whoſe Huſband being in *England*, and writing to her to come to him. . . .

In the other, and much earlier version, contained in the *Autofrag*, JS, himself, puts it this way:

> . . . when he was a year old, an event happened to him that seems very unusuell; for his Nurse who was a woman of Whitehaven, being under an absolute necefsity of seeing one of her relations who was then extremely sick, and from whom she expected a Legacy. . . .

> . . . as is usual among Irish nurses (continues Sheridan)[2] she bore such an affection to the child, that she could not think of going without him.

So, unknown to the widowed mother, she stole him on board ship, and brought him with her to that cross-channel destination, where he remained for about three years by the direction—strangely enough—of the distracted parent. The reason given for this surprising complaisance on the part of the mother was that she was so concerned for the health of her child, that she would not allow it to undergo the hazards of a return sea-voyage until it was of riper years. So the infant was left in the care of this kidnapper, who looked after it so well that on its return to Dublin, it could spell, and before the age of five, could read any Chapter in the Bible. For this the nurse[3]

---

[1]*Memoirs* vol. I, p. 68.
[2]Sheridan, *Life*, p. 20.
[3]*Memoirs*, vol. I, pp. 68-69.

. . . eafily obtained a Pardon, both on account of the Joy (the mother) conceived at feeing her only Son again, when fhe had in a manner loft all Hope of it ; as alfo, that it was plain, the Nurfe had no other motive for ftealing him, but pure Affection, which Women of *Ireland* generally have in as eminent Degree, for the Children they nurfe, as for their own Offspring.

There is some small disagreement over the age at which JS could first read any chapter in the Bible. In the Cobbe copy he apparently amended the " three " of the *Autofrag* to " two." Then he changed it to " almost three," and then finally crossed out the word " almost." Hawkesworth changes this figure to " five," and Dr. Lyon, in his amendments, takes a modest middle course and alters it to " four."

Duhigg,[4] without stating any authority, gives an entirely different reason for the abduction. He says that the nurse " was not paid by his impoverifhed parent ", and that this was why she took the child away to England.

Mrs. Pilkington is at variance with most of the other early reporters when she says that the mother was still in Dublin when the child was eventually brought back. Orrery states categorically[5] that Abigail

about two years after her hufband's death quitted *Ireland* and retired to *Leicefter*, the place of her nativity.

So that when the child of three or four was returned to Ireland . . . " in a Band-box ", to recall Deane Swift's whimsy, the anxious mother was already long gone to her old home, to which, one presumes, this unusually large receptacle containing the child could easily have been sent without the hazard of any second sea crossing whatsoever.

Deane Swift makes no mention of the return of Abigail to Leicester, but Hawkesworth[6] is quite definite about it, in words that he is not merely borrowing from Orrery. After mentioning Abigail's departure, he says

. . . but her fon was again carried to *Ireland* by his nurfe, and replaced under the protection of his Uncle *Godwin*.

---

[4]Duhigg, p. 220.
[5]*Remarks*, p. 6.
[6]Hawkesworth, p. 5.

Lyon evidently agrees, as he merely amends this sentence by writing " brought into " in place of " again carried to ", and he adds a long marginal note about the Dean's affectionate remembrance of Whitehaven which, if true, must mean that he was well past his third birthday before he was brought back. Forster—with Craik as usual following him—leaves the mother in Dublin until shortly after the child is returned, but in doing so they have only the authority of Mrs. Pilkington, and are flying in the face of everybody else who mentions the matter. So it seems reasonably clear that JS cannot have remembered having seen his mother at all before he reached the age of twenty-one, when, as will be seen, he first went to Leicester.

The truth of the matter seems to be that the child was shipped out of the country soon after it was born, and was not brought back again until after its mother had returned to her old home. The contradictory explanations of this significant incident that are presented to us by JS and his friends only serve to convince us finally that there is some secret about his birth, of vital importance to Swift, that is being concealed behind this accumulation of lies, exaggerations and plain nonsense. This is more than boasting or mere social snobbery. There is definitely something here that we are not supposed to find out for ourselves.

One immediate suspicion must be that it has got something to do with Swift's parentage. Why else should there be such shilly-shallying about both the place and date of his birth and the reason for the early removal of the child elsewhere? We have seen that Swift was in grave doubt about giving us the year of his birth. And this is no mere forgetfulness, for if we study the original holograph we must notice the heavily deleted marginal note opposite the reference to St. Andrew's Day. An examination of this will show that he originally wrote the page without giving any year. He then changed his mind and wrote 1667 in the margin. He then changed his mind again, and tried to render this date illegible. But he did not quite succeed in doing so, and one can still just make out the curves of the sixes and the downward strokes of the one and the seven. If the original is held up to the light this deleted date is more evident than in the photograph.

Why then was Swift in doubt about giving us so obvious a piece of information? It was because he did not know whether there was any extant public record that would disclose the date of his father's death. This is one of the reasons why he employed Lyon to search the Registers.

To his Grace the Lord Chancellor and the right hono[ble] the Judges and Benchers
of the honorable Society of the Kings Inns

The humble petition of Abigaill Swift widd

Humbly Sheweth

That it haue now pleased God to take away yo[r] pet[rs] husband the late Steward
of this honorable Society unexpectedly, and yo[r] pet[r] being left a disconsolate widdow
hath this affliccon added to her that there is due to her from the severall members
of this honorable Society viz Comons and Cast Comons aboue sixscore pounds
w[ch] money she is not wayes able to gett in w[th]out yo[r] honors assistance

That yo[r] pet[r] haue desired her late husbands brother Jo[hn] Swift to helpe her
in getting in her said money, who hath manifested himselfe very willing to
assist her but hath beene objected by severall persons vpon the like that he hath
not authority to receaue the same

Now for as much as yo[r] pet[r] hath not friend next to yo[r] honors, but
her said brother to rely vpon, and that he yo[r] pet[rs] said brother can not
be friend her w[th]out the be authorized by yo[r] honors orders to y[e] purpose

May it therefore please yo[r] honors to grant yo[r] pet[r] an order
wherein the said Jo[hn] Swift may be authorized and appointed
to colect and gather in yo[r] pet[rs] said money

And yo[r] petitioner shall euer pray &c

ABIGAIL SWIFT'S MEMORIAL

And when he was assured, in one way or another, that no such record could come to light, then and only then, did he willingly reveal to his friends the year of his own birth—1667.

The reason for this shiftiness is immediately understood if Jonathan Swift the elder was not his father. Indeed, once we have drawn our inferences from the Black Book, it must become perfectly evident that the Steward *could* not have been his father. A child born on the 30th November is hard put to it to claim a father who died prior to January the 23rd in the same year. And even if this deadline is still regarded as a matter of surmise, there is a further point that makes the matter conclusive. This concerns the state of affairs in early April, 1667, disclosed by Abigail Swift's Petition to the Benchers that appears in the Black Book, and was ruled upon on the 15th of that month.

A certain amount of nonsense has been written by several of the Biographers about the heartless treatment of this suffering widow by the authorities at King's Inns. This has been based upon a misunderstanding of the prayer of this memorial, and of her subsequent petition that was ruled on at a meeting on the 31st January, 1668.

As we have seen, it was amongst the duties of the Steward to collect the rents, subscriptions and dining fees from members of the Inns together with fees paid for admissions, and to account for these to his employers by means of terminal accounts. During the Hilary Term of 1667 nobody had collected anything. A new Steward, however, was not appointed until April, and he, of course, was not responsible for the collection of debts due to the Inns prior to his taking office. So naturally it was incumbent on the representatives of the late Steward to get this done—a task that was eventually undertaken by Uncle William, on behalf of his pregnant sister-in-law. The members of the Inns, however, showed some natural reluctance to pay subscriptions and arrears of commons to anybody who chose to demand them, and who was not in a position to give a valid receipt. So after some fruitless efforts on the part of William to collect these sums, the widow did the obvious thing. She applied to the Benchers for an order officially authorising William to demand these dues, which order she was given.

During the following Trinity Term (as appears from her second Petition) William collected as much of these arrears as he could, within the time he had to spare for such a task. He also prepared an account, which was filed in the Trinity Term, and a photograph of this account is here shown. However out of the sums in hand, belonging to the Inns, Abigail paid some of her late husband's personal debts and funeral expenses, with the result that when the account was made up, the estate was short in the sum of £12 18s. 11d. which was still due to the Inns. Over £100 of further arrears were still uncollected, and her second Petition, which must have been drafted in the Michaelmas Term, asked that the amount due from the estate be taken out of any further arrears yet to be collected by William or the new Steward, and that the estate of the dead man be relieved from the burden thereof. As the money that was due was at no time the property of the late Steward, but had been collected from the members of the Inn, and then applied improperly to the payment of debts and funeral expenses, it was not at all ungenerous of the Benchers to agree to such a proposal, which, in fact, amounted to a present to the estate of the balance not paid over.

As the second Petition has only been referred to in very general terms in those books that mention it at all, a transcript is here given, as some authority for these facts as above described. From the reference to the account having been presented " last term ", it must have been drafted before the end of the Michaelmas Term of 1667. Blanks are left at certain points where the holograph is difficult to decipher, and most of the abbreviations have been expanded for convenience in reading.

To his Grace the Lord Chancellor and the Right Honble the Judges & Benchers of y honble Society of the King's Inns
The humble Petition of Abigaill Swift Widdow Humbly Showeth
That your Petitioner's late husband Jonathan Swift being late Steward to this honble Society and dying suddenly your honours were pleased to authorise your Petitioner's husband's Brother William Swift to gather up for your Petitioner y Arrears of Comons & Cost Commons that were then due to your Petitioner and the Pensions Remaining then likewise in Arrear to this house and also to make up the accounts of your Petitioner's said late husband.
That the said William Swift hath last Term in obedience to the Commands of Sir Wm. Aston present Treasurer of this honble Society . . . . . . in y account of your Petitioner's said husband upon the Balance of which account your Petitioner appears to be indebted to this house in the sum of £12–18–11

An Account of what moneys were received
by Jonathan Swift Late steward of the
honoble sotiety of the Kings Innes upon the
acco:t of the house

Rents

		l	s	d
Received of my Lord Chancellor for a yeares rent ending		05	00	00
Rec:d of my Lord Cheife Baron for a yeares ending at Easter 1666		05	00	00
Rec:d of the Master of the Rolls for two yeares rent due ut supra		04	00	00
Rec:d of S:r William Aston for one yeare and a halfes rent due ut supra		01	10	00
Rec:d of m:r Carleton a yeares rent due ut supra		01	00	00
Rec:d of m:r John Brice for my Lords Loitg:ors Lodgings for a yeare due ut supra		01	00	00

—10—00

Admissions

		l	s	d
Ffor 5 admissions in Hillary dearme 1665 ab suppl: fol: 197		07	06	08
Ffor 4 admissions in Easter dearme 1666		05	13	04
Ffor 2 admissions in Trinity dearme 1666		05	00	08

6-8

Pensions

		l	s	d
Hillary dearme 1665 — 104 pensions		08	13	04
Easter dearme 1666 — 102 pensions		08	10	00
Trinity dearme 1666 — 098 pensions		08	03	04
Mickelmas dearme 1666 — 085 pensions		07	01	08
Ffillarey dearme 1666 — 079 pensions		06	11	08
		70	16	08

—00—00

That the said **Wm.** Swift Notwithstanding his more than ordinary endeavours hath gathered up for your Petitioner but a very inconsiderable sum of Money which your Petitioner hath been forced to expend in paying such debts as. . . . your Petitioner's late husband had contracted in his sickness and your Petitioner had contracted in burying him.

That there remains still due to your Petitioner from several of the Members of this honble Society for Commons and cost Commons near y sum £100 & in particular from the Honorable y (name cut out) about the sum of £76.

Now forasmuch as the said William Swift is much taken up with his own concerns as. . . . is not at leisure to gather and Collect up the remaining debts due to your Petitioner so suddenly as to raise money enough thereout for payment of the said £12–18–11 so due by your Petitioner as aforesaid in the short time of your Petitioner's . . . . will be expected from this honorable Bench.

May it therefore please your Honours to direct the new Steward of this honble Society to. . . . and choose out of such debts as still are remaining due to your Petitioner as aforesaid and particularly if your Honours so please out of those due from y honble y Benchers as being the most solvent and many indeed whereof might have been gathered before this time had the said William Swift had leisure so to do, so many debts as will suffice to pay the said £12–18–11 and to gather and Collect the same for that end also to further Impower the same William Swift to Collect for your Petitioner such debts as shall then be remaining so soon as he can be at leisure to attend the same. And your Petitioner as in Duty bound shall Pray.

It was a long and complicated proceeding, and anybody who has ever had any experience in the administration of an estate, even under modern conditions, must be aware of the labour and delays involved in collecting such debts and in preparing such accounts. A petition such as the one that was presented on the 15th April must have been prepared some time beforehand, and after at least some weeks of effort, firstly, on the part of Abigail and subsequently on that of her brother-in-law. The fact that the previous Steward (Wale's) widow was still in the same quandary is an eloquent confirmation of the amount of time required for such transactions.

When, then, must Jonathan have died, in order that the discovery of his indebtedness, and the winding up of his affairs, could be in the advanced condition shown by this first Petition in the early days of April ? At a very modest estimate, at least three months earlier, which precisely confirms our previous idea that he must have died before the 23rd January, and that this is why none of his duties were carried out during the Hilary Term. His death before this date is, in fact, the reason why these cost commons were not collected at the proper time.

If Jonathan's last act before he left this mortal sphere had been the begetting of this child—a virile gesture for a dying man with an itch— and if his sorrowing widow, hardly waiting to bury him, had first spent two weeks in promptly demanding these debts, and then if her brother-in-law had suffered rebuffs for an equally brief period before applying for the assistance of the Benchers, they might just have managed to draft and present this Petition in time to be ruled on by the 15th April. This is admitted. But how probable is it ?

The more reasonable answer is that the elder Jonathan was well and truly dead before the conception of the future Dean, and that this fact is at the back of all the dissimulation and contradictions that infest everything that we are told about his birth and background. This is why he was promptly shipped out of the country soon after he was born. This is how this cuckoo of incomparable brilliance appeared so strangely in a nest of Swifts. This is the only point from which we can start out to face what is yet to come, without finding the confusion becoming worse.

Who his father actually was, is quite another problem. It is here sufficient to submit that the father who could not have been his, was this obscure upper servant of the Benchers, Jonathan Swift, the elder.

SCHOOLBOY AND UNDERGRADUATE

WHOEVER the father may have been, it was to his Uncle Godwin that he was brought, and at six years of age he was sent from this foster-parent's home to Kilkenny College, where he had the benefit of what was probably the best teaching then available in Ireland, until the age of fourteen. Then he entered Dublin University as a Pensioner—that is to say as a paying pupil, in contradistinction to a Sizar, who would have to perform certain menial tasks in return for his education. At Kilkenny he had Congreve as a fellow pupil, two years his junior.

The official view is that it was this Uncle Godwin who provided for the cost of this expensive schooling. If this was so, Godwin must have been a man of unusual benevolence, because he had fourteen sons of his own to provide for, as well as three daughters ; and although his descendants tend to boast about the size of his income whenever they wish to boast, and deplore his hard-up condition whenever it suits them to pull a poor mouth, there is little indication that Godwin was a man of great wealth. He sent only three of his own sons to Trinity College, two of them from day-schools in Dublin, and it was only his eldest son, Thomas I, who enjoyed the privilege of attending both the University[1] and the " Eton of Ireland "—as Banim calls the school at Kilkenny.

As regards the education of Godwin's own sons, three of them died young—Robert (b. 1672), Joseph (b. 1677) and Dryden (b. 1680)—and are not included in William's Funeral Entry of 1698. Willoughby, Godwin II, Robert, Deane I, and Joseph, because of their ages, might have entered Kilkenny before the Registers began. There is no record one way or the

---

[1]Dublin University and Trinity College are synonymous terms, so far as this account is concerned. It is a University of one College. The original foundation of the school at Kilkenny in the 16th century was by Pierce Butler, eighth Earl of Ormond, and his wife. It came to an end about the beginning of the 17th century, but was reopened by the first Duke of Ormond in November, 1666. In 1684, when Lord Lieutenant, Ormond granted it a Charter, and provided for a register to be kept. Boys might enter from seven years of age, although not many as young as this actually did, and fewer still at the age of six. JS was there before the existing Registers commence.

other. But none of them was at the University. Meade and Michael went to Trinity, but got their secondary education in Dublin. Dryden, William, Christopher, Thomas II, Edward and John were neither at Kilkenny nor at College.

One might expect, therefore, a few friendly references to such a benefactor from JS in his later years. But just the opposite is the case. He never cherished the memory of his Uncle Godwin, and he blamed him in the *Autofrag* for his poor scholastic record—

> . . . by the ill treatment of his nearest Relations, he was so discouraged and sunk in his spirits that he too much neglected his Academick studyes . . .

and he even ran down his legal abilities, as we have seen.

In a note[2], Scott describes, on the authority of Theophilus Swift (a son of Deane Swift, the biographer), a nasty scene at a dinner party with Dr. Whittingham, the Archdeacon of Dublin, where JS remarked, in reply to an enquiry about his upbringing, " He gave me the education of a dog." Whittingham indignantly replied: " You have not the gratitude of a dog." It would seem from Swift's attitude towards his uncle that he must have been a peculiarly ungrateful person. Yet, strangely enough, we will shortly see that he did express some gratitude towards his Uncle William, who apparently did much less for him, and at a later stage of his career we will find him carrying gratitude and loyalty to fantastic lengths in regard to the fallen political leaders who had done nothing of consequence for him at all.

Mrs. Pilkington[3] reports :

> Doctor *Swift* very well obferves, that many Perfons have done a *juſt*, many a *generous*, but few a *grateful* Act.

The explanation for this inconsistency is, of course, that he owed his Uncle Godwin nothing. The latter did not stint himself to give the orphan son of a younger brother a better education than he gave his own family. He was merely an ungracious channel through which the cost of this child's upbringing was paid for by another source.

The records of Trinity College disclose JS as having been a very unsatisfactory scholar—a fact that he never attempted to deny or conceal,

[2]Scott, vol. I, p. 14.
[3]*Memoirs*, vol. III, p. 8.

whatever reasons he may have given for this phenomenon. In the *Autofrag* —writing of himself, as usual, in the third person—he says :

> . . . although he lived with great Regularity and due Observance of the statutes, he was stopped of his Degree for Dulness and Insufficiency. . . .

This matches up rather oddly with the report of that fantastic character, Jacky Barrett, Vice-Provost of the College, who, on the authority of the Buttery Books, stated in 1808,[4] that Swift's college life was studded with a long series of punishments for disciplinary offences, including " upwards of seventy weeks " of penalties over a period of less than two years. Whatever may have been his behaviour in his undergraduate days, as a graduate student he was given to neglect of compulsory Chapel, to the cutting of lectures, town-haunting, failing to turn up for evening roll-call, insolence and contumacious conduct towards authority, and—most probably—to some of his earliest exercises in the writing of abusive scandal. All of which culminated in his temporary suspension from Commons, and in a humiliating apology which he was forced to make on his knees in Hall before Dr. Owen Lloyd, the Junior Dean. He was granted his degree of B.A. *speciali gratiae*—that is to say, by special dispensation, a mark of dishonour that still remains upon the books, and for which he bore his Alma Mater an unquenchable grudge to the last.

> I am ashamed to have been more obliged in a few weeks to strangers (at Oxford) than ever I was in seven years to Dublin College.

is what JS wrote in a letter to his Uncle William.[5]

His well-wishers, from Lyon and Delany down to the present day, find it hard to believe that his limping degree was really the result of stupidity, and, even if they do not follow Forster's example by pooh-poohing Barrett altogether, they blame it on the curriculum of the day, in which they feel no high-spirited and original intelligence could possibly have been much interested.

> When Swift was entered at the University—says Scott[6]—the usual studies of the period were required of him, and of these, some were very ill-suited to his genius. Logic, then deemed a principal object of learning, was in vain presented to his notice ; for his disposition

---

[4]Barrett, pp. 11-15.
[5]*Correspondence*, vol. I, p. 10.
[6]Scott, vol. I, pp. 15-16.

altogether rejected the learned sophistry of Smiglecius, Keckermannus, Burgersdicius, and other ponderous worthies now hardly known by name; nor could his tutor ever pursuade him to read three pages in one of them, though some acquaintance with the commentators of Aristotle was absolutely necessary at passing examination for his degrees.

But Swift, himself, will have none of this, and when Mrs. Pilkington questioned his story that he had been stopped of his degree as a dunce, her report continues as follows[7] :—

> When I heard the Dean relate this Circumſtance, for I ſet down nothing but what I had from his own Mouth, I told him, I ſuppoſed he had been idle; but he affirmed the contrary; aſſuring me, he was really dull, which, if true, is very ſurpriſing.

To Deane Swift,[8] who alleges that he made the same denial of his idleness, JS is reported to have insisted " that he could never underſtand *Logick*, *Phyſicks*, *Metaphyſicks*, *Natural Philoſophy*, *Mathematicks*, or any Thing of that Sort."

Barrett's *Essay on the Earlier Part of the Life of Swift* was first published in Vol. I of Nichol's Edition of Swift's *Works*, and reissued the same year (1808) in separate form. Forster[9] devotes ten pages and a facsimile to a long attack on Dr. Barrett's work, which he describes as " rakings in the College books "—an expression that presumably means research resulting in facts that are not entirely welcome. Having disposed of the Vice-Provost, he then passes on to Taine's *History of English Literature*, the author of which is rash enough to show some regard for Dr. Barrett, and Forster then concludes with the hope that " students of English literature in that (Edinburgh) Academy have safer guidance than the brilliant but too often baseless fancies of M. Taine." Sir Henry Craik, following, as usual, the footprints in the snow, dismisses Barrett's book as " fruitless."[10] It might be truer to say that, like JS, they are both suffering from a surfeit of fruit. If Swift did not write the Tripos that Barrett prints, there must have been somebody else in College with an equal gift for powerful scurrility. And if it was not Swift, but his inoffensive cousin, who was made to suffer this humiliation in Hall, there must have been some other reason for the venom with which the Dean pursued

---

[7]*Memoirs*, vol. I, p. 69.
[8]*Essay*, p. 32.
[9]Forster, pp. 32-41.
[10]Craik, p. 14.

Dr. Lloyd for the rest of his life. See *A Short Character of the Earl of Wharton*[11] for an example of Swift's way with his enemies, and with Dr. Lloyd in particular. In this he alleges that Lloyd obtained his Deanery by marrying a whore of whom the Lord Lieutenant was tired. Dr. Baldwin, a contemporary who later became Provost, is reported as saying[12] that Swift was " remarkable for nothing else in College except for making a good fire." Dr. Baldwin, however, was a strong Whig.

Delany, in his *Observations*[13] agrees, and refers to Orrery's

> account of the uncreditable manner of taking his Bachelor of Arts degree . . . which he hath been often heard to ſay, was owing to his being a dunce. And he explained himſelf in the following manner : That he looked upon the ſtudy of Greek and Latin to be downright pedantry, and beneath a gentleman. That poetry and plays and novels, were the only polite accompliſhments.

In all of this, we can see an amusing and very human trait in JS, when accounting for an aspect of his past life which he was well aware could not be hushed up. His inferior degree stands upon the Trinity books for all to see. So he advertises the fact to all his friends, and turns it into a joke on both Trinity and Oxford. The Oxford aspect will be seen in a later chapter. For the moment it is sufficient to point out that he had no objection whatever to its being known that Trinity College considered him dull and insufficient ; because, whatever his other shortcomings may have been, Swift was obviously not a dunce, and to classify him so, reflects more upon the College than upon himself. But he has every objection to being described as insolent and undisciplined, because this is precisely what he was.

Orrery considers (on one of his interleaved pages already referred to) that JS qualified for his degree of Master of Arts in 1688. But " eighty eight being the year of the revolution and of particular confusion in Ireland, it is to be supposed that *Swift* could not take his Master's degree till the year 1692, the date of his letter to his Uncle William." This is probably based on some more misinformation from Swift to Orrery, intended to improve on his College record. As will be seen, he was in Dublin in 1690, and in a position to take his M.A. then, had he been qualified.

---

[11]Shakespeare Head SWIFT, vol. III, p. 182.
[12]Craik, p. 16 n.
[13]*Observations*, p. 48.

REFUGEE

THE next great upheaval in Swift's career comes during the latter part of 1688, or early in 1689, when the throne of James II was tottering, and attempts were being made to shore it up by the transfer of Irish Catholic Regiments into England. Panic was spreading amongst the Protestant minority in Ireland—a panic that culminated in a scare that there was a plan on foot to repeat the religious massacre of 1641 on the 9th December, 1688.

It is another curious feature of all of the early biographers that none of them mention the coming of the Williamite War as the immediate reason for Swift's first departure from Ireland. This is particularly odd as he mentions it himself in the *Autofrag*. Orrery writes as if he left Trinity in order to go to Oxford, while Deane Swift and Hawkesworth would both have us imagine that he went away in order to consult with his mother about his future career.

Deane Swift[1] puts it this way :—

> DR. SWIFT in the Year 1688 having obferved that his Fortunes began upon the Infanity of his Uncle to be clouded with a melancholy Afpect, took a Journey to *Leicester*, in order to confult with his Mother what Courfe of Life he had better refolve to purfue.

Actually, what was happening was as follows :—On the 5th November, 1688, the Prince of Orange landed in Devon, and began a circumspect and incredibly slow advance upon London, to the tune of Lillibulero. A little more than a month later, while he was still dawdling on his way, Derry slammed its gates in the faces of Lord Antrim's Papists, and from the less defensible parts of Ireland the steady drift of Protestant refugees into England swelled to a flood. William Swift went. Adam went—each with a distressed family, and each attainted by the Irish Parliament. Uncle Godwin, already sinking into a " lethargy " which is variously described

---

[1]*Essay*, p. 40.

as anything from mute speechlessness (Orrery) or insanity (Deane Swift) to actual death (Forster) remained behind in his arguable Dublin residence, and was not attainted.

Orrery is the originator of this expression " lethargy " in relation to Godwin Swift, and Deane Swift carries it on, suggesting that he was actually mad, but allowing him till 1693 before his death. Forster kills him off altogether in 1688. Yet in spite of whatever disorder Godwin may have had, he managed to propagate a final son in 1691, and according to his brother William—who ought to know—he died on the 7th December, 1695, and was buried two days later in St. Werburgh's.

Meanwhile the Prince of Orange entered London on the evening of the 18th December, and the King was encouraged to escape from Rochester to France four nights later. As it was reasonably certain that the coming conflict was going to take place in Ireland, the Board of Trinity College, on the 13th February, 1689, ruled that all those who thought fit to withdraw themselves from the College for their better security might have full liberty to do so.

It is uncertain when the future Dean joined in the flight, but it must have been after the 30th November, 1688, because on this date he celebrated his twenty-first birthday by a disciplinary row that ended in his suspension from his degree. Dr. Barrett thinks that he left with his cousin, Thomas, on or about the 26th January, 1689,[2] which does not seem at all unlikely. At any rate we know that he tramped from Holyhead to his mother's lodgings in Leicester, where he arrived at some date in the early part of 1689—let us surmise, early in February.

It will be recalled that at this stage of his life, Swift cannot have remembered ever having seen his mother before. Nor did he see her for very long now, because, after staying with her for some months, during which he passed the time in dalliance with one or two English country wenches, she sent him off with a letter of introduction to a certain Sir William Temple—a retired diplomat who lived at Moor Park, near Farnham in Surrey, but who was then temporarily residing at Sheen, close to Richmond.

His own reckoning of the number of journeys that he has made between England and Ireland by 1703[3] rules out any possibility of his having gone

---

[2]Barrett, p. 18.
[3]See pp. 133-134.

to see his mother during his school or college days. If, as Orrery[4] alleges, he visited his mother almost every year, it must have been after this date.

According to a letter which JS wrote to his Cathedral Vicar, the Rev. John Worrall,[5] he had some sort of an affair with an Innkeeper's daughter called Betty Jones during these Leicestershire days.

> My prudent mother was afraid I should be in love with her; but when I went to London, she married an Innkeeper in Loughborough. . . . This woman, my mistress with a pox, left several children, who are all dead but one daughter, Anne by name. . . .

The letter was written in 1729 from an address in County Armagh, and in it, JS instructed his Vicar as to what he was to do if this girl, Anne, turned up at the Deanery and asked for money. If Worrall was satisfied from his enquiries that the girl was really the daughter of Betty Jones, now Perkins, JS was agreeable to her being given a gift of five pounds. If Brennan, the servant, had known this tit-bit of information, it would have been a much better subject for scandal about his Master than his fanciful yarn about his having a child by Stella.

According to Lady Giffard's account of her brother's life[6], Temple left his own home at Moor Park, near Farnham, for that of his son at Sheen, in order to get out of the way of the opposing armies during the advance of the Prince of Orange upon London. This must have been in November or December, 1688. Whether or not he stayed there throughout the rest of that winter, or went back to Moor Park before returning to Sheen in April, 1689, is not clear. It is certain, however, that he was back at his son's home, winding up the latter's affairs, soon after the 14th April, on which date young John Temple had committed suicide.

This young man, his sole remaining child, had been offered to the new monarch as an adviser on Irish affairs, but unfortunately, almost the first piece of important counsel that John Temple had given to the Williamite government was to recommend the release of Richard Hamilton from arrest, and his appointment as a suitable emissary to the Jacobite Lord Lieutenant, Tyrconnel. Having been allowed to go to Ireland in

---

[4]*Remarks*, p. 21.

[5]*Correspondence*, vol. IV, p. 55.

[6]Never collated adequately until 1930, when it appeared in G. C. Moore Smith's *Temple. Early Essays and Romances*, pp. 3 et seq.

this capacity, under a pledge of loyalty to William III, Hamilton promptly changed sides, and accepted command of the besiegers of Derry on behalf of James II. This disaster is said to have been so discouraging to young Temple that he threw himself into the Thames on the 14th April, and drowned himself.

It is almost certain from the sequence of events, that it was shortly after this date that JS made his first appearance at Sheen, presenting himself to Sir William with an introduction from his mother. Indeed, it is not at all improbable that the death of the son had something to do with his visit at this particular time. However, this is not the reason that is given.

According to Deane Swift,[7] this is what Abigail said to her son, before sending him off:—

> I really cannot tell in your prefent Circumftances what Advice to give you, but fuppofe you would apply yourfelf to Sir WILLIAM TEMPLE, who is both a great and wife Man? I cannot but think he would at leaft give you fome Directions, and perhaps, if he were acquainted with your uncomfortable Situation, recommend you to fome kind of Employment either in Church or State. His Lady you know is a Relation of ours, and befides, his Father, Sir JOHN TEMPLE, had a Regatd and Friendfhip for your Father and for your Uncles until his laft Hour. Go your Ways in name of God to Sir WILLIAM TEMPLE, and upon afking his Advice, you will immediately perceive what Encouragement or Preferment you are likely to expect from his Friendfhip.

Whether or not this elaborate speech was ever made by the mother to her son, it contains, as Deane Swift reports it, a reason for the mission that had previously been given in Orrery's book, namely that Lady Temple was " a Relation of ours ". Orrery tells us[8] that Sir William's " Lady was related to Dr. Swift's Mother ". Abigail, like Uncle Godwin's first wife, is thus also credited with having influential connections for which there is no evidence whatever. And when we turn to the *Autofrag*, it is interesting to find that JS himself, at the time of writing, gave no such

---

[7]*Essay*, pp. 40-41.
[8]*Remarks*, p. 9.

reason for his having been sent to Sir William. According to this document, the only reason was that Temple's father "had been a great Friend to the Family".[9] Nor does Sir William give it as a reason for his interest in the young man, when recommending him to Southwell.

There is another feature of Temple's household that concerns his wife, and that should be noted as arising at almost exactly the same time. For the last five or six years of her life—that is to say, from about the time of the suicide of her last surviving child—Dorothy Temple drops out of the Moor Park picture, and her place as mistress of the household is largely taken by her sister-in-law, Lady Martha Giffard. This fact is commented upon by both Temple's and Lady Giffard's biographers, and it does not mean that Temple and Dorothy ever formally parted, or that JS never saw his patron's wife. What it amounts to is simply this, that from the summer of 1689 onwards, Dorothy Temple usually lived in their London home in Pall Mall, where she passed her remaining years as a friend and confidante of Queen Mary, while Temple's sister, Martha,—a woman to whom JS was deeply antagonistic—ran the establishment at Moor Park.

A possible reason for these odd family developments—which do not necessarily concern Swift's presence—will be found in the history of Temple and his wife, a matter which must be our next concern. To conclude the present chapter, it should be said that Temple apparently returned home to Moor Park in the early summer of 1689, having in his train Swift, Lady Giffard, a servant of Lady Giffard called Bridget Johnson, and three young children of the last-named.

In his essay, *On the Death of Mrs. Johnson*, the Dean wrote that Stella was born on the 13th March, 1681, and that he first knew her when she was six. Were this so, he must have arrived at Sheen before the 13th March, 1688. This, of course, is nonsense, as the Trinity books show that he was still at College for many months after this date. Elrington Ball in Appendix I to the fourth volume of the *Correspondence*[10] shows that Swift, in at least two other references to the length of his friendship

---

[9]This story of a family connection between the butcher's daughter from Wigston Magna and Dorothy Osborne of Chicksands could only have been communicated to Orrery either by Swift or by Mrs. Whiteway, who, as we will see, was the principal channel through which the Dean's later anecdotes about himself and his background reached both Orrery and Deane Swift. And it is just another example of the Dean's habit of producing facts in his old age that do not always agree with versions that he had already written down.

[10]*Correspondence*, vol. IV, pp. 450-451.

with Stella, implies two other dates for its commencement, namely 1691 and 1693. The Dean's record as a purveyor of accurate figures is already so bad, that we need not be surprised at there being three conflicting dates for this important event in his life.

As will be seen in the course of the next chapter, the most likely date for his first meeting with the Johnsons was during the removal from Sheen to Moor Park in the early summer of 1689. The probable membership of the party will be discussed in a later chapter. The date of the removal is based on the fact that Swift's Pindaric Ode to his new employer —dated by both Elrington Ball and Emil Pons in June, 1689—was composed at Moor Park.

Sir Harold Williams[11] questions this date for the Pindaric Ode, and maintains that it was written several years later ; but only because of the fact that at the date given in the Miscellanies and confirmed by Ball and Pons, Swift could only have arrived very recently in Temple's home. There seems nothing unlikely, however, in Swift gratefully apostrophising his new master in sycophantic verse, shortly after having been given the security of a bed in his household. In the absence of any better reason, the date placed upon the poem by these reliable sources should be accepted.

---

[11]Swift's Verse, vol. I, p. 26.

12

WILLIAM TEMPLE AND DOROTHY OSBORNE

HAVING eliminated the Steward of King's Inns as a possible father for the subject of our investigation, we should now be looking around for a possible alternative. It is also quite natural that the first subject for our suspicions should be this Sir William Temple, who plays so large a part in Swift's early life. In this, we would be going no further than many of Swift's own contemporaries, for it was commonly reported in the 18th century that such a relationship actually existed and that this was the reason for Temple's interest in the youth. Mrs. Pilkington refers to it in a brief footnote,[1] and Orrery mentions it several times as well :[2]

> Here it may not be improper to obſerve to you, that many of his friends imagined him to be a native of *England*, and many others, I know not whether to call them friends or enemies, were willing to ſuppoſe him the natural Son of Sir WILLIAM TEMPLE. Neither of theſe facts are true.

Now, although Orrery denies it, he then goes on to state :—

> I am not quite certain, that SWIFT himſelf did not acquieſce in the calumny. Perhaps, like ALEXANDER, he thought the natural ſon of JUPITER would appear greater than the legitimate ſon of PHILIP.[3]

It is this rumour—and in particular, Orrery's somewhat smug *snobisme* in his dismissal of it—that drives Deane Swift into the hysteria that is such a feature of his book whenever the subject comes up. For this Peer to have suggested that probably the Dean would have liked it to be true, is even more offensive to the writer's sense of family position, than the rumour itself which, if correct, would have meant that Swift was not a member of the family at all. He talks of a " Torrent of Scandal ",[4] and

---

[1] *Memoirs*, vol. III, p. 56.
[2] *Remarks*, p. 4.
[3] Ibid., p. 10.
[4] *Essay*, p. 37.

doubts that the calumny ever reached the Dean's ears as " there is no Record in the Annals of his Life that he ever cut any Man's Throat for an Infult of that Kind ".[5] It would be no elevation whatever in the social scale for a Swift to turn out to be a Temple, legitimate or otherwise, and the whole conception is too gross and absurd to merit any kind of an answer. So he answers it in approximately forty-five pages.

Our next task, therefore, is to look into Temple's history, which ought not to be difficult to do, in the case of a public figure of such eminence. Temple has been described in varying terms ; by Macaulay in one of his *Essays* as a vain, self-centred aristocrat with a lot of money, and a cold lack of interest in anything outside his own personal convenience ; by Clara Marburg, in a recent book that is a critical rather than a historical study, as " a 17th Century Libertin."

Neither description seems to be a fair one. It is true that he had social position, and as much influence and opportunity as a man could reasonably wish for. He also had money—though not so much as Macaulay's account would suggest—and if he was vain, his faults in this direction cannot have been of serious proportions, or they would certainly have aroused Swift's ire. His record actually shows him to have been a person of humane and generous temperament, selfish maybe, but disinclined to be the cause of pain to others, invariably conscious of the claims of his many dependants, and ill-suited to the rascality and cynicism of Restoration politics.

" Human life ", he is reported by his sister as saying, " is like a froward child that must be played with and humoured a little to keep it quiet, till it fall asleep, and then the care is over."

Of his wife, Sophie Shilleto Smith writes with a gush of enthusiasm :

> A history of her life and character would form one of the most desirable text-books to be placed in the hands of schoolgirls.

Whether or not this praise is true or even a recommendation, Dorothy wrote admirable letters, and her vigorous and somewhat officious sister-in-law refers to

> Queen Mary, with whom fhe had the honour to keep a *conftant* correfpondence, being juftly admired for her fine ftyle and turn of wit in writing letters and whom fhe outlived about a month ; the

---

[5]Ibid., p. 82.

deep affection for her Majefty's moft deplorable death having haftened her own.[6]

Temple's courtship of Dorothy Osborne is one of the best-loved romances of the colourful days of Cavalier and Roundhead, and is enshrined in her correspondence over a period of seven years from 1648 to 1654, which has survived to the present time and has been several times edited and published.

Dorothy's letters to William Temple were published in 1888 by Judge (afterwards Sir Edward) Parry. But the best-known details of their romance have been preserved for us in Lady Giffard's MS. *Life* of her brother, published only in part as a preface to various works on Temple (where it is attributed to " a particular friend "), until 1930, when—as already stated—it first made its appearance in full—or at any rate, all of it that is now left.

Bad as the muddle over the Swift chronology has been, it has been equalled, until quite recently, by the confusion over some aspects of Temple's history, thanks mainly to the aristocratic indifference to mere dates that is shown by Lady Giffard. This " particular friend " does not strike one as being a liar, except in her suppression of one or two aspects of the story. She is simply allergic to accurate figures, and in this she is not improved upon by her own biographer, Miss Julia Longe, whose *Life of Martha, Lady Giffard*, published in 1911, manages, for example, to be as much as five years out in reporting the death of Temple's daughter Diana.

However, reliable public records are still available for the purpose of checking the order of events, and in this task Professor Homer E. Woodbridge, in his book, *Sir William Temple, the Man and his Work*, published in New York in 1940, has performed a characteristic feat of careful American scholarship in clearing up most of it for us. Woodbridge's principal fault lies in his assessment of the relative values of other people's opinions on the subject of Swift—accepting that very readable compiler of popular books from secondary sources, Stephen Gwynn, as a genuine authority, while running down Churton Collins, Carl Van Doren and even Emil Pons for that very reason. What is more serious still is his recommendation of John Forster as " the best of the early authorities ".

---

[6]Temple's Works, vol. I, p. xxiv. Courtenay (vol. II, p. 227) thinks that this addition to the *Life* may have been made by Sir John Temple II.

However, his factual information about Temple appears to be uncontradicted, and is gratefully accepted by the present writer as the best reliable modern data, together with the Prefaces of G. C. Moore Smith, to the *Osborne Letters* (1928), and to Temple's *Essays* (1930).[7]

Temple first met the beautiful Dorothy in 1648 on the Isle of Wight, shortly after he had gone down from Emmanuel College, Cambridge. He was visiting his uncle, Sir John Dingley of Ventnor, on the first stage of the Grand Continental Tour that usually rounded off the education of young men of quality of his day. At that time, King Charles I was imprisoned in Carisbrook Castle, under the eye of the Puritan Governor of the island, Colonel Robert Hammond. Dorothy's father, Sir Peter Osborne of Chicksands, Bedfordshire, was Royalist Lieutenant Governor of Guernsey, and was under siege in Castle Cornet in the Channel Islands, an investment that lasted for the incredible period of about eight years, during parts of which the Governor managed to cross to St. Malo in order to plead with his superiors in England and in Jersey for stores and reinforcements. To this French port, Dorothy and one of her brothers (Robert) were on their way.

The Osbornes, according to Moore Smith, were suspect on the Isle of Wight, not only because of their father, but also because of the fact that another not very distant connection, Richard Osborne, had already been implicated in an attempt to organise the King's escape. But there is no reason to believe that Dorothy and her brother were not there in the course of a genuine journey to see their father. Having struck up an acquaintance with young Temple, Dorothy's brother could not, apparently, leave the island without making some sort of political demonstration, which is described in Lady Giffard's words as follows :—

> The spite he had to se the King imprison'd, and treated by the Goverour Coll. Hammond soe unlike what was due to him, provoked him to step back after all His company were gon before him out of the Inne to goe a shipboard and write theese words with a Diamond in the window, And Hamman was hang'd upon the Gallows he had prepared for Mordecai. Twas easy to imagine what hast he made after his company when he had done ; but he had no sooner overtaken them then he was seis'd himselfe, & brought back to the Governour, & only escap'd by his sister takeing it upon her selfe.

---

[7]Not all of the dates in Moore Smith's genealogical trees are correct.

Under these romantic circumstances " began an amour " (again to quote Lady G.) that was to last for seven years, and was vigorously opposed by the fathers of both parties. But in reporting this story in the light of events after the Restoration, Lady Giffard tends to gloss over the intimate family connections that so often existed between Cavaliers and Round-heads, in a manner that we have already noted in the case of William Swift, when referring to Admiral Deane.

Sir William Temple's uncle Thomas Hammond was one of the Court that tried Charles I (although he did not go so far as to sign the death warrant), and Colonel Hammond, who had arrested young Osborne, and was the King's jailer at Carisbrooke and the husband of John Hampden's daughter Mary, was actually Temple's first cousin. Sir John Temple—William's father—was violently opposed to the King's armistice with the Irish rebels in 1643, and was imprisoned by Ormond for almost a year on that account, until an exchange of Royalist and Parliamentary prisoners in 1644 procured his release. Thereafter he sat as Member for Chichester in the Long Parliament, until turned out in 1648 by the incident known as Pride's Purge. Even this did not permanently estrange him from the Government of the day, and in 1653 he was sent to Ireland as Commissioner for Forfeited Estates with a letter of recommendation from Cromwell to Fleetwood, the Lord Deputy. Both Peter and James Temple were regicides (the latter being a second cousin of Sir John). Another Sir Peter Temple was a Colonel in the Parliamentary Army, until he resigned his commission in protest against the execution of the King.

Nor is this Cromwellian connection confined to the Temples. Dorothy Osborne's uncle Sir Charles Danvers was another celebrated Roundhead, through whose introduction, Dorothy met Cromwell and his son Henry in 1644. She had many other suitors during the seven years of Temple's courtship and chief amongst these was this very son of the Lord Protector, who was William's principal rival for her hand, and had the support of her family. It was only after the death of her father that the negotiations for a marriage settlement were reluctantly entered into by her brother Henry and Temple's father. These discussions were interrupted by an attack of smallpox, from which Dorothy barely recovered, with—according to Lady Giffard—her beauty seriously impaired. Lady G. attributes her brother's readiness to go on with the marriage to the fact of

. . . his kindness haveing greater tyes than that of her beauty though that Loss was too great to leave him wholly insensible.

After Dorothy's recovery, the ceremony was performed on Christmas Day, 1654, without waiting for any Settlement, only to be followed by a lawsuit with her brother over her marriage portion, that was finally settled out of Court by the intervention of Sir John Temple in July 1655.

It is natural that after the Restoration the Temples should at first have been looked on with some suspicion by the new monarch, and Sir John at first refused to risk a snub by making any advances to the Court. But about five years later, William entered upon the diplomatic career that was to continue until 1679. The earlier dates are of importance, as they cover the period of the conception and birth of JS in February/March and November, 1667, respectively. In July 1665 Temple was sent to the Rhineland to implement a Treaty with the Bishop of Münster. For this successful but unprofitable service, he obtained a Baronetcy, and was afterwards moved to Brussels, where he conducted the negotiations that ended in the Treaty of Breda. His family—which now usually included his widowed sister, Martha Giffard—followed him to Brussels in April, 1666, and remained with him there until May, 1667, when, on account of Franco-Spanish hostilities in the Low Countries, he sent his wife and children home. The resolute Lady Giffard remained behind with him, and the only time that he appears to have seen England during this part of his life was for a period of five days at Christmas, 1667, when he returned briefly to London for instructions, before moving to The Hague.

As it is difficult to doubt any of these dates, and as by now JS is well established in the land of the living, and about to be dispatched to Whitehaven, we need not trace Temple's movements any further, until his final return from Nijmegen in or just before March, 1679. It is beyond the bounds of reasonable possibility that His Majesty's Ambassador in Brussels left his family there, and crossed two countries and two seas to Dublin, and there seduced the wife of the Steward of King's Inns, without leaving some record of so singular an excursion in the annals of the times. Nor is it any more likely that the lady was secretly conveyed to Brussels in February or March, for the purpose of insemination. We may therefore, rule out Sir William Temple as a possible father for Jonathan Swift. But this does not necessarily mean that his private affairs are finally and wholly eliminated from the life story of the Dean. So, before filling in the gap between 1667 and his last retirement to Moor Park in 1689, let us turn our attention to the group of people, already mentioned, that accompanied him there after the death of his son.

13

THE JOHNSONS

In the letter by the anonymous correspondent C. M. P. to the *Gentleman's Magazine* for November, 1757, that has already been referred to, we read :

> When Sir William Temple left Sheen to reside at Moor Park in Surrey, he brought down with him, one summer, a gentlewoman in the character of a housekeeper whose name was Johnson.

As Temple's first change of residence from Sheen to Moor Park was not in the summer, but in November, 1686, this account must refer to his second removal, which *did* take place in the summer—that of 1689. The woman referred to is Bridget Johnson, who has already been mentioned as a servant of Lady Giffard and who, with her three children, must have appeared at Moor Park—if this account be true—at about the same time as JS. It is of importance to note on the evidence of her grand-daughter, Mrs. Hearn, who corresponded from Brighton with Monck Berkeley,[1] that her first introduction to the household was as a factotum of Lady Giffard, and not as housekeeper to Sir William, himself.

> Whilſt Mrs. Johnſon lived at Richmond, ſhe had the happineſs of firſt becoming acquainted with Lady Giffard, the ſiſter of Sir William Temple. . . . As they ſeldom were apart, and Lady Giffard lived much with her brother Sir William, it was through her that Mrs. Johnſon and her two daughters (her ſon dying young) were brought to the knowledge and friendſhip of Sir William Temple and his lady. . . .

At Moor Park she did not live in the principal residence, but was accommodated with her family in a cottage on the estate that still bears the name of her more celebrated daughter. Of the other two children, very little is known except that their names were Anne and Edward, and that they were most probably the children who were respectively baptised in these names in the Parish Church of Richmond on the 12th August, 1683, and the 8th July, 1688 ; that Anne married a baker (or possibly a butcher) called Filby ; and that this Filby had another married brother

---

[1] *Relics*, p. xxix.

who lived near Farnham, whose wife must not be confused with Anne. All that we ever hear of Edward is that he was put to school at Farnham, and then went abroad, where he died young.

This Mrs. Filby of Farnham is probably the same person (misread as " Kilby ") who is referred to in a letter from Swift to either Stella or her mother when in London, and which is considered by Elrington Ball to have been written in 1698. If it refers to Anne, she must have been older than Stella, and the Richmond Register must refer to somebody else.

The only knowledge that we have of Edward comes from C. M. P.'s article in the *Gentleman's Magazine*, which, however much despised, is made use of by most writers for any information fitting into the standard picture that is not available elsewhere.

Nichols, in a note to Sheridan's *Life*[2], refers to Anne's baptismal entry, which he has found in the Register, but he fails to notice Edward's. Nor is he certain that Anne is any relation, as he does not know the first name of Stella's father. Stella's entry, he states, is not to be found in the Register, which only commences in 1682. In Vol. I of the Publications of the Surrey Parish Register Society it is explained that the earlier records from 1583 to 1682 were only brought to light in 1796, when the son of Clement Smith, an earlier Vestry Clerk, returned them to the Church.[3]

The eldest child, Esther, was baptised in the same Richmond Parish Church on the 20th March, 1681. But when we come to enquire as to who she was, we are at once treated to the familiar double exposure by the earlier writers, none of whom knows her mother's maiden name, nor any name at all for her father, except, presumably, that as her surname was Johnson, his must have been Johnson too. Swift, in his paper, *On the Death of Mrs. Johnson*, informs us that he was a younger son of a Nottinghamshire family. Elsewhere we learn that he was a merchant of London " who having been unfortunate in trade, afterwards became master of a trading sloop which ran between England and Holland ", in which latter country he died. Scott's *Memoirs*[4] add that this death occurred " soon after Esther's birth." On the other hand, Orrery describes him as Sir William Temple's Steward without giving his name, and the fact that Stella's mother did in fact marry Temple's Steward lends support to this

---

[2]Sheridan, vol. I, p. 55.

[3]For the entries relating to these three Johnsons see pp. 75, 78 and 85, respectively. of the published Register.

[4]Scott, vol. I, p. 55.

last statement, until we discover to our annoyance that these nuptials did not take place until after 1722, when Bridget was about sixty years old, and that the name of the bridegroom was not Johnson, but Mose.

This Augean stable, with which we must now be becoming familiar, is ingeniously cleaned up by the second bank of biographers, who have no longer any original sources of information of their own. So rather than adopt the cynical solution that somebody has been lying, they create an earlier Steward, prior to Mose, of whose existence there is no evidence whatever, and tell us that this must have been Johnson the Merchant, at some other stage of his career. Here Forster is well in the fore. He says : " Mrs. Johnson's husband had been closely in the confidence of Temple."[5] In which embellishment he is immediately echoed by Craik— so creating two eminent authorities for this single piece of surmise.

The fact of the matter is that, here again, there are originally two contradictory stories. The first concerns a Nottinghamshire man of good family, who failed as a merchant in London, and was then the master of a trading sloop. This is launched by Swift in 1728, and is confirmed and elaborated by those who actually knew the Johnsons in Farnham. The second concerns Sir William Temple's Steward, and this version was evidently put about by Swift at a later date for reasons that will appear. This last is the story that is told by those who have no information at all on the subject, except what they have heard in Dublin from the Dean in his later years. Those in the first category are at one in avoiding any suggestion that the man was ever in Temple's employment. Those in the second category do not even know the name of the man they are writing about ; and it is a significant fact that the only evidence of this name that we have to the present day comes from the Richmond Parish Register, which nobody referred to in full until 1875.

In this dilemma, fortunately, it is unnecessary for us to flounder for very long, as there is a third alternative that makes it quite immaterial to decide as to what or who this Johnson was. It was commonly reported from an early date that Esther was Sir William Temple's child. As early as July, 1723—almost five years before her death—John Evans, the Bishop of Meath, in a letter to Archbishop Wake, printed in Temple Scott's edition of Swift's *Prose Works*[6] described her as " a nll. daughter of Sir Wm.

---

[5]Forster, p. 85.
[6]Temple Scott, vol. XII, p. 95.

Temple, a very good woman ". Mrs. Pilkington knew of the alleged connection,[7] and Swift's sister Jane is reported to have made the somewhat acid denial that would have been expected of her as a pensioner of JS but an enemy of Stella. Dr. Patrick Delany, a constant visitor at the Deanery, and a close friend of both Swift and Stella, was quite satisfied that both Stella and her duenna, Rebecca Dingley, were " relations " of Sir William, although he was not so certain as to what the relationship actually was.[8]

But much the fullest—in fact the only circumstantial account of any kind that we have of the Johnsons comes from exactly where one would expect it to be found—from a neighbour and friend of some of the parties in their latter days in Farnham. As early as 1757 in the November issue of the *Gentleman's Magazine*, there appeared the long letter signed C.M.P. G.N.S.T.N.S. already referred to, which professes to correct errors in Lord Orrery's exceedingly brief reference to the Johnsons. From internal evidence and another article with the same signature, this C. M. P. appears to have been a gentleman of the neighbourhood, possibly a Roman Catholic, interested in coin collecting, who obtained his information from a lady, most probably a Mrs. Mayne of Farnham, in whose house both Stella's mother and Swift's sister resided for some years before their deaths.

Although—like everybody else—he does not know Johnson's first name, it is he who gives the only account of the place of his death. He is also the only person, prior to the 19th century, who can tell us the name of Stella's brother—on which point he turns out later to be perfectly correct. In the course of his letter he refers to Stella :

> who was no otherwife related to Sir *Wm. Temple's* fteward, than by her mother's marriage with him many years after the death of Sir *William*.

He then goes on to say :

> . . . This gentlewoman was the widow (as fhe always averred) of one *Johnfon*, a merchant, who having been unfortunate in trade, afterwards became mafter of a trading floop, which ran between *England* and *Holland*, and there died. He left her, as fhe faid, three children ; the

---

[7]*Memoirs*, vol. III, p. 56 n.
[8]*Observations*, p. 54.

eldeſt a daughter, was brought up in *London*, and there married one *Fillby*, a baker, by whom ſhe had 18 or 19 children ; and living in a genteel manner, he was ſoon ruined, and was ſent by their friends into the weſt of England, as a ſalt officer, whither she accompanied him, with ſuch of her children as lived.—The ſecond of her children was a ſon, *Edward* Johnſon, who was put to ſchool at *Farnham* ; and, when of a proper age, was ſent abroad, in order to qualify him for trade, but he died there young. The third and laſt was her daughter *Eſther*, who only, of all her children, was permitted to reſide with her at *Moor Park*, where ſhe was educated ; and her appearance and dreſs ſo far exceeded the rank and fortune of her mother, and the reſt of the children, that the world ſoon declared Miſs *Johnſon* to be Sir *William's* daughter. . . . And could the ſtriking likeneſs have been overlooked, Sir *Wm's* uncommon regard for her and his attention to her education, muſt have convinced every unprejudiced perſon, that Miſs *Hetty Johnſon* was the daughter of one who moved in a higher ſphere than a *Dutch* trader.

In the order in which he places the children, he is, of course, wrong unless we ourselves are wrong in our surmise that the Anne and Edward Johnson appearing in the Richmond Register are children of the same Edward Johnson who appears as Stella's father (on which point there is no further evidence). But in other respects C. M. P. appears to be much nearer the truth than Orrery, in spite of the fact that his reliability is officially condemned, while Orrery's—in this particular matter—is generally accepted. What Orrery says is[9] :—

> She was the daughter of Sir WILLIAM TEMPLE'S ſteward. . . . Sir WILLIAM TEMPLE bequeathed her in his will one thouſand pounds as an acknowledgment of her father's faithful ſervices.

It is this considerable legacy to the housekeeper's child that provides us with our most substantial reason for raising our eyebrows. But even this is not conclusive by itself. It might have been, as Sheridan suggests, that little Esther's outstanding merits had so charmed Sir William in his later years that he decided to endow the child for life, and we might—like Orrery—have rested content with this misinformation about the £1,000, had his informant been able to keep his or her mouth shut as to the reason

---

[9]*Remarks*, p. 14.

for it all. But such discretion in letting a minor misstatement ride without making it worse by an explanation, was evidently impossible—as so often is the case when lies are being told. And when we look at the will itself, we find at once that it was not £1,000 that was left to Stella, but a valuable leasehold property in County Wicklow, while the widow of this supposedly faithful servant only got £100.[10] In other words, as a reward for the services of the father, the daughter was left about ten times as much as the widow—surely an odd way of accomplishing such a purpose. Not, of course, that any such nonsensical reason is given in the will. The purpose of the legacy is a gloss invented by Orrery's source of information —Swift, I suggest—who rightly felt that some sort of explanation might be needed to lull our suspicions.

In a footnote on p. xxv of Vol. I of his edition of the *Journal to Stella*, Sir Harold Williams tells us that, according to Nichols,[11] C. M. P's., letter to the *Gentleman's Magazine* was " probably communicated by Dr. Hawkesworth." If so, it would imply a complete reversal of the view taken by Hawkesworth only a few years earlier.

Lady Giffard's will contains this provision :—

> I give ten pounds to Mrs. Hester Johnson I give ten pounds with y hundred pounds I put into y exchequer for her life and my owne and declare y hundred pounds to be hers wch I am told is there in my name upon y survivorship and for wch she has constantly sent me her certificate and received y interest. I give her beside my silver chocolate pot.

It is not often mentioned that Lady Giffard also made a small settlement on Stella for no apparent reason (since the Irish Sea had been between them for about ten years). And if this is not enough, we have finally the significant fact that, shortly after Temple's death, Esther left her mother for ever. Bridget Johnson remained in a menial capacity with Lady Giffard, while her daughter went to Ireland in the care of Temple's ex-Secretary, Swift, where her chaperone and lady companion for the rest of her life was Rebecca Dingley, a first-cousin-once-removed of Sir William —the relation of the head of the family in attendance upon one of the

---

[10]Temple's will is printed in T. P. Courtenay's *Life of Temple*, vol. II, p. 484. Lady Giffard's will and codicil (the latter misdated) can be seen in *Martha, Lady Giffard* by Julia G. Longe, p. 345.

[11]*Literary Illustrations*, p. 380 n.

servant's children. The other two children, be it added, received neither attention nor legacy, notwithstanding their supposed identical relationship to the faithful steward.

Nothing can be more tiresome than to go on elaborating a point that is already accepted, so the following chapter should be passed over by anybody who is satisfied that by any recognisable pattern of human behaviour, Stella was, of course, Temple's daughter. But in spite of the fact that she has been sensibly recognised as such by a succession of writers including Thackeray, Hay, Moriarty, Hone and Rossi, Emil Pons, W. D. Taylor and even by Sir Shane Leslie, this line has not yet been adopted as the orthodox view, and its supporters are liable to be classified amongst " those who spend their time washing up in an obscure light in the back kitchen of history." The expression is that of Miss Sophie Shilleto Smith who, in 1911, was no more outspoken in her denunciation of " greasemongers " than are the more sophisticated holders of the same view today. For example, Mr. Bernard Acworth in a recent book,[12] writes that this inference about Stella's parentage has been " started by the Paul Prys, the gossips and the slanderers," but that the old " story is accepted by the straight-forward ever since."

High feeling in the matter has driven even Professor Woodbridge to add a footnote to page 221, that is a little reminiscent of the style of Forster :—

> There is not a particle of evidence to support the story that she was Temple's natural daughter. It is a piece of malicious gossip. . . .

The reader, however, need not be intimidated by any literary steam-rolling. Whatever reasoned conclusions he may reach on the subject may be legitimately held without any hanging of the head. In support of which statement, the present writer, whether a Paul Pry or not, will now proceed to review the history of this non-existent evidence regarding Stella's parentage, and to show the ' straightforward ' manner in which it has been handled.

The fact that there should be any heat engendered by the subject is all the more ridiculous when we realise that it is now a purely academic question, that nobody's feelings or reputation are going to be hurt at this distance, and that there is nothing whatever to Stella's discredit in her having been born without the permission of the Church.

---

[12] *Swift*. Bernard Acworth. London, 1947, p. 115.

14

STELLA'S PARENTAGE

THERE is no mention whatever of Stella in the *Autofrag*. This side of his life is completely ignored by Swift in providing us with information about himself. But in the paper that he began on the evening of Stella's death, cited above, he tells us that

> Her father was a younger brother of a good family in Nottinghamshire, her mother of a lower degree ; and indeed she had little to boast of her birth.

This last sentence is usually interpreted as referring to the mother's birth, but grammatically it is just as likely to refer to Stella's. If it applies to the mother, it seems to carry an unnecessary social slur on a woman whom Swift was always careful to say nothing against. If it applies to the daughter, it may be taken as a hint that all was not well with her genealogically, and that an occasion of deep emotion for Swift was also the moment for an unusual regard for the whole truth.

Our next informant is Orrery, whose brief comment has already been quoted. Orrery, it will be remembered, was quite satisfied that Stella was not Temple's child because he believed that she was Swift's wife, and had she been a Temple—legitimate or otherwise—Swift would have been the first to boast about it. So Orrery was not interested in her father—not even in his name—and was quite happy to accept fully whatever his informants told him on the subject. He had not seen Temple's will, and was unaware that his source of information was in error about the legacy. Nor was he aware of any further overriding reason that Swift might have had for concealing any relationship between Esther Johnson and Temple.

Orrery's Sources

We are fortunate in having Orrery's own statement about his sources of information on this particular subject, since he has left us a marginal note in one of the copies of his own book in the Library of Harvard University, which runs as follows :—

> My accounts of Stella are drawn in general from anecdotes sent to me by *Mrs. Whiteway* or *Mr. Swift.* . . .

By " Mr. Swift " he means Deane Swift, with whom he was in correspondence at the time of his publication, in spite of the latter's furious objection to some of his views. And Deane Swift, as an authority on this aspect of Stella, is simply echoing Mrs. Whiteway,[1] who in her turn can only have got her information from the conversation of JS himself.

If Mrs. Whiteway was ever at Sheen or Moor Park, which is most improbable, it must have been as a mere child. She knew Stella, but there is no evidence that she ever met any of the other participants in the Surrey drama. Nor is there much reason to suppose from her movements that she even met Swift's sister, Jane Fenton.

According to her son-in-law's book[2] the Swift family in Ireland was

> . . . upon no Terms of Friendſhip with the Doctor, nor he with them ; at leaſt after his return to Ireland upon the Queen's (Anne's) Death.

So her information—which also must be the basis of most of what her son-in-law has to tell us—is really that of the Dean.

Swift's attitude towards the Swifts

As an illuminating example of the way in which JS ignored the Swift family from the time of his appointment to the Deanery, we have the petulant statement of Deane Swift,[3]

> The only Preſents which Doctor SWIFT ever made in his Life, beſide what hereafter ſhall be acknowledged, to any Man of his Name and

---

[1]Mrs. Whiteway was a daughter of JS's Uncle Adam, and was born in Chester in 1690, during the flight of her family from the Jacobites. She was brought up in County Down, married a clergyman called Harrison at the age of seventeen, and lived with him for about seven years, mainly in County Meath. Harrison died in 1714, and two years later she married Edward Whiteway, who lived in Dublin till his death in 1732. During her second widowhood, and in Swift's old age, she became one of his regular visitors at the Deanery. Lyon states in one of his marginals that she " . . . came from her own house at the other end of Dublin three days in each week to read and chat with him after Stella's death being y principal female that frequented his Table for many years while his memory remained."

[2]*Essay*, p. 372.

[3]Ibid., pp. 372-373.

Family, were a Bundle of Osiers, and Half a Dozen young Cherry Trees to his Cousin DEANE SWIFT (the biographer's father), when he was planting his Garden near fifty years ago ; and an ELZEVIR VIRGIL, in the Year 1738, to one of the present Generation. However indeed, there were some three or four, among the Women of the Family, whom the DOCTOR greatly regarded : But excepting to that one Person (Mrs. Whiteway), whom every Body knows to have been his intimate Friend ; and who upon all Occasions acknowledges her Obligations to him, and is pleased in doing so ; he never gave to the Value of Ten Pounds to all the rest ; unless it were a Seal, a Ring or some little Toy, which he thought would be acceptable to a young Person.

In a note on p. xlii Deane Swift continues :

. . . sure it is, that Dr. SWIFT never loved his Uncle, nor the Remembrance of his Uncle, to the Hour of his Death ; so deep were the Characters this Want of Money in the University of *Dublin* had engraven upon his Mind. And this in all Probability was the Reason, that he never would vouchsafe the least interest in any of the Posterity of GODWIN throughout his whole Life.

So when we come to study the account of Stella's father that Mrs. Whiteway gave to Orrery, it is interesting to find that here again, JS has evidently told her a different story from the one that he had previously written down at an earlier period of his career. We have found him doing this sort of thing before—over the supposed relationship of his mother to Lady Temple, for example. So it is not very surprising to find him doing it again. This is how Orrery's marginal note continues :—

Stella was the daughter of Sir William Temple's Steward. She was allowed by the Dean's sister (a bitter enemy of her's) to be the very picture of her mother's husband ; and this *Mrs. Fenton* would insist on whenever she heard the aspersion of her being *Sir William Temple's* daughter mentioned, because, as she expressed herself, ' she ought to give the devil his due.'

The Surrey Sources

This disclosure of Orrery opens up the next source of information on the subject—namely, the ladies in Surrey. After Temple's death, Stella's

mother remained on in the same office that she had always held in that
household—as a servant of Lady Giffard. On the death of her patroness
in 1722, she returned to the Farnham area where she lived for a time with
her daughter Anne's brother-in-law, Filby. Soon, however, she married
Ralph Mose, the man who had been Sir William Temple's Steward, and
was the widower of his cook, and who had also remained on in the service
of Lady Giffard after the death of Temple. It is reported by C. M. P's
informant that this marriage was very distasteful to her, but that she
consented to marry again at this advanced age because of the fact that
Mose had some information about her that might have been disclosed had
she refused his offer. After Mose's death, she lived for a time with Mrs.
Mayne of Farnham, before returning to Filby's house, where she died
soon after 1742.

Jane Swift was brought up in Dublin, most probably in the household
of her Uncle William. At any rate, her marriage licence describes her as
" of Bride Street." Like her brother, she never saw her mother during her
youth, after the age of about three, but apparently visited her at Leicester
in 1692, during which summer a letter of JS to their uncle shows that
she must also have visited Moor Park at the time.

Her marriage to Joseph Fenton, also of Bride Street, took place in 1699,
and the fact that the bridegroom is supposed to have been a tradesman is
the usual reason given by the Biographers for the fact that after this
marriage Swift " would never be ſo far reconciled as to ſee her Face."[4]
Jane's deplorable social lapse could hardly have carried such weight after
she had parted from Fenton in 1710, and still less after the death of this
" old tyrannical, vicious Rake " in 1720 ; and Dr. Delany[5] expresses some
of the doubts that we may all feel as to whether the social condition of
her husband was Swift's real reason for cutting himself off completely
from his sister. It is not even certain that Fenton was a " currier." Craik,[6]
refers to a story that he had been a student at Trinity College. Elrington
Ball[7] denies this, but then takes back his denial in his Corrigenda,[8] having
found what he is satisfied is a reference to Fenton in the Matriculation
Book, under the name of ' Penton.'

---

[4]*Essay*, p. 110.
[5]*Observations*, p. 72.
[6]Craik, p. 82.
[7]*Correspondence*, vol. I, p. 3
[8]Ibid., vol. VI, p. 241.

But whether or not Swift approved of the marriage—and Deane Swift[9] alleges that he offered her £500 provided she would turn Fenton down— Jane actually received a dowry of £300 from some unknown source—a mystery on which Deane Swift speculates.[10] Furthermore, during the latter part of her life, she received a substantial annuity of £20 a year from JS on condition that she remain out of Ireland. The authority for this is again Deane Swift,[11] who does not understand the reason for it. It is doubly peculiar to find JS supporting somebody else's wife at a time when he is supposed to have been too badly off to acknowledge his own.

This odd combination of circumstances could, of course, be explained very simply by the fact that Jane was one of the few who knew the details of her brother's birth, and was paid to stay away from the Dean's circle, and to keep her mouth shut. Her removal from the Irish scene and from her husband took place in 1710, just about the time when Swift was becoming a public figure, and also the year of their mother's death. As with Bridget Johnson, it was Lady Giffard who gave her employment as an upper servant at £12 per annum, and at her mistress's death she received a bequest of clothing, her bedroom furnishings, a saucepan, a small silver cup, and twenty guineas, being referred to in the will as " Fenton "—a form of address that is hardly applicable to anybody except a servant or an author. She then went to Farnham, where she boarded with Mrs. Mayne—the same lady who provided a home for Bridget Johnson— where she died in 1738.[12]

She can hardly have had any personal knowledge of Temple affairs prior to 1710, when she entered Lady Giffard's service, except for whatever she may have picked up in the course of one visit to Moor Park in 1692, at which date no Edward Johnson the elder could have been around if Bridget was already a widow. She had, on the other hand, almost twelve years of association with Lady Giffard, and even longer with Bridget Johnson, from which sources it may be assumed she derived her line with regard to Stella's parentage. In her reference to the latter's resemblance to " her mother's husband," already quoted, it will be seen that she does not mention him by name, and the insinuation can hardly apply to any " husband " except the only one she knows—Ralph Mose. He was the

---

9*Essay*, p. 108.
10Ibid., p. 107.
11Ibid., p. 110.
12Monck Mason, p. 227.

" devil " who had blackmailed her friend into marriage—not Johnson. If she is insinuating anything about Stella, it is that Mose was her father. But just as likely, she merely is supporting the story of Lady Giffard and Bridget against widespread gossip to the contrary.

The Evidence of the Portraits

This evidence of physical resemblance is actually very deceptive. One of the points made in Mr. Maxwell Gold's book—the only seriously documented exposition of the official view—is that none of the surviving portraits of Stella bear any likeness to those of Sir William Temple, thus —as he says—confirming Mrs. Whiteway[13]. However, a glance at the few surviving portraits of Stella will support the contention that they do not even resemble each other. We are, here, in a deplorably bad period of portrait painting.

Nor is it clear how Mrs. Whiteway, who never saw Sir William, can be regarded as good authority for the fact that Stella and Temple bore no resemblance to each other, when we have evidence from Surrey that they did.

Neither Lady Giffard nor Bridget Johnson could be expected, for a moment, to admit that Stella was Temple's child. They are both interested parties. But the person who appears to have no interest in the matter whatever, except to explain the peculiar behaviour of her friends, is Mrs. Mayne, the lady in whose home Bridget and Jane both resided during their latter days. She might well be expected to have picked up some hints about the matter over the years, and these, apparently, she communicated to C. M. P.

Delany and Deane Swift

Dr. Delany,[14] who is next in the list of printed commentators, expresses a firm conviction that there was some relationship between Stella and Sir William, although he does not know what it is.

We are told (and I am satisfied by SWIFT himself) at the bottom of a Letter to Dr. SHERIDAN, dated Sept. 2—1727, that Mrs. JOHNSTON and Mrs. DINGLEY, were both relations to Sir

---

[13]Gold, p. 23 n.
[14]*Observations*, p. 54.

WILLIAM TEMPLE; at whoſe houſe SWIFT became acquainted with them, after he left the Univerſity of *Dublin*, Mrs. JHONSTON then was not the daughter of Sir WILLIAM'S menial ſervant; at leaſt if ſhe was, that ſervant was his relation.

This clumsily expressed statement refers to two quite independent sources of information (1) a letter to Dr. Sheridan printed by Faulkner, and (2) the Dean himself. Deane Swift is quite right in pointing out that it is only a marginal note by Faulkner that refers to Stella's parentage, and that there is nothing in the letter itself to lend support to the Temple connection. But the bracket—" I am satisfied by Swift himself "—does not mean that Swift has said so in the letter, although awkwardly inserted into the middle of the other sentence. And it stands as an independent reason for Delany's belief in the relationship.

Deane Swift, who comes next, devotes several pages of almost incoherent abuse to Orrery's reasons, while unfortunately having to agree with Orrery's conclusions. The source of his knowledge is precisely the same as the source of Orrery's—Mrs. Whiteway. Indeed, he is, himself, one of Orrery's two informants. But a social slur has been cast on the Swift family by this irritating suggestion that Swift would have been proud of an alliance with a Temple—even if marred by a bar sinister. Nevertheless, he believes in the marriage, and—honest man that he is—he can think of no other credible reason for his relative's refusal to acknowledge the ceremony except the nonsensical one that Stella was a girl of very humble origin.[15]

If Dr. SWIFT had acknowledged his Marriage even with this improved, this adorable Creature, he would in Spight of his Genius, and all the Reputation he had acquired in the Days of King WILLIAM and Queen ANNE have immediately ſunk in the Eſteem of the World.

Edward Johnson

It will be seen that there is still no knowledge on anybody's part either of the names of Stella's Nottinghamshire father or of Sir William's Steward. So there is no reason for anybody to believe that they are not one and the same person. It is Hawkesworth, when he comes to edit the

---

[15]*Essay*, p. 88.

Works ten years after Swift's death, who inserts into his opening reference to Stella a gloss on Deane Swift, whom he quotes as his only authority.[16]

> . . . ſhe was the daughter of his ſteward, whoſe name was *Johnſon*. . .

This very reasonable conjecture on Hawkesworth's part—for, after all, was not Stella's name Johnson?—is nevertheless a gloss, because Deane Swift gives no such name, and like Orrery, is referring to an unknown Steward slipped into the record by Swift, in contradiction of his earlier story, in order to justify the legacy—" as an acknowledgement of her father's faithful services." However, all is well until the steward's name turns out to be Mose, and somebody looks at Sir William's will.

This useful piece of research, however, was not undertaken for another fifty years. Meanwhile the next development comes in 1757 in the *Gentleman's Magazine*, already quoted. If purely fiction, this account is a remarkable piece of invention, and it is doubly curious that it was never contradicted, although published during the lifetime of many of Sir William's near relatives, including his nephew, John Temple, who was always most vocal on the subject of Swift's affairs. The fact that it is wrong in some particulars is used as the pretext for its general condemnation today. What these particulars are, will be pointed out presently. For the moment it is sufficient to say that the fact that Orrery and Swift himself can be shown to be wrong in a great many facts is not made use of as a reason for disregarding their accounts in other respects. The interesting thing about the story told by C. M. P. is the number of details, not given elsewhere, in which it subsequently turns out to be perfectly right.

Dr. Johnson has nothing more to say on this subject, while Sheridan does not even trouble to repeat Hawkesworth's gloss, and is still labouring under the same mistake as to the nature of Temple's legacy. This, he adds, was also given for Stella's " own rising merits," a statement that proves that he never saw the will. But just about the turn of the century we get two refreshing touches of original enquiry. The first comes in 1792 in Monck Berkeley's *Literary Relics*[17] and is contained in a letter which Berkeley says he had received from Mrs. Hearn, a niece of Stella, who was still alive, and was then living in Brighton. Mrs. Hearn, who is, presumably, a granddaughter of the man in question, says

---

[16]Hawkesworth, vol. I, p. 16.
[17]*Relics*, p. xxix-xxx.

Her father was a merchant, and the younger brother of a good family in Nottinghamſhire. He died young, and left his widow with three children, a ſon and two daughters . . . Stella's own fortune being only £1,500, one thouſand of which, as a further mark of friendſhip, was left her by Sir William Temple himſelf.

It will be seen that, although Mrs Hearn quite naturally does not allege that her aunt was Temple's byblow, thereby scandalising the name of her own grandmother, this account is in accord with the *Gentleman's Magazine* in so far as it deals with her grandfather's background. He was a merchant from Nottinghamshire, and there is no indication whatever that he ever worked for Temple. Nor do we as yet hear his first name.

The other comment is a marginal note by Malone in the Victoria and Albert Museum copy of Hawkesworth, and it entitles him to our congratulation for being the first in the field to look at Temple's will. This note opposite the reference to the will reads, with perfect truth :—

Not one word of her father's valuable services in Sir William Temple's Will, nor is her father mentioned, nor did he leave her £1,000 but a leasehold farm in the Co. of Wicklow which perhaps she sold for that money.

Next comes Scott in 1814, who seems to have observed the thickening fog with some distaste, and then swept it aside with an authoritative (and quite unsubstantiated) generalisation. After stating that her father " died soon after Stella's birth " (which is unlikely), he adds[18] :—

The birth of Stella has been carefully investigated, with the hopes of discovering something that might render a mysterious and romantic history yet more romantic. But there are no sound reasons for supposing that she had other parents than her imputed father and mother, the former the younger brother of a good family in Nottinghamshire, and by profession a merchant in London.

It need hardly be said that on the date on which he writes, neither Scott nor anybody else—with the possible exception of Malone—had " carefully investigated " Stella's birth. Nor had they yet discovered her supposed father's name. Scott's contribution is merely to throw some

---

[18]Scott, p. 55.

doubts on the merits of her education to the detriment of Deane Swift's praise of the same. And on this slender foundation, the further glosses now begin to fall thick and fast.

Forster, of course, is in the vanguard, as we have already noted, with Craik close upon his tail, describing Bridget as the

" widow of a confidential servant of Sir William's,"[19]

and it would be tedious to enumerate the elaborations on this theme down to the present day that culminate in Julia Longe's description of Johnson, not only as a " cadet of a good old Nottinghamshire family," but also as " a distant relation of Lady Temple."[20]

So, although some of the more recent commentators have begun to show signs of a healthy independence, the most weighty view today is still ponderously opposed to any doubts on the subject of Stella's legitimacy, for the same reason incorrectly pontificated by Scott :—that the circumstances have been carefully investigated, and there are no sound reasons for supposing anything else.

Maxwell Gold

Actually, it is an illuminating and rather amusing fact that the best scholarly examination of the record in support of the majority standpoint comes from one who was, at the time of writing, an undergraduate at Harvard—Mr. Maxwell Gold—in an excellent little book, *Swift's Marriage to Stella*, published by the Harvard University Press in 1935. Several of his points have already been touched upon. To continue with them, he comments on the fact that none of the Temple papers that we know about lend the slightest colour to the suggestion that Sir William had an illegitimate daughter. Except, one might add, the not unimportant will. He omits to mention, too, who it was that had charge of these papers after Temple's death, and who was employed to edit them—Jonathan Swift. He assumes, of course, that Jane Fenton is speaking of Johnson and not of Mose in her remarks upon Stella's appearance. And he dismisses C. M. P. because of the fact that he " smacks too much of gossip," and must " undoubtedly " be wrong on the point of resemblance, because he does not agree with Mrs. Whiteway's surmise to the contrary.

---

[19]Craik, p. 25.
[20]Longe, p. 179.

But, as might be expected, he is both fair and informative in his recital of the facts on both sides, and shows a fitting respect for the work of Mr. Emil Pons of the University of Strasbourg, who is a leading exponent of the opposite view. What is more, he is frank enough to admit that one of the things he finds most damning about the information in the *Gentleman's Magazine* is not its accuracy, but its motive.[21]

> In fact the reason he (C.M.P.) attempts to prove that Temple was Stella's father springs from a desire to prove that, since Temple was Swift's father as well, the marriage of Swift and Stella could not take place.

This, of course, is the basis of a widespread objection to C. M. P. It is not primarily on account of Stella, but because of the rumour that he reports concerning Swift. But to wave aside all that C. M. P. tells us about Stella and her mother, because of the fact that he is wrong about Swift, does not establish any contrary thesis. It merely creates a vacuum around the Johnsons, as there is no contrary thesis, apart from what Swift and Lady Giffard have chosen to say on the subject.

What is more, this introduction of the subject of motive is a little dangerous, since it might be applied with even greater force to the conclusions reached by Mr. Gold himself, in the course of a book dedicated by its very title to the proposition that such a marriage *did* take place.

Other Comments on C. M. P.

What is more questionable than Mr. Gold's well reasoned remarks, is the footnote—already quoted—that one is disappointed to find coming from so well-informed a biographer as Professor Woodbridge. In line with this, we have another footnote by the most distinguished English contemporary authority, Sir Harold Williams, who in the Introduction to his superb edition of *The Journal to Stella*,[22] adopts the whole sequence of uncorroborated glosses that we have outlined above, and then goes on to dismiss the *Gentleman's Magazine* in the following terms :—

> It is, perhaps, needless to labour the presumption against a story which appeared seventy-six years after Stella's birth.

---

[21]Gold, p. 23 n. Mr. Gold is not always accurate in his quotations in this section.
[22]*Swift. Journal to Stella*, vol. I, p. xxvi.

This is a most surprising remark, as it seems calculated to convey the impression that for nearly a century, nobody ever thought of questioning Stella's parentage, until C. M. P. or his informant invented the gossip, long after the death of everybody concerned. Such an interpretation of Sir Harold's purpose is, of course, absurd, and it would be highly impertinent to suggest that so eminent an authority had any intention of misleading us by his footnote. However, the alternative is the astonishing conclusion that he has forgotten about Bishop Evans's letter, and Dr. Delany's comment, and the contemporary reviews of Orrery's book, and Jane Fenton's remark. Nor is he apparently aware that such scandal—whether we accept it or not—was well known in Stella's lifetime, and was actually twice referred to in print in advance of any biography save that of Orrery.

Sir Harold also tells us that the correspondent in the *Gentleman's Magazine* is of "dubious credit." He gives us no particulars of any matters on which he bases this judgment, but presumably refers to the same aspects of the letter that Leslie Stephen is thinking of when the latter tells us[23] that the communication "includes such palpable blunders as to carry little weight."

It is true that C. M. P. is probably in error in three of his checkable statements. First of all, he gets the order of the birth of Esther and her brother and sister the wrong way round. This is to say, they are the wrong way round if we assume that the Anne and the Edward appearing in the Richmond Register are, in fact, children of the same Edward Johnson who is stated to be Stella's father. Not a very serious blunder, when one considers that no writer on Swift except Sheridan and Malone ever looked at the Registers before 1875.

Secondly, he is under the impression that Stella was first brought over to Ireland by Swift while Sir William Temple was still alive. "But of this," he adds with a frankness rare amongst our informants, "I am not so positive as I am that her mother parted with her as one who was never to see her again." What a help it would be if all our commentators were as refreshingly straightforward whenever they have no substantial grounds for what they are saying.

Lastly, we come to his real offence. He has heard this story that Swift, also, was Temple's child, and he includes it in his account, not as something

---

[23]Stephen, p. 29 n.

on which he has any positive information apart from hearsay, but as a possible explanation for the behaviour of the principals. In this is he "undoubtedly" wrong. But after all, he is only professing to put on paper the beliefs and information current around Farnham, which are of considerably greater interest on the subject of the Johnsons than anything that might be picked up by Mrs. Whiteway in Dublin. And perhaps it may turn out in the end to be not quite so grave an error as might be supposed.

If biographical information on Swift is going to be dismissed *in toto* because of some errors of the above calibre, it is not with the *Gentleman's Magazine* that we should begin. And now that it is clear that C. M. P. is not going to be used in the present instance as an argument to support any thesis that Swift and Stella were brother and sister, his information on the subject of Stella may, perhaps, be re-examined with a friendlier eye. After which, it may be appropriate to turn from this interminable pointing out of inconsistencies, to show, not only that Sir William Temple could have been Stella's father, but that, if one accepts this conclusion, there are no longer any serious inconsistencies.

We cannot put the matter further than this. No positive proof can ever be forthcoming about matters of historical paternity. One can only go so far as to say that physically, geographically, and psychologically a certain solution could be the correct one. And that if it is not correct, some other explanation ought to be found for the known behaviour of the persons concerned.

15

TEN YEARS RECONSTRUCTED

In reconstructing what I suggest to be the actual course of events in Temple's life between 1679 and 1689, I am accepting in their entirety the dates that have been ascertained and corrected by the valuable labours of Professor Woodbridge. The fact that I do not also follow him in some matters of opinion arising from the sequence of events that he describes, may perhaps be attributed to the fact that he is himself unaware of the significance of the clues that are to be found in the pages of his useful book.

In the footnote regarding Stella's paternity that has already been partially quoted, he continues as follows :—

> It is extremely improbable that Lady Temple would have tolerated as a member of her household a woman who had been her husband's mistress, or that Temple would have expected her to do so. The story gained currency through an article in the *Gentleman's Magazine* for November, 1757, (Vol. XXVII, pp. 487–491) which attempts to solve the problem of Swift's later relation to Stella on the theory that both were illegitimate children of Temple. M. Pons, who accepts the part of the story relating to Stella, pointedly ignores the even more absurd part concerned with Swift.

Now, actually C. M. P. propounds no " theory," and is not attempting to solve anything. He is merely trying to correct certain errors that he has read in Orrery's book, from information that is current around Farnham. This information he reports with so many qualifying phrases such as " as she always averred " and " as she said " that he must be fully aware of the doubtful veracity of some of the things that he has been told, and is sometimes rather a bore in making this clear. He is not, as Maxwell Gold suggests, trying to prove This, in order to prove That. He is telling us what he has heard, and in telling us that he has heard it, he is probably being perfectly accurate.

The first part of Woodbridge's note, however, presents us with a good point, which must be considered in relation to the background as we find it in the pages of his own book.

When Sir William Temple returned to England in March, 1679, after his last mission to Nijmegen, the country was boiling with excitement over the Popish Plot. The king was pressing Temple to accept the job of Secretary of State, but in the same month—March—his beloved daughter, Diana, died at the age of fourteen. She was the sixth of his children to be lost to him, and now the only survivor of his nursery was John, his eldest son.[1]

Temple was now within a month of his fiftieth birthday, and his wife was a year older, and past the age of any further child-bearing. His father had died two years before, and life was turning sour on Temple. Indeed, as Lady Giffard reports, he was afterwards heard to say how happy his life would have been if only it had ended before the age of fifty.[2]

Elected to the House of Commons for a brief period as Member for Cambridge University, his disgust for public life under the Stuarts finally overcame him, and when a new Parliament was elected next year, he refused to stand again, and retired permanently to his house at Sheen, fronting the river on the site of the present Observatory—a house that he had owned since Spring, 1665.

As a punishment for this reluctance to continue in the royal service, he was struck off the roll of the Privy Council, and it must now have seemed to Temple that his public life was virtually ended. His prospects of family life were hardly in a better condition.

In such a period of despair and disgust, it would not be surprising to find him turning for some consolation to a woman of neighbouring Richmond. And such a woman, by name Bridget, surname unknown, was in fact pregnant in June, 1680—whether or not by Temple. The fact that we can find no record of her marriage to the merchant, Edward Johnson, is not inconsistent with the idea that the wedding took place in private, shortly after the pregnancy was discovered.

In the *Monthly Review* for November, 1751[3] appears the following paragraph, which may or may not be correct about Temple, but which gives a good illustration of the matter-of-fact attitude of the times towards

---

[1]Lord David Cecil in 'Two Quiet Lives,' 1947, credits him with six children altogether. Julia Longe, who is usually wrong in her figures, alleges that he had nine. I do not know which is right, nor does it matter, since they were all dead but John after March, 1679.

[2]Moore Smith, *Temple. Early Essays*, p. 21.

[3]*Monthly Review*, November 1751, p. 416.

bastards, and of a common practice of the upper class in dealing with such contingencies :—

> It is well known that Sir *William Temple* was a very amorous man, and much addicted to intrigue with various women ; and it is not improbable that ſuch a man as Sir *William* ſhould take uncommon precautions to provide well for his natural children, without letting the public, or even themſelves, know that they were ſuch.

Temple was clearly a humane and well-intentioned person. His constancy in his courtship, his marriage to a woman disfigured by small-pox, his obedience to his father, his provision of a home for his widowed sister, and finally, his treatment of Swift, all bear this out.

So it is suggested that he then followed the better practice of the age, and provided a husband for the woman whom he had got into trouble, and a name for the child that was on the way. It was not difficult, in an age of universal patronage, to find a suitable man ready to oblige. And who better than a decent younger son of a middle-class family from the Midlands, who had failed in business, and who could be provided with a trading sloop in return for his willingness to accommodate a lady in a difficulty ? Temple had been Ambassador at The Hague, and still had useful contacts in Holland. Where, more naturally, would Johnson take his ship than on the Dutch run ? Or indeed, it is equally possible that he was already engaged in this trade, and had had dealings with Temple in the Low Countries. Thus Temple provided for his child in a satisfactory manner.

Woodbridge is perfectly right in what he says. Temple would never have wished to bring this woman into his house, or have expected his wife to accept her. So he accommodated her and her baby in other ways. A special licence enabled the ceremony to be performed in private, with no embarrassing calculations over dates later on, after the child was born. And so the affair seemed to have ended with a husband for Bridget, soon to be followed by two other children, in the course of her lawful marriage.

But what about seven years later, when Temple's last legitimate child had committed suicide under tragic circumstances, and Johnson had died abroad, leaving his wife destitute, with three young children to support ? It would not be so easy to get another husband for her now—nor so urgent. Yet Temple could hardly be expected to leave his only surviving child in the lurch. Once again the solution—it is suggested—was precisely what one would expect. Not Temple, but his managing, loyal sister, his standby throughout his life, took the woman into her service, just as she later took charge of the dangerous Jane Fenton by giving her a similar post. And when they went back to Moor Park in the Summer of 1689, Bridget accompanied them with her young family, exactly as C. M. P. tells us, and was accommodated—not in the house—but in a cottage in the neighbourhood.

Probably Lady Temple did not like this arrangement very much, but if so, what could she do, except exactly what she did do? She retired from the establishment at Moor Park, leaving its management to her sister-in-law, and took herself to the family house in Pall Mall, London, where she devoted her remaining years till her death in 1694 to attendance on her friend Queen Mary. As Julia Longe has put it[4]:

> . . . the five last years of Lady Temple's life are a closed book to us . . . What records Lady Giffard may have left, undoubtedly have been destroyed; and life at Moor Park, from the day of the family's return thither until Lady Giffard breaks the silence in a letter to Lady Berkeley in 1697, is unknown.

Could she have put it any more plainly, even if she had known the reason?

Almost a year after these upheavals of 1689, Lady Giffard wrote her account of her brother's life—a document that was treated with some reserve by other members of the family, who amended and partially suppressed it, so that it was never actually published in full until 1930. Even now we have no means of being certain that what is before us is all that Lady Giffard originally wrote. But whatever she wrote, it would never have disclosed that Stella was her brother's child, although this discretion did not prevent her from leaving her a legacy. Nor would her servant Jane Fenton—however spiteful—reveal such a fact while Lady Giffard lived, or while her main source of income, afterwards, was a pension from Swift. Nor would Bridget herself talk, except in so far as a hint or two might be dropped from time to time in the presence of her landlady, Mrs. Mayne, who—as might be expected—was C. M. P.'s source of information.

---

[4]Longe, p. 190.

But Mose knew something, and used his knowledge to force Bridget to marry him. And Stella knew, and proudly pulled up her roots and left it all, to go to Ireland. And Dingley, the poor relation, knew, and found no social difficulty whatever in attending on her cousin's child abroad—a situation that she might well have demurred at, had Stella been merely a housekeeper's daughter.

If the above is not the missing piece of the jig-saw that fits all these divergent aspects, it will be necessary to provide a better one. But at any rate let us express the modest hope that it will never again be said, that " there is not a particle of evidence to support the story."

16

AN OXFORD DEGREE

ALTHOUGH Abigail's appeal to Temple on behalf of her son was not unsuccessful—whatever its grounds may have been—it is of interest to note that Sir William's first reaction to the arrival of the young man at his house was, not to keep him there, but to get him back again to Ireland as soon as he could. While the greater part of that country, including JS's native city, was still in the hands of the Jacobites, this was hardly possible. But in May, 1690, when the new King was preparing an expedition to reconquer the neighbouring island, and almost two months before it was clear that he would succeed, Temple took the opportunity to ship JS off in the train of that monarch, by finding him a job with his friend, Sir Robert Southwell.

Southwell had been appointed Secretary of State to attend on the King in this campaign, and to him young Swift was sent with a letter of recommendation dated the 29th May, 1690, which is the first item in Volume I of the *Correspondence* edited by Elrington Ball. In this letter Temple wrote :—

> . . . he has lived in my house, read to me, writ for me, and kept all accounts as far as my small occasions required. He has Latin and Greek, some French, writes a very good and current hand, is very honest and diligent, and has good friends, though they have for the present lost their fortunes, in Ireland, and his whole family having been long known to me obliged me thus far to take care of him. If you please to accept him into your service, either as a gentleman to wait on you, or as a clerk to write under you, and either to use him so if you like his service, or upon any establishment of the College to recommend him to a fellowship there, which he has just pretence to, I shall acknowledge it as a great obligation to me as well as to him. . . .

Southwell was still at the Custom House, London, on the 30th May, 1690, and from the diary of the movements of William III,[1] it appears

---

[1]See the Southwell papers in Trinity College Library.

that he was with the King when he landed in June at Carrickfergus in County Antrim. So that, in all probability, this landing was also the date and occasion of Swift's return to his own country, although there is no indication in any of his works or conversations that he was a witness of the stirring events that culminated in the Battle of the Boyne. Nor is it otherwise certain what happened when he turned up again in Dublin, where his Uncle Godwin—whether in a lethargy or not—was still propagating children, in accordance with his habits for the past thirty-four years. All that we know is that Southwell neither retained him in his service nor did he obtain for him the suggested Fellowship in Trinity College. Apparently, Ireland did not want any further part in Jonathan Swift at this time, and in the summer of 1691 we find him back again in Sir William's household—this time to stay.

What is noteworthy about the whole matter is that none of the early biographers comments upon the fact that Temple tried, at first, to get rid of the young man, while Swift himself enlarges the length of his original visit to Temple, and then describes in the *Autofrag* the reason for his early return to Ireland in the following fanciful way :—

> . . . he was received by Sir William Temple . . . where he continued for about two years. For he happened before twenty years old, by a surfeit of fruit to contract a giddyness and coldness of stomach, that almost brought him to his Grave ; and this disorder pursued him with Intermissions of two or three years to the end of his Life. Upon this Occasion he returned to Ireland by advice of Physicians, who weakly imagined that his native air might be of some use to recover his Health. But growing worse, he soon went back to Sir William Temple ; with whom growing into some confidence, he was often trusted with matters of great Importance.

Shortly before the composition of the *Autofrag*, he also writes somewhat facetiously to Mrs. Howard in a letter dated August, 1727 :—

> About two hours before you were born, I got my giddiness by eating a hundred golden pippins at a time at Richmond.

Here is more of the usual double-talk. In the first account, he acquired this peculiar complaint at the latest in 1687, and of necessity in Ireland. In the second, his over-eating was in Richmond in the Spring of 1689— the only time when he was living near that place.

Actually, this quotation from the *Autofrag*, in which the words " in 1690 " are said to be added in the Cobbe copy, seems to be another of the elaborate explanations to which JS is prone, whenever he is describing something that bothers him. As originally written, he must have intended to convey that his return to Ireland did not take place until about 1691 or 1692. Then realising that this could be shown to be untrue, he inserts the correct date, 1690, in the later copy, but omits to alter the earlier part of the text. He also tells us, confidently anticipating his last days by seventeen or eighteen years, that this surfeit of fruit affected his constitution " to the end of his life "—a statement that presumably was not supposed to be read until after his death.

The fact that he could not say simply that he was given a job with Southwell that came to nothing, must be bound up with some unpleasantness about the incident, that he does not wish to remember.

On his return to Moor Park, his precise position in the household was whatever the reader likes to make of these two superbly contradictory descriptions :—

(a) Deane Swift :[2]

> . . . it amounts to fomewhat more than a bare moral Impoffibility that fo great and wife a Statefman, thoroughly verfed in all the Windings and Turnings of human Nature, as Sir WILLIAM undoubtedly was from his great Experience both at Home and Abroad, fhould not immediately perceive what a Treafure was offered to his Friendfhip by this amazing and exalted young Genius, whofe Abilities had been employed for feven Years in all the nobleft Refearches both of *Greek* and *Roman* Literature, whether among Poets, Hiftorians, or Philofophers. And accordingly we find that his Talents were foon remarked, and his Perfon highly efteemed by that fagacious Minister.

(b) Samuel Richardson :[3]

> Mr. Temple, nephew to Sir William Temple . . . declared to a friend of mine, that Sir William hired Swift, at his first entrance into the world, to read to him, and sometimes to be his amanuensis, at the rate of £20 a year and his board, which was then high preferment to him ; but that Sir William never favoured him with his conversation because

---

[2] *Essay*, p. 42.
[3] Scott, vol. I, p. 26 n and Richardson's *Correspondence*, vol. VI, p. 173.

of his ill-qualities, nor allowed him to sit down at table with him. Swift . . . had bitterness, satire, moroseness, that made him insufferable to his equals and inferiors, and unsafe for his superiors to countenance. Sir William Temple was a wise and discerning man. He could easily see through the young fellow, taken into a low office, and inclined to forget himself. Probably, too, the Dean was always unpolite, and never could be a man of breeding.

The statement of Richardson comes from a letter to Lady Bradshaigh, and is quoted by Scott from Richardson's *Correspondence*. It probably errs too much in the opposite direction to Deane Swift, as Jack Temple, who made the sour remark, was always an enemy of JS. Nevertheless it has been made the basis of Macaulay's equally sour description in his essay on *Sir William Temple*, where we hear of " an eccentric, uncouth, disagreeable young Irishman, who had narrowly escaped plucking at Dublin" and who " attended Sir William as an amanuensis for board and twenty pounds a year, dined at the second table, wrote bad verses in praise of his employer, and made love to a very pretty, dark-eyed young girl who waited on Lady Giffard ". Anybody who ever humiliated JS was pursued by his malevolence for ever afterwards. It was the unpardonable offence. Yet wherever Swift may have sat at table, he never expressed any hatred for Sir William Temple ; from which fact we may assume that his treatment was reasonably civil.

Whatever may be the truth behind these conflicting views, there is every reason to believe that, with the passage of time, Swift's presence became acceptable—and indeed, essential—to Sir William, who sent him to Oxford in the summer of 1692, where he was admitted to Hart Hall— now Hartford College—and obtained his degree of M.A.

He was actually at Hart Hall for less than a month, and not from his leaving Trinity until 1691, as Orrery[4] implies. Both Orrery and Deane Swift[5] relate JS's story that the University authorities there were deceived by the words " *Speciali gratiae* " in the Certificate of his Dublin degree, which they imagined to be a mark of merit, rather than the reverse. Deane Swift then cites the Certificate in full on pp. 45 and 46, and is honest enough to point out that the qualifying words are not, in fact, in it.

---

[4]*Remarks*, p. 8.
[5]*Essay*, p. 32.

Indeed, he shows a very endearing distress in trying to reconcile the evidence of his eyes with what was evidently just another of the Dean's good after-dinner stories.

Returning to Moor Park from Oxford, Swift worked as Temple's secretary until the death of his patron in 1699, with the exception of a period of about two and a half years, when he took holy orders and obtained a prebend in the north of Ireland—an interlude that will be dealt with in the next chapter. During this period of his life in Surrey, he met King William III, who instructed him in the art of cutting asparagus, and offered him—of all things—a commission in a troop of cavalry, " an offer "—as Orrery says—" which in fplenetic difpofitions, he always feemed forry to have refufed ". On his own part, Swift is said to have offered some advice to His Majesty on the subject of the Triennial Bill, which gesture was similarly refused, so leaving the score all square.

It is Deane Swift[6] who introduces the subject of asparagus, in which anecdote he is confirmed by Lyon. Scott[7] tells an amusing story, said to have come from George Faulkner, JS's Irish publisher. When Dr. Leland called Faulkner a blockhead for allowing himself to be bullied by Swift into eating the stalks of his asparagus, Faulkner replied :

> Yes, Doctor, and if you had dined with Dean Swift, *tête-a-tête*, faith you would have been obliged to eat your stalks too !

Before finally passing on from the subject of Oxford, it is necessary to touch on the vexed question of who paid for him there. According to Deane Swift,[8] Uncle William Swift and Cousin Willoughby Swift of Lisbon contributed to the support of their penniless relation not only during the early part of his residence with Temple, but also at Oxford— in fact, up to the somewhat unadolescent age of twenty-seven.

In this contention he has some independent support from Lord Orrery,[9] who writes :

> But I muft not omit to tell you, that another of his father's brothers, WILLIAM SWIFT, affifted him when at *Oxford*, by repeated acts of

---

[6]*Essay*, p. 114.

[7]Scott, vol. I, pp. 29-30.

[8]*Essay*, pp. 52-53. Lyon is "certain" that both William and Willoughby sent JS remittances to Moor Park.

[9]*Remarks*, p. 10.

friendſhip and affection. I have a letter now before me, which, tho'
torn, and imperfect in ſeveral places, ſhows his gratitude and devotion
to the uncle, whom I have juſt now mentioned, and whom he calls
the beſt of his relations.

It should be remarked, however, that all that Orrery alleges is " friendship and affection "—not any financial assistance, and that all that Swift
actually says in this letter[10] is to refer to himself as " one who has always
been but too troubleſome to you", before going on to say :

I am sorry my fortune should fling me so far from the best of my
relations, but hope that I shall have the happiness to see you some
time or other.

An expression of the hope that he might see him some time or other
can hardly be taken as thanks for an Oxford degree, and may better be
accounted for by the fact that Uncle William helped his mother, as we
have seen, in the harassed early days of her widowhood. Nor is Deane
Swift entirely certain about what he alleges, and is frank enough to admit it.

In his *Essay*[11] he goes on to say that it must have been "the ſame generous
Benefactors, the Family of the Swifts " who got together the sum of £300
as a Fortune for JS's sister Jane " to puſh her into the World." But he
admits that this is based on speculation, and he must be regarded as not
entirely disinterested in reaching the above conclusions. Terrified that
this benevolence on Temple's part might give weight to the rumour that
JS was Temple's son, Deane Swift then devotes page after page of his
book to proving, in almost incoherent language, that his great relation
was not in any way financially obliged to Sir William, either for his
education or for his early support. And his argument simply amounts to
this :—that if it did not come from Temple, it must have come from the
Swift family. And that is the end of it.

---

[10]*Correspondence*, vol. I, p. 10.
[11]*Essay*, p. 107 n.

17

KILROOT

SWIFT's departure to build a future for himself independently of his patron was not achieved without some ill-feeling. This can be gathered from his letter to Deane Swift I (his cousin, and the father of his bothered biographer) written from his mother's home in Leicester on the 3rd June, 1694.

> . . . I forgot to tell you I left Sir William Temple a month ago, just as I foretold it to you; and every thing happened thereupon exactly as I guessed. He was extremely angry I left him; and yet would not oblige himself any further than upon my good behaviour, nor would promise any thing firmly to me at all, so that everybody judged I did best to leave him. I design to be ordained September next, and make whatever endeavours I can for something in the Church. . . .[1]

However, on returning to Ireland he found himself confronted with the same kind of difficulty that he must have experienced when there with Southwell four years earlier. A great chasm lay between these prosperous Protestant days and the Dublin that he had known before the Williamite wars. New faces were everywhere—particularly on the Bench of Bishops— and few of them professed to know him, or to be ready to help him. If this young man—last known around the town during the panic before the War—wished to be ordained, he must first produce some certificate from his most recent employer to show that he was a person of good character, suitable for the Ministry. So in October, Swift had to swallow his pride and write to Sir William for his help and recommendation. And it is to the latter's credit that he provided it promptly, without deigning to take out any resentment on the young man for having left him.

As a result of Temple's help, Swift received Deacon's Orders in October, 1694, and Priest's Orders in the January following. In the same month in 1695 he was presented to the Living of Kilroot in County Antrim by Lord Justice Capel—at one time a neighbour of the Temples at Sheen. And so JS began his brief residence as a Parish Clergyman on the shores of Belfast Lough.

[1]*Correspondence*, vol. I, p. 12.

The prebend comprised three small Parishes in a strongly Presbyterian area, with a parsonage on the principal living where, however, the church was in ruins. This meant that Swift had to conduct his services in the two secondary buildings, a fact that did not disgust him nearly as much as the preponderance of Scotch-Irish nonconformists in the area, which included many of the local gentry, and presented a much more difficult problem to a parson of the Established Church than the usual dumb mass of Catholic peasantry.

Sheridan[2] gives the month of his ordination wrongly as September, 1694, and Lyon—presumably on Swift's instruction—adds the words " by Doctor William Moreton, Bishop of Kildare " to the reference in the *Autofrag*. But Forster[3] here again knows better. Contradicting Lyon— and presumably Swift himself—he insists that the Orders " were un- doubtedly conferred by King, then Bishop of Derry". The use of this word " undoubtedly" should put us on our guard. Justifiably so in the present case, for Forster is mistaking " Gug. Darensis", in the original document, for " William Derry", when what it means is " William Kildare". In this, he is at last deserted by Sir Henry Craik, who corrects him.

Varina

There are three stories of his life in County Antrim that must be referred to, although two of them are almost certainly apocryphal. The first of these—and the acceptable one—concerns his courtship of Miss Jane Waring, a daughter of the Archdeacon of Dromore, and a cousin of two of his contemporaries at Trinity.

She was a sister of Westenra Waring, stated by both Forster and Craik, on the authority of Deane Swift, to have been at College with JS. Deane Swift actually describes him as " Chamber Fellow". But Elrington Ball has pointed out[4] that this Waring did not enter Trinity until 1691. JS's actual contemporaries were two cousins, William and Richard Waring.

This " Wassendra Warren (*sic*)", . . . " a Gentleman of undoubted Veracity", assured a female relation of Deane Swift that he had seen the completed MS. of *A Tale of a Tub* when the author was but nineteen years old, and presumably still at Trinity College.[5] This is odd, as Warren (Waring) was not at Trinity College himself until fours years later.

[2]Sheridan, p. 37.
[3]Forster, p. 15 n.
[4]*Correspondence*, vol. I, p. 16 n.
[5]*Essay*, p. 33.

Swift called Jane Waring, Varina, and she passes unnoticed by all the biographers prior to Monck Berkeley, except for a couple of brief references by Deane Swift, and a marginal note by Lyon. But as her refusal of his offer of marriage has been made much of by some recent writers, it is of importance to refer to his final appeal for this lady's affections, dated the 29th April, 1696, and written to her shortly before he left the district on his return to England. She had evidently been flirting with him, but did not think that his prospects as a young parson were good enough to put him into the category of a possible husband. In bidding her farewell, he wrote an extremely long letter, now occupying six pages of Elrington Ball, only two brief extracts from which are given here :—

> . . . I am once more offered the advantage to have the same acquaintance with greatness that I formerly enjoyed, and with better prospect of interest. I here solemnly offer to forego it all for your sake. I desire nothing of your fortune ; you shall live where and with whom you please till my affairs are settled to your desire, and in the meantime I will push my advancement with all the eagerness and courage imaginable, and do not doubt to succeed[6]. . . . the love of Varina is of more tragical consequence than her cruelty. Would to God you had treated and scorned me from the beginning. It was your pity that opened the first way to my misfortune ; and now your love is finishing my ruin. . . . [7]

It is now necessary to skip a few years in order to finish this part of the story. In 1700, after Swift had returned to Dublin as Chaplain to the Earl of Berkeley, one of the Lords Justices, and had been presented to the living of Laracor, Varina changed her mind about his prospects, and indicated that, as he had now more of the qualifications of a husband, she might be persuaded to give him a different answer. Swift, by letter of the 4th May, 1700,[8] which has been variously described as a model of " meanness, selfishness and brutality " and as the answer of an honourable and straightforward man, by no means refused to repeat his offer, but asked her in effect whether she, on her part, was aware of some of the qualifications of a wife—which he thereupon set forth. If the answer was Yes,

---

[6]*Correspondence*, vol. I, p. 18.
[7]Ibid., p. 19.
[8]Ibid., pp. 31-35.

he would be glad to have her in his arms. To this not unreasonable query, he seems to have got no reply. So there the matter ended.

As an entertaining example of the conflicting views of various writers on this letter, compare Jeffrey's hostile comments in Vol. XXVII, p. 28 of the *Edinburgh Review* with those on page 37 of Churton Collins' book on the Dean.

Swift's earlier letter is stated by Elrington Ball[9] to have been in the possession of a Dr. Saunders of Dublin at the time when it was first printed by Monck Berkeley in his *Literary Relics* (1789). The second letter is apparently unknown to Monck Berkeley, and is printed by Elrington Ball from Nichols' Edition of the *Works*,[10] where it made its first appearance without any reference as to where it came from, or where the original was to be found. It would be interesting to know what possessed Miss Waring to keep so crushing a communication, much less to allow it to fall into anybody else's hands.

In a footnote to p. 14 Nichols says that he has the dates of three earlier letters which he, himself, has not seen, and which are still unknown.

Rape

Now for the second incident. In 1786 a story appeared in No. 188 of *The Tatler*, on the authority of a "Reverend Mr. P—", stated to have been one of JS's successors in Kilroot. This was to the effect that JS had been charged with an attempted rape on a farmer's daughter in the neighbourhood, and that information had been laid before a local magistrate called Dobbs, whose family still held all the papers relating to the indictment. This, it was alleged, was the reason for Swift's hurried abandonment of his prebend and his return to England.

Monck Berkeley[11] and Scott[12] refer to the story in order to denounce it, and Scott adds that this Mr. P. died insane in St. Patrick's Hospital, Dublin, (Swift's foundation). But Forster,[13] while agreeing that the scandal was apocryphal, proceeds to render it lethal by pointing out that there was, in fact, a local magnate called Dobbs in the district, and by adding that Swift himself had referred to the incident in letters to his immediate

---

[9]Ibid., p. 15.
[10]Sheridan, vol. X, p. 27.
[11]*Relics*, pp. xlv-lii.
[12]Scott, vol. I, pp. 40-42 n.
[13]Forster, p. 80.

successor in Kilroot, the Rev. John Winder. What Swift actually wrote to Winder from Moor Park on April 1st, 1698, was as follows :—

> Since the resignation of my living and the noise it made amongst you, I have had, at least, three or four very wise letters, unsubscribed, from the Lord knows who, declaring much sorrow for my quitting Kilroot, blaming my prudence for doing it before I was possessed of something else, and censuring my truth in relation to a certain lady. . . . For what they say relating to myself, either as to my prudence or conscience, I can answer sufficiently for my own satisfaction or for that of anybody else who is my friend enough to desire it. . . .[14]

Whether this justifies Forster's assertion that it shows a knowledge of a criminal charge of rape, is a matter that each of us can judge for himself. To my eye, it refers to his leaving Varina, and to some local resentment of that fact. But the story is probably disposed of by the fact that nothing more was ever made of this scandal during his life, even by his most venomous enemies, and that no indictment was ever proceeded with on his return to Ireland only a few years later.

It is also reported by Scott that, after the appearance of this tit-bit in the magazine, Dean Dobbs, then head of the family, was challenged by Malone to produce these alleged papers from his archives, but Dobbs denied that he possessed any such documents.

The whole matter is of interest more as an amusing instance of unpoetic justice than as anything else. Swift was not at all averse to flinging this very charge at other people. In the original edition of the third of *The Drapier's Letters* he brings it against John Browne of the Neale, and in a letter to Harley[15] he does it again at the expense of Sawbridge, Dean of Ferns. Indeed, he elaborated the latter charge into one of his less edifying Ballads.

> A holier priest ne'er was wrapt up in crepe ;
> The worst you can say, he committed a rape.

If, as Scott says, Wharton was at the back of this attack on Swift it was only a fair return for some of the scurrility that was levelled at him by the Dean—in particular the celebrated pamphlet called *A Short Character of His Excellency THOMAS Earl of Wharton.*[16] After reading this libel, it is illuminating to turn to Forster's argument that Swift could not possibly

---

[14]*Correspondence*, vol. I, pp. 22-23.
[15]Ibid., vol. IV, p. 161.
[16]Shakespeare Head SWIFT, vol. III, pp. 177-184.

have written the scurrilous Tripos of 1688, that got him into trouble in Trinity College.

Salter, the Master of Charterhouse, says in a letter to Nichols, quoted by Monck Berkeley,[17] that the origin of Swift's hatred for Wharton lay in the latter's refusal of Somers' request that JS be appointed Chaplain to the Lord Lieutenant when Wharton assumed that office. " Oh my Lord ", Wharton is reported as having replied, " we muſt not prefer or countenance theſe fellows ; We have not character enough *ourſelves*." Actually, this is rather an unassuming remark on the part of Wharton.

Mr. Winder's Black Horse

The last fable also concerns his departure from Kilroot, and is mentioned by Deane Swift, although Sheridan[18] is the one to elaborate it on what looks very like the authority of another good after-dinner tale told by the Dean himself. It seems that Swift one day met an elderly clergyman " of near sixty years of age " riding along the road, and invited him to dinner. So moved was he by the hard-luck story of this impoverished Mr. Winder —the sole support of a wife and eight children—that he offered to ride to Dublin in order to use his influence on Winder's behalf, if the latter would lend him his black horse. This, the parson gratefully agreed to do ; so the generous young man rode off for the capital, where he made the best arrangement that could be managed for his poor old friend ; namely, that he would surrender his own living of Kilroot to him, and return to England to hitch his fortunes once more to the star of Sir William Temple. On his return to the north, Swift put the Presentation into the hands of his new acquaintance, while keeping his eyes

> steadily fixed on the old man's face, in which the joy of finding that it was a presentation to a living, was visibly expressed ; but when he came to that part of the writing which mentioned the name of the living, and found that it was Swift's own which he had resigned in his favour, he looked at him for some time in silence, with such a mixed emotion of astonishment and gratitude in his countenance, as presented to Swift one of the most striking pictures of the mind expressed in the face, he had ever seen ; and he said, that he never before had felt such exquisite pleasure of mind as he did in that hour.

---

[17]*Relics*, pp. xl-xli.
[18]Sheridan, vol. I, pp. 39-41.

. . . The old man, before his departure, pressed him to accept of his black mare . . . as a small token of his gratitude; and Swift was too well acquainted with the sensibility of a generous heart, under obligations, to hurt him by a refusal.

Orrery, Delany, Deane Swift and Hawkesworth give a less amusing account of his going. He was too far from the City, and there was nobody to talk to except Presbyterians. Sir William, meanwhile, was pressing him to return, promising him a Prebend in England if only he would come and help him with his papers during his declining years. So he resigned Kilroot " in favour of a friend ". But it is left to Monck Mason,[19] who married Winder's great-grand-daughter, to mount the most scathing assault on this yarn, with all the vigour of an indignant connection of Winder's family.

He tells us that so far from Winder being an aged and indigent clergyman with a large family, he had a respectable estate of his own, and his eldest child was not born until August 1697. And so far from Swift resigning the living in his favour before returning to England, he left Winder to look after it for nearly two years, until he had finally decided to remain in Moor Park. This last fact is confirmed by the date of the Collation of Winder to the Prebend, which is 11th March, 1698, from which it will be seen that Swift actually held Kilroot for over three years, for the greater part of which he was an absentee.

It is possible that the whole Kilroot interlude, and Swift's desire to leave Sir William's household, followed by his early readiness to return there, may have had something to do with Lady Temple, and her very natural attitude towards some of her husband's dependants. Had she been averse to associating with certain of them, and made Swift self-conscious about his position there, it would have been a strong incentive to him to go away and to establish an independence of his own. This feeling would not, of course, become acute while Lady Temple remained a resident of Pall Mall; but when Temple fell ill late in 1693, Dorothy returned from London to look after him, and according to Mundt's *Lettres sur les Anglais*, she was still there in the summer of 1694. It is significant that this is the very period when Swift decided to leave. But Dorothy died in February, 1695, and was buried on the seventh of that month in Westminster Abbey " within a month of Her Majesty out of sheer grief for her loss "

[19]*History of St. Patrick's*, p. 235.

—as JS sycophantically and inaccurately reports in his Memoir of Temple. Soon after this, Temple seems to have begun pressing him to return to Moor Park. And the fact that Sir William was now a widower, with nobody left in his family but Lady Giffard, may have weighed as heavily with Swift in deciding to reverse his previous decision, as it did with Temple, in persuading him to do so.

In any event, Swift decided to give it another trial in the Spring of the following year (1696). He returned to Moor Park after bidding farewell to Varina, swearing that

> if I leave this kingdom before you are mine, I will endure the utmost indignities of fortune rather than ever return again, though the King would send me back his Deputy.[20]

Although he did leave before she was his, and he never returned to Kilroot, he was actually back in Ireland, in a little more than three years' time, for what turned out to be permanent residence.

Before leaving Kilroot and passing on to the major problem of Swift's life—his relations with Stella—let us pause for a moment to underline one other important feature of the record, as it appears down to this point. Whatever we may feel about some of JS's peculiarities, there is nothing, so far, to indicate anything odd in his attitude towards women or marriage.

His dossier as a student " town-haunter ", the affair with Betty Jones that so worried his mother, and lastly, his very orthodox proposal to Varina, have all the marks of a man who likes women, and who gives every indication of looking forward to a normal married life, as soon as he can afford a wife and a home of his own. Accepting the official parentage as correct, his relatives are healthy and extremely philoprogenitive. Three of his uncles had nine or ten wives between them, and produced thirty-six children. And if an " itch " had not killed his supposed father, there is every reason to believe that the latter would have continued in the same tradition.

Nor does JS give any indication, either in his correspondence or in his behaviour, that he is afraid that an overdose of fruit, eaten in adolescence, was likely to affect his marriage chances later on—much less result in insanity during his sere and yellow, as seems to have been W. B. Yeats' conclusion.[21]

---

[20]*Correspondence*, vol. I, p. 19.
[21]*The Words upon the Window Pane.*

18

LARACOR

The child from the cottage on the estate—the dark-eyed daughter of Lady Giffard's housekeeper—was now a girl in her 'teens. There is little evidence, apart from Macaulay's fertile imagination and an expression in Temple's will, that she was ever treated as a servant, or waited on Lady Giffard. On the other hand, there is evidence that she enjoyed the special attention of the master of Moor Park, and was taught her lessons by the Secretary.

Scott[1] considers that she was very poorly educated, and deduces from the fact that some public matters of great simplicity were explained to Stella and Dingley by Swift in some of his letters, that the two ladies were gravely deficient in matters of common knowledge. Whether or not this conclusion is justified, she was uncertain of her spelling to the last. But she was also destined to become as good a poet as her celebrated Tutor. Indeed Yeats considered that she was a better one.[2]

Sir William died early in the morning of the 27th January, 1699, leaving to Stella the legacy already mentioned, and to " Mr. Jonathan Swift now dwelling with me " the sum of £100, and the task of editing and publishing his collected Works.

He died on good terms with his spirited secretary, a fact that disproves the widespread belief that the proud spirit of JS could never endure any patronage. We must find a better reason for his hatred of Uncle Godwin.

While quarrelling with Martha Giffard over problems of editorship, Swift hoped for a time that the King would honour what he considered to be the promise of a prebend in the Church of England. But nothing came of it. Now that Temple was dead, a chill had settled on London, and the compliments and easy pledges, that had been his whenever he had visited the Court of St. James on behalf of Sir William, suddenly ceased. The best that he could do was to obtain the job of chaplain and secretary

---

[1]Scott, p. 56 n.
[2]*The Words upon the Window Pane.*

to the Earl of Berkeley,[3] when this peer was appointed as one of the Lords Justices for Ireland.

It was during this period of service with Berkeley that he wrote his celebrated parody of a religious pamphlet, *A Meditation on a Broomstick*, as a gentle hoax on Lady Berkeley for the amusement of her daughters.

But even this appointment turned out to be disappointing, for on arriving at Dublin in Berkeley's suite, he was argued out of the secretary-ship by a man named Bush, and found that he had nothing to his name but the chaplaincy. The Deanery of Derry, which then fell vacant, was sold to a higher bidder by the same Bush, and all that he could obtain from his new employer was the triple living of Laracor, Agher and Rathbeggan in County Meath, where, for the second time, he entered upon the life of a country parson, in February, 1700.

He returned to England for a few months in the Spring of 1701, when Berkeley lost his appointment, during which visit Swift saw his mother in Leicester, and had some highly important discussions in Surrey, that were to have a profound bearing on the rest of his life. As a result of what-ever was said there, Stella—now just turned twenty—decided to leave Farnham and her mother, and to trust her fortune and her future to Swift in Ireland, in the company of Temple's relation, Rebecca Dingley—a granddaughter of Sir John Dingley of Ventnor, a local magnate whom we have already come across during the Isle of Wight episode.

JS tells us in *On the Death of Mrs. Johnson* that he persuaded Stella to remove her residence to the sister island because of the high rate of interest prevailing there, which would mean that her fortune would go further. Others archly insinuate that she crossed the sea because she was after Swift. But the reason that probably carried the most weight with Stella was her own wish—now that she was old enough to do so—to get away from Farnham.

Deane Swift[4] considers that her real " Intent was to captivate the Heart of Dr. SWIFT ", and quotes a portion of a letter from Thomas Swift, the

---

[3]There are too many Berkeleys in Swift's life, and most of them are not even related. This one is Charles, 2nd Earl of Berkeley, who is not to be confused with the Lords Berkeley of Stratton, two of whom married nieces of Sir William Temple. Nor, of course, with Berkeley the philosopher, who was later Bishop of Cloyne and one of Vanessa's Executors. Nor with the latter's grandson, Monck Berkeley, the compiler of the *Literary Relics*.

[4]*Essay*, pp. 91-92.

Vicar of Puttenham, JS's first cousin and companion at Trinity, in which the Vicar enquires of the unknown recipient

> whether JONATHAN be married? or whether he has been able to refift the Charms of both thofe Gentlewoman that marched quite from *Moor Park* to *Dublin* (as they would have marched to the *North* or any where elfe) with full Refolution to engage him.

This Thomas Swift was an intimate contemporary of JS during his adolescence, and, according to Elrington Ball, took his place as companion and chaplain to Temple while JS was in Kilroot. His enquiry is of importance in showing that he had no knowledge of any impediment in the way of a marriage between JS and Stella, or indeed of any circumstances that might suggest that his cousin was not the marrying type. Nor could JS be regarded any longer as an impoverished parson, for in the autumn of 1700, Narcissus Marsh, the Archbishop of Dublin, gave him the Prebend of Dunlavin in St. Patrick's Cathedral. With these four sources of income, together with a Chaplaincy in Dublin Castle, it is hardly surprising that Varina decided to reconsider him as an eligible husband.

It is not unreasonable to suppose that Sir William on his deathbed entrusted the future of his only remaining child to the young man for whom he, himself, had done so much, and that this was the basis of Swift's assumption of a position *in loco parentis* that was afterwards taken for granted by Stella's suitors.

As to the date of the coming of the ladies to Ireland, JS does not remember it, and leaves the last figure a blank when writing *On the Death of Mrs. Johnson*. Nichols in his Edition adds a note " probably in 1700 "[5] which Forster incorporates in a misquotation from Swift's text, and then contradicts his own misquotation in a note on p. 126. All agree now that 1701 is the correct date for Stella's first arrival in Dublin.

From the start of this adventure the utmost discretion was shown. Rebecca Dingley took on the role of chaperone, and the two ladies travelled to Dublin in advance of Swift's return, in order to forestall any gossip that might arise from the fact of their all arriving together. Dingley had less to live on than had the housekeeper's daughter—an annuity of about £27 a year[6]—and it should be noted that JS's account books disclose that for the greater part of their remaining years, Swift supplemented

---

[5]Sheridan, vol. IX, p. 344 n.
[6]Hawkesworth, vol. I, p. 16.

both ladies' incomes from his own, pretending that he was collecting and paying Dingley only the profits of her own investments. Stella, on the other hand, was fully aware that the pretence that both she and her companion were living on their own incomes was only a pious fraud. Yet she accepted this situation without any apparent comment.

Lyon, in a note on Hawkesworth's page 27, gives Dingley's income as only £16 a year, to which JS secretly added £52 a year. Hawkesworth, on the same page, says that he always acted as though he were merely her Agent,

> and fometimes would pretend with great feeming vexation, that fhe drew upon him before he had received her money from *London*.

Assuming the prevailing view to be right, that there was no secret tie or other obligation between Stella and JS, one might conclude that she cannot have been a very proud young woman to have accepted support for the rest of her life from a man who was actually a stranger, but who perhaps reluctantly married her at a later stage of their life together, while going to enormous lengths to avoid being compromised by her embarrassing presence. Swift, too, must have been an extremely prudish parson, where she alone was concerned. For the circumspection continued. Often when JS was away in England, Stella and Dingley would take up residence in his vicarage. But whenever he came back, they moved either to Trim, or to Dublin, or to a cottage near Laracor that still bears Stella's name. Never could it be said that Swift and Stella were living together in the same house, even under the respectable chaperonage of Dingley. Indeed, it is constantly alleged that, henceforward, they were never seen together except in the presence of a third party—a fact that can hardly be literally true, but which argues an extraordinary care on the part of Swift, where Stella was concerned.

The reviewer of Orrery's book, writes on p. 415 of *Monthly Review* for November, 1751 :

> We will not take it upon us to affirm, whether our noble author or ourfelves have been mifinformed in this particular; but we are credibly affured, that the dean, who certainly was exceffively fond of his *Stella*, frequently vifited her in private. An honeft fober woman who lived in the fame houfe with that unfortunate lady, declares that the dean particularly vifited her very often when fhe was ill, and

uſually devoted the time to RELIGION; and that ſhe frequently, in an adjoining room, overheard him praying extempore. . . .

It might also be expected that so charming a girl would have offers of marriage. And so, of course, she had. For example, the Rev. William Tisdall, whose family Swift had known when he was in Kilroot, was a friend of the ladies from soon after their appearance in Dublin, and corresponded with JS during the latter's visit to England during the winter of 1703–4.

From this point onwards the relevant dates begin to fall thick and fast, and are increasingly easy to ascertain. Most of those relating to his journeys to and from England are to be found in his Account and Note Books, and can be accepted in their most accessible form from Craik. But before passing on from this winter visit of 1703–4, it is interesting to refer to a statement by Forster,[7] confirmed by one of Lyon's MS. notes to Hawkesworth, that " in his notebooks now in my possession " there is a reference to the return portion of this journey as his tenth voyage between the two countries.

According to the record which is mainly provided by Swift himself, this was not his tenth, but his fourteenth crossing of the sea, which must mean that in making the entry he either forgot, or wished to forget, both the Whitehaven incident and his unprofitable trip with Southwell.

(1) To Whitehaven soon after his birth.
(2) To Dublin from Whitehaven probably about 1672.
(3) To Leicester early in 1688.
(4) To Ulster with Southwell in June, 1690.
(5) To Leicester in late 1690.
(6) To Dublin in the Summer of 1694.
(7) To Moor Park from Kilroot before the end of 1695.
(8) To Dublin with Berkeley, Summer, 1699.
(9) To England with Berkeley, May, 1701.
(10) To Laracor, September, 1701.
(11) To England, April, 1702.
(12) To Ireland, October, 1702.
(13) To England, November, 1703.
(14) To Ireland, May/June, 1704.

---

[7]Forster, p. 131.

For the convenience of future reference, this list is continued as follows :—

(15) Ireland to London, March, 1705. (Stella was in England too.)

(16) London to Laracor, Autumn, 1705.

(17) Laracor to London, November/December, 1707. To begin with, Stella was again in England—her last visit.

(18) London to Laracor, June, 1709.

(19) Laracor to London, August/September, 1710. His mother had died at Leicester in the previous April.
The Whigs fell shortly after his arrival, and he remained in London to edit *The Examiner*.

(20) London to Dublin, June, 1713, to be installed as Dean of St. Patrick's.

(21) Dublin to London, September, 1713.
Harley fell in July, 1714, and Queen Anne died on the 1st August.

(22) London to Dublin, August, 1714.
On this occasion he was soon followed by Vanessa.

(23) Dublin to Twickenham, March, 1726.
About the publication of *Gulliver*.

(24) Twickenham to Dublin, August, 1726.
Stella was ill.

(25) Dublin to London, April, 1727.

(26) London to Dublin for the last time, in mid-September, 1727.
Stella died about three months after his return.

During the early spring of 1704, Tisdall evidently enquired about Swift's intentions with regard to Stella, in order to ascertain whether it would be proper for him to pay his own addresses to her. The whole of the correspondence has not survived, but in Elrington Ball[8] can be found JS's reply from London, dated the 20th April, in which he writes :—

> . . . First, I think I have said to you before, that, if my fortunes and humour served me to think of that state (matrimony), I should certainly, among all persons on earth, make your choice ; because I never saw that person whose conversation I entirely valued but hers ; this was the utmost I ever gave way to. And secondly, I must assure you

---

[8]*Correspondence*, vol. I, pp. 45-47.

sincerely, that this regard of mine never once entered into my head to be an impediment to you ; but I judged it would, perhaps, be a clog to your rising in the world ; and I did not conceive you were then rich enough to make yourself and her happy and easy. But that objection is now quite removed by what you have at present. . . .

The letter continues in the same reasonable vein, and is difficult to match up with Deane Swift's story[9] of his having insisted that Tisdall keep a coach for his wife, and settle a hundred pounds a year upon her for pin money. If such conditions were ever suggested, no evidence of them has survived apart from Deane Swift's account of the matter, which seems acutely at variance with the letter that we do possess. Nor can it be seen how such a letter as the one we have read could have, in the words of Sir Henry Craik[10], " the desired effect of closing the episode."

Deane Swift[11] alleges that he has obtained his additional information about JS's terms to Tisdall from some further correspondence which he has seen, but was not allowed to copy. It is a pity that he did not at least let us know in whose hands it was, because it has never since come to light.

What is of interest is Tisdall's evident assumption that Swift was the appropriate person to forward his proposal to Stella's mother, and that Swift frankly accepted this anomalous position, only demurring at doing what Tisdall asked without Stella's express consent. Both Deane Swift and Sheridan believe—not without some reason—that the whole episode was promoted by Stella herself, in order to bring Swift to the point of declaring his own intentions. Furthermore—according to Sheridan—it was her action, and not anything that Swift said or did, that finally gave Tisdall his congé. But what actually did pass between Swift and Stella is just another question-mark in the mystery of the relationship of these two extraordinary lovers.

A little more than a month after the date of Tisdall's last letter, Swift returned from London to Dublin, and evidently reached some permanent understanding with his woman friend. One might imagine that the outcome of such a crisis, which she may indeed have engineered herself, would have been marriage for Stella—if not with Swift, then with Tisdall.

[9]*Essay*, p. 94.
[10]Craik, p. 118.
[11]*Essay*, p. 93.

But, whatever took place between her and JS, no such solution was reached. She married neither. Tisdall was dismissed, and as far as can be judged, Swift and Stella continued their relationship under precisely the same anomalous conditions as before, with this solitary difference—that there were now no more suitors.

And, strangest of all, Stella appeared to be quite content with this situation, and made no further move, either to graduate from the tutelage of her *de facto* guardian, as most normal women of full age would do if baffled in an attempt to raise the issue of marriage, or to regularise her position in the eyes of the world in any other way.

From this behaviour springs the widespread conception of Stella as an extremely compliant and submissive young person—an ingénue, so loving and so meek in her disposition that she never could bring herself to demand marriage or a home from her adored one, so long as he did not choose to offer them. What did she care if Dublin buzzed with rumours that she was his kept woman? Or even that she was his secret wife?—a wife so deplorable socially, that their marriage had to be hushed up. She had the companionship of her wonderful man—and that was sufficient on any terms for a woman who truly loves.

It is hardly surprising that several generations of male Victorians have wept their great hearts out over Stella.

> Who hasn't in his mind the image of Stella? Who does not love her? Fair and tender creature; pure and affectionate heart! Boots it to you now, that you have been at rest for a hundred and twenty years, not divided in death from the cold heart which caused yours, whilst it beat, such faithful pangs of love and grief—boots it to you now, that the whole world loves and deplores you? Scarce any man, I believe, ever thought of that grave, that did not cast a flower of pity on it, and wrote over it a sweet epitaph. Gentle lady, so lovely, so loving, so unhappy! you have had countless champions, millions of manly hearts mourning for you. From generation to generation we take up the fond tradition of your beauty; we watch and follow your tragedy, your bright morning love and purity, your constancy, your sweet martyrdom. We know your legend by heart. You are one of the saints of English story.[12]

[12]*English Humorists*, pp. 45-46.

This is Thackeray—the creator of that best of all Victorian vixens, Becky Sharp, but who is evidently in a highly emotional condition when he contemplates Stella.

But if millions of manly hearts feel this way about the state of Stella's organs, is the same true for the ladies? What do they think about this delineation of one of their sex, who, when some fool remarked in her presence that Miss Vanhomrigh must have been a very remarkable woman to have inspired so fine a poem as *Cadenus and Vanessa*, tartly replied that " it was well known the Dean could write finely upon a broomstick."[13]

And how does Thackeray's picture match up with another view of Stella that is given in Swift's Essay?

> She and her friend having removed their lodgings to a new house, which stood solitary, a parcel of rogues, armed, attempted the house, where there was only one boy. She was then about four-and-twenty; and having been warned to apprehend some such attempt, she learned the management of a pistol; and the other women and servants being half dead with fear, she stole softly to her dining-room window, put on a black hood to prevent being seen, primed the pistol fresh, gently lifted up the sash, and taking her aim with the utmost presence of mind, discharged the pistol, loaded with the bullets, into the body of one villain, who stood the fairest mark. The fellow, mortally wounded, was carried off by the rest, and died the next morning.[14]

This lack of consistency between the resolute character of this acid-tongued young woman as depicted in Swift's *Bon Mots de Stella*, and the meek little piece that one might visualise from her behaviour with her Dean, is another part of the problem that is going to become even worse when we get to 1716. For the moment, she must remain as a courageous girl with a sharp tongue and an excellent aim, who was content to forgo matrimony with an eligible clergyman in order not to marry the Vicar of Laracor.

---

[13]*Observations*, p. 58.
[14]Temple Scott, vol. XI, p. 130.

19

LONDON

WE have now reached the beginning of Swift's life as a public figure—a well documented period, throughout which there can be little serious controversy over the principal facts. He was in the public eye. His activities and sayings were of sufficient importance to be widely noted. And if this is not enough, there is *The Journal to Stella*, which—whatever may have inspired its preservation, and however one-sided are some of the views therein expressed—was not written for the purpose of hoaxing biographers.

As the books become correspondingly reliable about dates and details, the controversy shifts from facts to motives. We may therefore hasten through his life in London, which has been most adequately described, and come to the next vexed question—that of his supposed marriage.

Between March 1705 and the summer of 1709, JS had two spells of residence in England, during each of which Stella also returned for a brief visit. During the first, which lasted for rather more than six months, he became widely known as the Mad Parson of the Coffee Houses—the shadowy author of *A Tale of a Tub*, and, as such, he laid the foundations of most of his literary friendships. The second visit lasted over a year and a half, and had a political purpose—to persuade Queen Anne's Government to grant the First Fruits to the clergy of Ireland, as had already been done for the Church of England. The Whigs, however, were still in power, and little progress was made towards this end, until the Tories came in under Harley and St. John during the summer of 1710, and JS returned to London once again.

This third period, until the death of the Queen in the summer of 1714, was Swift's great era of political power, during most of which he remained permanently in England, as the principal pamphleteer for the Government. Except for the last year, it is also the period covered by the *Journal to Stella*, and the heyday of his affair with Vanessa.

The most vivid objective description of JS in the flood-tide of his power is to be found in the MS. diary of White Kennett, Bishop of Peterborough, which is amongst the Lansdowne papers in the British Museum. It was first printed by Nichols, but can most conveniently be found in Elrington Ball.[1] It also has been reprinted by Carl Van Doren and Bertram Newman in their biographies of the Dean.

But, although he was eminently successful in obtaining the First Fruits for his fellow clergy, and in getting financial backing for his friend Pope's translation of Homer, and in influencing the Ministers over innumerable appointments, he failed singularly to obtain anything of real value for himself. Patent after patent for bishoprics passed before his eyes, but they were always for others—never for him. It is usually said that Queen Anne, herself, was behind this opposition to his advancement. She would not make a bishop of any parson who had written such a book as *A Tale of a Tub*. If this is the true explanation, she must have been a woman of even more profound stupidity than is usually supposed, for the *Tale* is one of the best apologies for the Anglican position that has ever been written.

It is just as likely, however—as Deane Swift very properly points out[2] —that his employers, the Ministers, never pressed his claims upon the Queen, in spite of their protestations to the contrary, preferring to retain his febrile pen in a dependent position rather than make him a bishop, and so have him permanently in the House of Lords, where he would have been a power to reckon with in his own right. When the twilight of the Tories was at hand, all that Swift could obtain as a reward for his services was the Deanery of St. Patrick's, Dublin, which, of course, for a man in his position, amounted to banishment. And many a noble politician—both Whig and Tory—must have breathed a sigh of relief as soon as he was safely back across the Irish Sea.

Yet JS, himself, never seems to have been fully alive to this duplicity, and he stuck resolutely to the adventurers who had made use of him, throughout their exile or imprisonment under the first Hanoverian King. In this respect he proved himself to be capable of both gratitude and loyalty to an absurd degree, refusing all advances from the Whigs for the rest of his life—a fact that disproves another popular misconception, that he was an ungrateful political turncoat, who had only attached himself to Harley and the Tories for purely selfish reasons.

It is, however, his social relationships in London that concern us at the moment, more than his political. Oddly enough, while the ladies in Dublin

[1]*Correspondence*, vol. II, pp. 414-415.
[2]*Essay*, p. 163.

came from England, the ladies in England had come from Dublin. Bartholomew Vanhomrigh, Merchant (and probably also a Shipowner), was originally of Amsterdam, and the Special Licence for his marriage to a Dublin lady named Hester Stone, is addressed to the Vicar of St. Andrew's and dated the 7th December, 1686.

Bartholomew Vanhomrigh

Orrery[3] mistakenly supposes that he first came to Ireland at the time of the Revolution, and adds that Vanessa's mother " whose name I forget, was born in Ireland of very mean extraction." He afterwards learns that her name was Esther (*sic*) Stone, and adds this detail in a holograph note to one of the copies of his book which is at present in Harvard (opp. p. 105). But he does not bother to rehabilitate her socially. In actual fact her father, John Stone, was a Revenue Commissioner and a person apparently of both good standing and education. And the celebrated Miss Long, the toast of London in her day, used to refer to Vanessa as her cousin.

Vanhomrigh, although a Protestant and a foreigner, was sufficiently acceptable to the authorities in Dublin, as late as October, 1687, to be made an Alderman of the city on that date, and his infant daughter, Esther, in common with the other Aldermen's children, was " enrolled free of the City " on the second Friday after Easter in 1688, as appears from the Dublin Assembly Roll for that year.[4] In a document amongst the Southwell MSS., which is to be found in Trinity College, there was originally a star opposite his name, intended as a mark of approval for those who had not been friends " to the Lord Chancellor and his late Government." But this star was subsequently deleted—an indication that, perhaps, Vanhomrigh may have been over-prudent in his relations with James's government, prior to the arrival of the Prince of Orange, a suspicion that also is in the mind of Gilbert, the editor of the Dublin Calendar. Nevertheless, he took flight in 1689, and according to Luttrell's diary, he arrived in London " from the English camp in Ireland " in October of that year. He was included in the list of those attainted by the Jacobite Parliament before the Battle of the Boyne, and was back in Schonberg's camp at Lisburn before the end of the same year, as one of the two Commissaries General for the Army. Subsequently, he was made

[3]*Remarks*, p. 69.
[4]*Calendar of Ancient Records of Dublin*, vol. V, pp. 472-473.

a Commissioner for Revenue, sat for Derry City in the Williamite Parliament, and in 1697 became Lord Mayor of Dublin, in which last office he obtained from the King the handsome SS collar or chain that is still worn by the chief city official. He died, a reasonably wealthy man, on the 29th December, 1703, and was buried in St. Andrew's Parish Church on the 1st January following.

St. Andrew's Parish

So far, we have not heard much of St. Andrew's Parish, but hereafter, we will find it assuming a certain importance as the parish of the residents of the area east of the Castle. So it is now appropriate to say something about its history. The Church was originally in Dame Street, close to the gate of the Lower Castle Yard. In 1554, during the period of the Reformation, the parish was amalgamated with St. Werburgh's by George Browne, Archbishop of Dublin, and the church was turned to various secular uses, becoming in turn a Mint and a Viceregal stable. It eventually fell into complete decay, and its site became that of a City Market.

In 1665, about two years before Swift's birth, the parish was reconstituted by Act of Parliament, and from 1670 till 1674 a new church—popularly known as the Round Church—was in the process of erection further east, more or less on the site of the present Parish Church in Suffolk Street. As a corrupt contractor was given the job, this edifice soon began to fall down, and had to be rebuilt on the old foundations in the latter part of the 18th century. This new building was burnt in 1860, and the present Victorian church was then put up " a few yards to the south."[5]

The Registers of the new Parish began in 1670, but were unfortunately the first to be deposited for safe keeping in the Record Office, where they were blown up in 1922. To add to our difficulties the Parish Register Society has unluckily here confined its selection to Marriage Entries only, from 1672. However, I am indebted to a memorandum made in 1906 by Mr. H. S. Guinness, a copy of which has been kindly supplied to me by Mrs. Kennedy, the widow of a recent Rector—a memorandum which is silent on the subject of any Swifts, but which happily provides some useful information about the Vanhomrigh family.

---

[5]Much of the above information can be found in the Rev. S. C. Hughes' *Church of St. Werburgh, Dublin*, and in H. A. Wheeler's and M. J. Craig's informative handbook, *The Dublin City Churches of the Church of Ireland*, published in 1948.

Examining the Registers in 1904 in search of some traces of Vanessa, Mr. Guinness found and noted the baptisms of Ginkel and Mary Vanhomrigh on the 27th January, 1693, and the 7th September, 1694, respectively. These are Vanessa's younger brother and only sister.[6]

Guinness also found the burial of Bartholomew, the father, on the 1st January, 1704, and of Mary on the 3rd March, 1721. No record could be found of Esther's baptism—which occurred before the Revolution—or of that of her brother Bartholomew, who was probably born before the end of the upheavals caused by the War. At any rate he was of sufficient age to make a will on the 3rd March, 1714. From this will, Mr. Guinness is satisfied that both the mother and the son, Ginkel, were buried in St. James's, Westminster. The son, Bartholomew, was probably buried in England too, although his will was admitted to probate in Ireland on the 6th July, 1715.

This left only Esther unaccounted for, and after a further search, the page containing her burial record was found, bound up amongst the baptisms. The edge of the page was mutilated, so obscuring the day of the month, but the entry was the third for the month of June, 1723. And in one of the Vestry Books he also found the following corroboration :—

June 4, received for breaking ground in the Church for Mrs. Esther Vanhomrigh, £2. 0. 0.

From the above it seems clear that she died very early in June, 1723, and was buried, like her father, under the floor of the old Round Church. But where precisely her remains now lie in relation to the present Church, it is impossible to say. Vanessa's grave is irretrievably lost.

As to her birth on the 14th February, 1688, it is clear from the *Journal to Stella* that this was the day of the month that was celebrated as her

---

[6]Elrington Ball, on p. 456 of Vol. III of the *Correspondence*, gives the year of Ginkel's baptism as 1693/4, which places it only a little more than eight months before the baptism of the next child, Mary. If we explain away this physiological anomaly by saying that Ginkel's ceremony must have been considerably delayed, we then find ourselves placing his birth within a distance almost equally perilous of that of the previous son, Bartholomew, who—according to Ball—was fifteen in 1708. If we accept these figures as correct, it means that the longest possible period over which Mrs. Vanhomrigh could have given birth to three children was twenty months—no mean feat. So I am accepting the figures that are provided by Guinness in preference to those that are Ball's. As Guinness has clearly corrected his dates to the modern usage in the case of Bartholomew's and Mary's burials, it may be assumed that he has also done so in the case of Ginkel's baptism, and that 1693 means what it says.

birthday by the household in London, and from the other figures mentioned above, no other year is possible, unless she was conceived before her parents' marriage—a hypothesis that nobody has had the temerity to urge.

Elrington Ball's excellent summary of the result of his researches into the Vanhomrigh history is to be found in Appendix III to Volume III of the *Correspondence*. It may be accepted as the best account that we have, with only two or three reservations. The first of these is with regard to the birth dates of Vanessa's brothers and sister, already referred to. The second concerns Ball's idea that Vanessa may have invented St. Valentine's Day as her birthday in order to impress the Dean, or to appeal to his sympathies in some obscure way. If so, her whole family must have been party to this somewhat pointless hoax, as the *Journal to Stella* makes it clear that her birthday was celebrated in her home on the 14th February as early in their acquaintance as 1711.

The third is another slightly far-fetched theory that an elaborate fraud was practised on Swift in order to deceive him about her age. On the strength of a reference in Letter XXVIII of the *Journal*: " Her eldest daughter is come of age, and going to Ireland to look after her fortune and get it in her own hands," Ball suggests that JS was led to believe that Vanessa was only twenty-one at a time when she was actually sinking into the sere and yellow of twenty-three. It does not follow, of course, that Swift believed she had only just come of age at the time of writing. The purport of his remark was to explain why she was going to Ireland.

In December, 1707, four years after her husband's death, the widow Vanhomrigh brought her family with her to London, in order presumably to cut a better social dash on her late husband's money than could ever be managed in Dublin. Elrington Ball reports as follows :—

> In the letter to Dawson she remarks with a note of triumph that she had already seen several friends and acquaintances at her lodgings. . . .
> There is reason to believe that Swift was amongst the acquaintances who waited upon Mrs. Vanhomrigh on her arrival in London.[7]

Indeed, as Ball suggests, JS himself travelled to London early in the same month, so it may be that they first became acquainted on the journey,

---

[7]*Correspondence*, vol. III, p. 457.

and that this is what is referred to in the allusive passage in Swift's letter to Vanessa of August 13, 1720, during one of the great crises in their friendship :

> What would you give to have the history of Cad—— and ———— exactly written, through all its steps, from the beginning to this time ? I believe it would do well in verse, and be as long as the other. I hope it will be done. It ought to be an exact chronicle of twelve years from the time of spilling of coffee, to drinking of coffee, from Dunstable to Dublin, with every single passage since.[8]

This does seem to suggest that Dunstable saw the beginning of their friendship with a spilling of coffee, just as Dublin was to see its climax, with a drinking of this enigmatic beverage.

The visit to England that is described in *The Journal to Stella*, opens with a return to London in August/September, 1710. Although there are many references to " Mrs. Van " and her hospitable home in the course of the *Journal*, Vanessa is only mentioned three times, and never actually by name. These references come on the 2nd and 14th February, 1711, and on the 14th August in the same year.

As at Moor Park, the prospect of instructing an intelligent and amusing young girl proved irresistible to Swift—" a Man beyond all others upon Earth, whoſe Delight was to give Instruction to young People and especially to young Women,"[9] and before long he had assumed an informal appointment as her Tutor. She was almost seven years younger than Stella—a fact that is often forgotten in the popular picture of the two women—and the course of their growing attachment is convincingly described in the poem *Cadenus and Vanessa*—" Cadenus " being an anagram for Decanus the Dean, and " Vanessa " being the name that he invented for the purposes of the poem, and that he thereafter applied to her. It was written for her private eye alone, and could hardly have strayed too far from the recognisable facts, if it was to mean anything to her.

Most of the early biographers minimise the apparent enormity of Swift's conduct towards this young and eager pupil by insisting that she was a forward hussy, and that all the advances came from her. Orrery describes her as follows :

VANESSA was exceſſively vain. . . . She was fond of dreſs : impatient

---

[8]Freeman, p. 121.
[9]*Essay*, p. 257.

to be admired ; very romantic in her turn of mind : ſuperior in her own opinion, to all her ſex : full of pertneſs, gaiety and pride : not without ſome agreeable accompliſhments, but far from being either beautiful or genteel . . . happy in the thoughts of being reputed SWIFT'S concubine : but ſtill aiming and intending to be his wife.[10]

Then he takes the opportunity of warning his dear Hamilton against the dangers involved in preferring wit to religion, and concludes with the gloomy epilogue :

> Thus periſhed, at *Selbridge*, under all the agonies of deſpair, Mrs. ESTHER VANHOMRIGH ; a miſerable example of an ill-ſpent life, fantaſtic wit, viſionary ſchemes, and female weakneſs.

His Lordship's mother in a letter commenting on her son's book which has been copied out on pages 72–73 of one of the copies of the *Remarks* in the Harvard Library writes :

> Tho' Vaneſsa was very unfortunate, ſhe does not ſtir up one Sentiment of Pity for her hard fate in our breaſt : whereas no eye can read the misfortunes of Stella without a tear.

Dr. Delany firmly challenges Orrery's description of the lady, which he describes as " utterly inconſiſtent with the endowments beſtowed upon her, both by VENUS, and PALLAS,"[11] but he cannot refrain from prefacing this gentlemanly defence by the disclosure that she " certainly gave herſelf up (as ARIADNE did) to BACCHUS, from the day ſhe was deſerted." Delany, of course, at the time of writing was not aware of any particular need to defend his old friend, JS. He had not read the correspondence with Vanessa, and had been falsely assured by Dr. Berkeley that the letters " contained nothing which would either do honour to her character, or bring the leaſt reflection upon CADENUS."

In the present century, Sophie S. Smith provides us with an amusing example of the lengths to which the abuse of this unfortunate young woman can be carried in an effort to make Swift out to be a kind, middle-aged gentleman, horrified by her exhibitions of affection, and writing *Cadenus and Vanessa* with the benevolent intention of showing her that " all hope of love between them was impossible." Vanessa's " misfortune

---

[10]*Remarks*, p. 70.
[11]*Observations*, p. 121.

lay purely in her own character ". She was ill-suited to become Swift's pupil, and " entirely unsuitable for friendship with him or any other man."

It is only the despised Deane Swift,[12] in his zealous defence of whatever he conceives to be the truth, who comes to the rescue of the unfortunate Vanessa.

> I have been affured, that Mifs VANHOMRIGH was in her general Converfe with the World, as far from encouraging any Stile of Addrefs, inconfiftent with the Rules of Honour and Good-breeding, as any Woman alive. Neither can it be faid, if any Conclufions may be drawn from her Appearance and Behaviour in Ireland, that fhe was either a vain Woman, or fond of Drefs ; although fhe was extremely nice and delicate, as well in the Cleanlinefs of her Perfon, as in every Thing fhe wore. Her only Misfortune was, that fhe had a Paffion for Dr. SWIFT, which was not to be conquered ; although it is a Point inconteftable, that Dr. SWIFT, had never once made her the moft diftant Overtures of Marriage. And this Paffion (her Friends, I hope, will excuse me for afferting it) was in all Probability the remote Cause of her Death. She languifhed, I think, for fome Years, and fell into a Confumption ; neither, as I have heard, was fhe convinced that Dr. SWIFT was married to Mrs. JOHNSON, until about two Months before her Deceafe.

And then he concludes, in an amusing parody of Orrery :

> Thus died at *Cellbridge*, worthy of an happier Fate, the celebrated Mrs. ESTHER VANHOMRIGH, a Martyr to Love and Conftancy.

In this gallant defence of a much-maligned woman, Deane Swift is half-heartedly supported by Monck Berkeley,[13] who says that no apology can be offered for the Dean's conduct towards her, and very fairly points out that she " knew of no engagement to prevent their union." Nevertheless, he has to add :

> the encouragement she gave to Swift might be rather inconfiftent with the etiquette observed by all *prudent* and *experienced* women when in a ftate of courtfhip.

It is patently obvious that whatever may have been the attitude of this

---

[12]*Essay*, p. 277.
[13]*Relics*, p. xxxviii.

girl hardly out of her teens, she could have made no advances to the Vicar
of Laracor—a man-of-the-world in his forties, who was soon to become
the mainstay of the Government—that he did not make possible by his
own behaviour. Furthermore, it is not any defence of Swift, but an insult
to his intelligence, to suggest that he was made a fool of against his better
judgment by this hoyden of St. James'. As Elrington Ball demonstrates
in the Appendix above quoted, it was Swift who made the first advances
to the family in 1708, and who renewed the acquaintance in 1710. It was
he who called upon the household in St. Jame's, and invited her visits to
Chelsea and Kensington. If the Vicar was soon to be regarded—as he was
—as a possible suitor for Miss Vanhomrigh, he had nobody to blame but
himself. And to try to get him out of this position by saying that it was
all the girl's doing is to imply that JS must have been a simpleton.

What the present writer is going to imply is the solution that is the only
justification for Swift—namely, that he loved this girl, and that she was
probably his mistress. This last point, however, is not necessary to any
thesis, and is purely a matter of opinion, to be deduced or not from what
they wrote to each other.

Would the following arch verse be more likely to be written for the
private eye of a woman with whom Swift had had sexual relations, or to
one with whom he had not?

> But what Success *Vanessa* met,
> Is to the World a Secret yet :
> Whether the Nymph, to please her Swain,
> Talks in a high Romantic strain ;
> Or whether he at last descends
> To like with less Seraphick Ends ;
> Or, to compound the Business, whether
> They temper Love and Books together ;
> Must never to Mankind be told,
> Nor shall the conscious Muse unfold.

If this is not enough on which to form any opinion, perhaps a few
extracts from the correspondence, that Dr. Berkeley described as " containing nothing ", will be of interest.

Why then, you should not have come, and I know that as well as
you. . . . I doubt you do wrong to go to Oxford ; . . . and if I do not

inquire for acquaintance, but let somebody in the inn go about with you among the colleges, perhaps you will not be known. (Sept. 28th, 1712.)

If you are in Ireland while I am there I shall see you very seldom. It is not a place for any freedom, but where everthing (*sic*) is known in a week and magnified a hundred degrees. (August 12th, 1714.)

I wish I were to walk with you fifty times about your garden, and then—drink your coffee. (October 15th, 1720.)

Cad— assures me he continues to esteem and love and value you above all things, and so will do to the end of his life, but at the same time entreats that you would not make yourself or him unhappy by imaginations. . . . Without health you will lose all desire of drinking your coffee. . . . I can say no more, being called away, mais soyez assurée que jamais personne du monde a été aimée, honorée, estimée, adorée par votre ami que vous. I drank no coffee since I have left you, nor intend till I see you again. There is none worth drinking but yours, if myself may be the judge. (July 5th, 1721.)

. . . remember that riches are nine parts in ten of all that is good in life, and health is the tenth. Drinking coffee comes long after, and yet it is the eleventh ; but without the two former you cannot drink it right ; (June 1st, 1722.)

The best maxim I know in this life is, to drink your coffee when you can, and when you cannot, to be easy without it. . . . This much I sympathise with you, that I am not cheerful enough to write, for I believe coffee once a week necessary to that. (July 13th, 1722).

These appeals for caution, the use of the third person—a trick also used in the *Autofrag*—the switching into French to defeat the eye of any casual reader, are hardly the ways of a disinterested tutor holding off an affectionate pupil at arms length. And Horace Walpole was one of the first to comment on the recurrence of these references to drinking coffee. Perhaps opinions may differ as to what precisely Swift is referring to, but whatever it is, one must surely be a little naive to believe that it is a beverage.[14]

---

[14]My friend, Sybil LeBroquey, has drawn my attention to *A Foreign View of England in the Reigns of George I and George II*, by Cesar de Saussure, translated by Mme. van Muyden in 1902, from which it appears that at this period one could "easily recognise" a brothel in England because "they frequently have as a sign a woman's arm or hand holding a coffee pot."

Finally there is the poem entitled *To Love*, in Swift's handwriting, that was found in Vanessa's desk after her death, which—together with the rest of the Correspondence from which the above extracts are taken— is printed in full in A. Martin Freeman's *Vanessa and her Correspondence with Jonathan Swift*. Here are the first ten lines of the poem:

> In all I wish, how happy should I be,
> Thou grand deluder, were it not for thee!
> So weak art thou, that fools thy power despise
> And yet so strong, thou triumph'st o'er the wise.
> Thy traps are laid with such peculiar art,
> They catch the cautious, let the rash depart.
> Most nets are filled by want of thought and care;
> But too much thinking brings us to thy snare,
> Where, held by thee, in slavery we stay,
> And throw the pleasing part of life away.

The scribe is the man of whom Mrs. Pilkington said: " I really believe it was a Paſſion he was wholly unacquainted with, and which he would have thought it beneath the Dignity of his Wiſdom to entertain."

Sir Harold Williams, in a note on p. 717 of his edition of Swift's *Poems*, disposes of this poem, by saying that the style is obviously not his. " If a draft of the poem in his hand was found in Vanessa's desk it is most likely to have been a composition by her, touched up by the Dean." It may indeed have been a poem by anybody one likes to suggest, copied out by JS in his spare time in order to confuse us. The thing that we can be sure of is that it was not written by someone in his capacity of a young lady's personal chaplain, or by a minx engaged in trapping a simple-minded Vicar.

In 1713 came Swift's appointment to St. Patrick's, and next year saw the death of the Queen, which was promptly followed by the fall of the Tories and the new Dean's hurried return to Dublin. At some time in the midst of these upheavals, both the Widow Vanhomrigh and her only surviving son, Ginkel, died. And soon after this, Vanessa and her sister, now parentless, also returned to Ireland, ostensibly to see to their property in Celbridge. Orrery states that the purpose of this move was to escape from the Bailiffs; but as both young ladies still had considerable fortunes, and were not personally responsible for their mother's debts, there are no grounds for accepting this ungallant suggestion, doubtless invented by somebody to cover up a much more likely reason—that they went there because it was the direction in which Swift had vanished.

At any rate, from some date in the latter part of 1714 onwards, until Vanessa's death in 1723—a period of about nine years—we find JS in the equivocal position of having both his women friends of indeterminate status, living within a few miles of each other and of his Cathedral—a state of affairs that he clearly did not enjoy, although any distress in the situation did not result in his crossing either of them off his visiting list.

For a short period after their arrival in Ireland, the Vanhomrigh sisters apparently lived close to the Deanery in Turnstile Alley, presumably while their late father's house, Marley Abbey in Celbridge, was being prepared for them. Bertram Newman[15] on the strength of this address—or absence of address—in some of Swift's letters to Vanessa, mistakenly extends this period of their residence in the City until 1720. The sisters were actually to and fro from Celbridge almost from the time of their arrival in Ireland, as may be gathered—for example—from Swift's letter of November, 1714, where Celbridge may not be recognised under its parochial name of Kildrohod.

Had Stella and Vanessa both been residing in Dublin during the ensuing six years, it is hard to believe that they would never have met. Yet there is certainly no evidence of any such meeting.

The same impenetrable barrier applies to Swift's friends. Many of them knew one or other of the ladies very well indeed, but it is difficult to find anybody who knew them both. Even Dr. Berkeley, who was one of Vanessa's executors, can hardly be said to have been acquainted with the testatrix. The only friend who ever moved in the circle of both women was Charles Ford, who was " Don Carlos " to Stella, and " Glassheel " to Vanessa. But Ford, alas, has never given us his views.

---

[15]Newman, p. 257.

20

THE SUPPOSED MARRIAGE

FOR a prominent clergyman to live for nine years in close proximity to two spirited young women, each of whom presumably expects him to marry her, without an explosion or an angry parting until the end of that time, is a feat that is almost impossible to visualise. In a sounding-board like Dublin, it was inevitable that each woman must have known about the other—Vanessa, that there was already a hostess in the Deanery; Stella, that a part of the Dean's London life had followed him across the sea. Could two such women, in a position like this, be expected to accept such a situation for long?

The story goes, of course, that Stella did not accept it, and that some time in the year 1716 she was privately married to the Dean by St. George Ashe, Swift's old tutor in Trinity, who was then Bishop of Clogher. As early as July, 1723, this information was reported to Archbishop Wake by Dr. Evans, Bishop of Meath, in the letter previously quoted where he describes Stella as " a nll. daughter of Sir W. Temple". Then in 1751 Orrery calls her " the concealed, but undoubted wife of Dr. Swift ", and adds :[1]

> . . . if my informations are right, fhe was married to Dr. *Swift* in the year seventeen hundred and sixteen, by Dr. *Ashe* then Bifhop of *Clogher.*

Mrs. Pilkington and Dr. Delany each agree with this, and Deane Swift declares that he is " thoroughly perfuaded ". Dilworth and Hawkesworth join in the unanimous chorus, without adding any further details to the story, although the latter sagely observes :[2]

> Why the dean did not fooner marry this moft excellent perfon ; why he married her at all ; why his marriage was fo cautioufly concealed ; and why he was never known to meet her but in the prefence of a third perfon, are enquiries which no man can anfwer.

---

[1]*Remarks*, p. 14.
[2]Hawkesworth, vol. I, p. 49.

This paragraph of Hawkesworth neatly sums up the secondary aspect of the problem—the fact that not only was the marriage performed in secret, but that it was also *kept* a secret. It will also be noted that, although few incidents in the Dean's life are reported with such unanimity by the early biographers (as distinct from the Dean's factotums), not one single commentator down to this point gives us the source of his information, or any indication of the evidence upon which he has been so " thoroughly persuaded ". It is Dr. Johnson in 1781 who is the first to throw any light on the source. After stating that the ceremony was performed by the Bishop of Clogher " as Dr. Madden told me, in the garden", he concludes his account by saying :[3]

> . . . this marriage is mentioned as fabulous, or doubtful ; but alas ! poor Stella, as Dr. Madden told me, related her melancholy story to Dr. Sheridan".

Without pausing here to enquire why the Dean's crony, Thomas Sheridan, is in the odd position of being the sole person to claim any direct knowledge of the matter, and also the person whom nobody else will quote as an authority, let us continue the history of the " tradition "—as it is soon to be called—down to the present day.

The next development comes, as might be expected, from Sheridan's son Thomas, who in his *Life* of the Dean gives a circumstantial account of how Ashe came to perform the ceremony—without witnesses he adds— which account is repeated almost verbatim by George Monck Berkeley, five years later in 1789. This story stood, without much further elaboration, until 1908, when Dean (afterwards Archbishop) Bernard wrote an Essay of singular unreliability, which appears in the Index Volume of Temple Scott's edition of Swift's *Works* under the title, *The Relations between Swift and Stella*.[4]

Bernard is another of these historians who sometimes proves a point by stating that there is no informed opinion to the contrary, thus leaving his reader to discover for himself that this roadblock is a dummy. As an example of this lamentable practice, he does not say that he, personally, does not believe that Stella was a child of Sir William Temple—which would be fair. He prefers to tell us that " there is no shadow of evidence

---

[3]*Lives of the English Poets*, vol. II, p. 215.
[4]Temple Scott, vol. XII, pp. 85-106.

for the unworthy suggestion." As another example, on his last page he says that " Swift was buried beside her "—a matter on which he must have been aware that his Cathedral books contradict him. And although there is plenty of room for a difference of opinion on this second point, he does not indicate that there is any doubt about the matter at all.

Taking the line that that master of syntax, Dr. Johnson, meant that the marriage and not Dr. Madden was " in the garden", Dean Bernard adds that the garden in question was that of the Deanery at Clogher. Finally, about 1937, Sir Harold Williams reported to Maxwell Gold of Harvard that he had been pointed out the actual " old chestnut tree " in the Bishop's —not the Dean's—garden at Clogher, under which it all took place. So now we have not only the unanimous consent of the contemporaries, but also one—if not two—definite locations for the event itself—a fascinating example of a process that is known in the language of the Church as the Growth of Tradition. Yet this is a marriage that is categorically denied by the party principally concerned—the supposed bride herself—when, in anticipation of her death, she described herself in her will as " Esther Johnson . . . Spinster".

According to Bernard, she did this because of a compact with JS, " if marriage there was, that it should never be avowed ". But she would have been making no avowal of the wedding if she had made her will without adding any such description or misdescription whatsoever. The addition of the word " Spinster " to her name was not required for any legal purpose[5] and, even if it were, this very purpose would have been defeated had the addition been relevant and untrue.

It seems much more like what we know of Stella that in this solemn moment, shortly before her death, her last public act contained an open avowal of the truth about herself.

Nor did the bridegroom give the marriage any countenance either. Rather than give any answer at all, he preferred to administer a death blow to the person most entitled to know whether he was a married man. The implication behind his refusal to answer Vanessa will be discussed at a later stage. It is sufficient here to suggest that it is better evidence that there was no marriage than that there was one. Had there been a marriage, all that Swift would have had to do in order to end an intolerable situation

---

[5]It may be noticed that Lady Giffard, in her will, does not call herself, " Martha Giffard, widow" (Longe, p. 345). Stella's will can be read in Wilde, pp. 97-101.

was to admit it privately to Vanessa ; and it is useless to argue that this might have given away any secret, since half the town and all his friends believed in it already.

In short, this is a situation that it is impossible to get out of except by facing up to the fact that somebody is lying. If it is not Sheridan, then it is Stella ; and although it is not uncommon for couples to lie about being married when, in fact, they are not, we should be very reluctant to believe in a married couple that is falsely claiming to be single, without some good authority and several excellent reasons for such unusual behaviour.

Therefore, if the reader is satisfied that a lady's own assurance is usually the best authority as to whether she is married or not, he need not waste his time in studying the following subsection. But for those who can face without tedium another brief review of the evidence that has already been analysed in print on many occasions, let us return once more to 1784 and Dr. Sheridan. ˙

The Evidence Analysed

In this crucial investigation, which is much the most difficult in the whole tangled story of Swift, we must be prepared to put into practice all the lessons that we have learned in the course of solving earlier and simpler riddles. We must recognise the fact that, for all its impressive appearance, the printed word carries no greater guarantee of accuracy than the spoken word. Nor does it gain weight by antiquity. Men and women lie when they have got something to conceal, and the truth is not necessarily to be found in some middle ground between contradictory statements. Nor must we fall into the easy trap of imagining that an error gathers some sort of sanctity by repetition, or that six authorities, however eminent, are any more than one authority if each is merely repeating what the other has said.

Furthermore, we should recognise that a witness who is not speaking from personal knowledge, and does not report the source of his infor-mation, is not a witness at all, except to the fact that he has heard such a story. Thus, Orrery is telling us nothing of value when he calls Stella the " undoubted wife " of Dr. Swift, unless he was himself present at some part of the ceremony, or tells us how he knows. Finally, we must regret-fully take notice of a widespread human tendency to believe that evidence is good if it fits into a picture that we already possess, and bad if it does not. For example, Bishop Evans is regarded as a good authority when he states his belief in the marriage, but a bad authority when, in the same letter, he describes Stella as Temple's child.

It is understandable that all Swift's contemporaries wanted to believe that he and Stella were man and wife. Apart from the question of secrecy, it dispensed with the need for some other explanation of his highly anomalous treatment of her. Even more powerfully, it gave some sort of reason for Stella's complaisant behaviour in her very peculiar position. Therefore it was easy for everybody to accept any evidence that supported the marriage, and when there was no such evidence—or evidence only from an unapproved source—to fall back on that verbal danger-signal, " undoubtedly". Actually the reason for this undocumented dogmatism that is started by Orrery becomes increasingly plain when we realise that the solitary root from which these tales originally drew their sustenance was Thomas Sheridan—a man whom everybody despised.

Variously described as a fool, a fiddler, and a punster, this is the man of whom Dean Ward wrote the following uninspiring squib, which has been copied out opposite p. 84, *et seq.*, of one of the copies of Orrery's book in the Houghton Library at Harvard :—

> Tom was a little merry grig,
> Fiddled and danced to his own jigg.
> Good natured, but a little silly,
> Irresolute and shally shilly.
>
> . . .
>
> He writ the wonder of all wonders.
> He writ the blunder of all blunders.
>
> . . .
>
> Swift puts a bit upon his snout.
> Poor *Tom*, he dare not look about :
> But soon as Swift once gives the word
> He snaps it up, tho' it were a xxxx.

And it is a lamentable fact that the only authority that the first tier of biographers had to go on was Sheridan's word that Stella had confessed the marriage to him on her death bed. This was doubly irritating, since Sheridan was also the source of a further story, that Stella had asked Swift to acknowledge the marriage before she died, but that the Dean had most cruelly refused his consent. This half of the story was quite unacceptable to Orrery, Delany, Deane Swift, etc. So the half that was wanted was taken without acknowledgment, and the only begetter thereof was then roundly abused, discounted and dismissed for having perpetrated the other half.

Not even Sheridan's son cites his father as his authority for the marriage. It is a more distant party, Dr. Johnson, who first discloses the source of the story that was told to his friend, Madden. The younger Sheridan, on the other hand, attributes his knowledge to a friend of his father and of the Dean called Mrs. Sican, who does not claim to be more than a mere retailer of hearsay, and whose knowledge of the matter is unknown—unless it, too, comes from the older Sheridan.[6]

> The whole account of this transaction was given me by Mrs. Sican, a lady of uncommon understanding, fine taste, and great goodness of heart ; on which account she was a great favourite both with the Dean and Mrs. Johnson.

No reason is given why Mrs. Sican should know anything about it, nor is there any indication—apart from the above—that she ever told such a story to anybody else. As any evidence of the marriage, it is as if one said, " Mrs. X knows all about it ; therefore it must be so." This is all the more peculiar, since the authority that one imagines that Sheridan should have cited, was his own father. But the only material point on which he does cite him is in connection with the plea for acknowledgment.

So we find ourselves with this extraordinary paradox, that as far as the early witnesses are concerned, the only person prepared to state from personal information that the wedding was admitted by one of the parties is a man whom nobody will quote, because most people violently disagree with the second half of what he says. This is why nobody will give any indication of how they know that JS and Stella were married. It would mean quoting Sheridan.

However, as is usually the way, the story becomes more—not less—circumstantial, as Time moves further away from the events described. Young Sheridan, for example, gives us a wealth of detail that we never had before ; and then Monck Berkeley follows, in an interesting and significant manner. He repeats the same details in what is clearly a précis

---

[6]Sheridan, vol. I, p. 318 n.

of Sheridan's words, but attributes his knowledge to an entirely new and different authority. Here, to begin with, is how young Sheridan has put it :[7]

> Thus oppressed at once by love, jealousy, and disappointment, her spirits sunk, a settled melancholy . . . impaired her health to such a degree, as to give the most alarming symptoms of an approaching dissolution. Shocked with the apprehension of so fatal an event, whereof he must be conscious to himself he was the cause ; and moved with compassion at the state to which he saw her reduced, all Swift's former tenderness and affection for her revived in his breast. . . . He employed a common friend to both learn from her the secret cause of that dejection of spirits, which had so visibly preyed upon her health ; and to know whether it was by any means in his power to remove it. . . . Upon this application Mrs. Johnson opened her mind fully to this friend. She told him, " that from the peculiarity of her circumstances, and the singular connection she had with Swift for so many years, there had been great room given for the tongue of slander to exert itself. . . . That she had learned to bear with this patiently, as she had reason to expect that all reports of that sort would be effaced by marriage, as soon as Swift should be in circumstances to make her a proposal of that nature. That she now saw with the deepest concern, ever since his promotion, his behaviour towards her had been wholly changed, and a cold indifference had succeeded to the warmest professions of eternal affection. That the necessary consequence would be, an indelible stain fixed upon her character, and the loss of her good name, which was much dearer to her than life."
>
> Swift, in answer to this, said, " that he had early in life laid down two maxims with regard to matrimony, from which he was determined never to depart. One was, never to marry, unless he was before hand possessed of a decent provision for a family ; another was, unless this should be the case at a time of life when he might reasonably expect to breed up his children, and see them properly entered into the world. . . . That of all women upon earth, could he have entered into that state consistently with these principles, she should have been his choice. And as her apprehensions about her character's suffering seemed to weigh the heaviest on her mind, he was ready to go through the ceremony of marriage with her upon two conditions. The first

---

[7]Sheridan, vol. I, pp. 315-318.

was, that they should continue to live separately, exactly in the same manner as before : the second, that it should be kept a profound secret from all the world, unless some urgent necessity should call for the discovery."

However short of Stella's expectations these conditions might be, yet as she knew the inflexibility of Swift's resolutions, she readily embraced them. And as it is probable that her chief uneasiness arose from jealousy, and the apprehensions she was under that he might be induced to marry miss Vanhomrigh, she would at least have the satisfaction, by this measure, of rendering such a union with her rival impracticable.

In other words, what we are to believe is that at the time of the Tisdall episode, Swift probably promised marriage at some future date. When growing gossip about Vanessa began to make Stella's position intolerable, she indicated that he should now carry out his promise. But Swift would only do so on condition that she remain in precisely the same anomalous position in the eyes of the world as she was in already.

In spite of the fact that such an arrangement would be of no benefit whatever to Stella, either socially, economically or in any other way, save in the eyes of Heaven—where she was blameless anyhow—she agreed to this insulting proposition, because at least it prevented the Dean from marrying Vanessa. And this Vanessa was never told—a monstrous state of affairs, reflecting no credit on either JS for proposing it, or on Stella for having agreed from so mean-minded a motive.

When we turn to what Monck Berkeley has written on the subject,[8] we will see that his is not a new version of the story, coming from an independent source, but is a summary of Sheridan, often in almost the same words :—

Swift, fhocked at the effects his own inconftancy was likely to produce, requefted Bifhop Afh, the common friend of *both*, to inquire from Stella what could reftore her former peace of mind. Her anfwer was to this effect, " That for many years fhe had patiently borne the tongue of flander ; but that hitherto fhe had been cheered by the hope of one day becoming his wife : That of fuch an event fhe now faw no probability ; and that, confequently, her memory would be tranf-mitted to pofterity branded with the moft unmerited obloquy".

---

[8]*Relics*, p. xxxv.

Swift, in his reply to this declaration, obferved, that " in early life he had laid down two maxims with refpect to matrimony : The *firft* was, never to marry unlefs poffeffed of a competency : the *fecond*, unlefs that was the cafe at fuch a period of life as afforded him a probable profpect of living to educate his family ; but yet, fince her happinefs depended on his marrying her, he would directly comply with her wifhes on the following terms : That it fhould remain a fecret from all the world, unlefs the difcovery were called for by fome urgent neceffity ; and that they fhould continue in feparate houses."

It becomes even more difficult to swallow this account, when we study the reasons that are given by the biographers for Swift's insistence on secrecy. According to Orrery :—[9]

> . . . the flaw, which in Dr. SWIFT'S eye reduced the value of fuch a jewel, was the fervile ftate of her father . . . thus the vanity of boafting fuch a wife was fuppreffed by the greater vanity of keeping free from a low alliance.

Delany,[10] on the other hand, has been assured by Swift himself that Stella was a relation of Sir William Temple, so he does not hold with his Lordship's magical notions on the subject of birth. Delany attributes the development of the situation to economic causes that carry more conviction than Orrery's reasons, but still seem very odd in the case of a man in Swift's position, who was probably much better off than Delany himself.

> He waf in debt, and Mrs. JOHNSTON's fortune fmall ; he could not in those circumftances, live up to the dignity of his ftation. Nor would his honour allow him to run the leaft rifque of hurting her fortune ; and therefore, he chofe rather to lie by, and fave, till he had wherewithal to enable him to appear as he ought. And this, alfo, I take to be the true caufe of his abftaining (as undoubtedly he did) from all marital commerce with that Lady for a confiderable time ; to prevent the increafe of a family under fuch circumftances. And before their joint views and interefts could be fully anfwered and adjufted, various accidents intervened ; which rather confirmed than ftaggered them, in their refolutions of living feparate.

[9]*Remarks*, pp. 15-16.
[10]*Observations*, pp. 55-56.

> The Dean's difappointments . . . death of friends, and total overthrow
> of all his ambitions, profpects, inftead of calming his paffions, un-
> happily fermented, and foured them, by a ftrange fingularity of temper,
> the withdrawing of the fewel enflamed the fire. This gave STELLA
> inexpreffible uneafinefs : and I well knew a friend to whom fhe
> opened herfelf upon that head ; declaring, that the Dean's temper
> was fo altered, and his attention to money fo increafed : (probably
> increafed by his follicitude to fave for her fake) her own health at the
> fame time gradually impaired ; that fhe could not take upon herfelf
> the care of his houfe and oeconomy : and therefore refufed to be
> publicly owned for his wife, as he earneftly defired fhe fhould.

Delany then goes on somewhat ingenuously to deplore this decision,
showing how it would actually have been cheaper for them to have had
one house instead of two, and mentioning how the cost of constant
chair-hire could have been avoided had they only decided to live together.
He does not attempt to deal with the fact that all these disappointments
and frustrations of his ambition occurred several years before the supposed
marriage, and not after it.

Mrs. Hearn, Stella's niece, has nothing to add from Johnson family
lore, except that " why that marriage was not owned to the world has
never been thoroughly explained." But the height of fantastic nonsense
is probably reached by Deane Swift, who, during JS's lifetime it should
be noted, did not originally believe in the marriage, and wrote to Orrery
in an otherwise unknown letter quoted by Craik[11] that it was based only
" on a buzz and rumours". It was only in the 50's, when he came to write
his book on JS, that he changed his mind and accepted the story, the
secrecy for which he explained in this manner :

> In one Word, if Dr. SWIFT, whofe Ambition was not to be gratified
> without fome uncommon Degree of Admiration, had acknowledged
> Mrs. JOHNSON for a Wife, he would on all Sides have been fo
> perfecuted with Contempt and Derifion . . . that unable to fupport
> himfelf under the Burthen of his Affliction, he would have loft his
> Spirits, broken his Heart, and died in a Twelvemonth. And accordingly
> we find he had more Wifdom than to acknowledge this beautiful, this
> accomplifhed Woman for his Wife.[12]

[11]Craik, p. 529.
[12]*Essay*, pp. 89-90.

It need hardly be argued that, if they were really man and wife, some better explanation for the secrecy must be sought for than any of these absurd and contradictory reasons.

There are only two other candidates besides Sheridan for the position of a direct authority on the fact of the marriage. The first of these is the indefatigable Mrs. Whiteway who was, we know, one of the informants of her son-in-law, Deane Swift, as well as of Orrery. Thanks, however, to the careful researches of Maxwell Gold amongst the Orrery papers in the Harvard Library, we are now aware that the story she told to them was also hearsay from Sheridan. It is Scott in 1814 who develops Mrs. Whiteway into an original witness in her own right. This he does on the word of Theophilus, son of Deane Swift, who alleges he had it from Mrs. Whiteway herself. According to Scott[13] when Stella was on her deathbed, Mrs. Whiteway overheard from the next room a portion of a conversation that Stella had with the Dean.

" Well, my dear, if you wish it, it shall be owned " said Swift. To which Stella answered with a sigh,

" It is too late."

The interesting thing about this conversation is that, although it is generally taken as referring to the marriage, it could equally well refer to some secret by reason of which there was no marriage. This is a pity, as the incident is the first occasion on which Mrs. Whiteway is anything more than a mouthpiece for others. So we are still back with Sheridan, on the main question. There is, however, one other channel that professes to provide us with direct evidence of the marriage, apart from the lucubrations of this joker. This was first mentioned by Monck Berkeley in 1789. According to him, St. George Ashe admitted to George Berkeley (later one of Vanessa's Executors) that he had performed the ceremony, and Berkeley told this to his wife, who was Monck Berkeley's grandmother and informant.[14]

It is strange that neither Ashe nor Berkeley ever told this to anybody else who has reported it, and much argument has taken place as to whether Ashe could, in fact, have told it to Berkeley, who, as Churton Collins alleges, was abroad at the time of the supposed wedding, and never return-

---

[13]Scott, vol. I, pp. 355-357.
[14]*Relics*, p. xxxvi.

ed until after Ashe was dead. However, from an article by Marguerite Hearsey,[15] it now seems clear that, unless the wedding took place late in the year, Ashe could actually have seen Berkeley afterwards, or alternatively could have mentioned the matter in a letter to Berkeley while the latter was abroad with Ashe's son. So the channel of information is a possible one, and the testimony of Monck Berkeley's grandmother as to what she says her husband was told by Ashe, might properly be added to that of Sheridan, if in fact Monck Berkeley had done more than merely mention it. But, as we have seen, the details of his account are not his grandmother's, but are derived from young Sheridan, who in his turn attributes them to this Mrs. Sican.

It will be seen, therefore, that the difficulty in ascertaining what the evidence for the wedding actually amounts to, is the difficulty of trying to find out from this babel of voices how many people are actually speaking. It sounds like a host of witnesses, all clamouring to contradict Stella, and to explain the purposes of this extraordinary transaction. But it turns out to hang solely on the word of Thomas Sheridan, corroborated by Monck Berkeley's grandmother as to the fact of the marriage, but not as to its reason.

On the other hand, in support of Stella's truthfulness we have some significant testimony. We have Stella's Executors, Rochfort and Corbet, both of whom had legal inducements for being sure that she was right, and indeed for being certain that she was entitled to make a will at all. We have the person who, above all others, might be expected to be in the forefront of those who insisted that her friend was legally married— Rebecca Dingley. We have both of Swift's housekeepers, Mrs. Brent[16] and Mrs. Ridgeway. And lastly, we have Dr. Lyon, whom we have already come across as one of the Dean's most faithful utility men in later life, and probably the guardian of his person during his senility. In the V. & A. copy of Hawkesworth already referred to, there is a lengthy holograph note entitled *Of the Report about Dr. Swift's Marriage*. For some reason, the title is deleted, and the text that follows also contains a number of amendments and additions. This note is in the same handwriting that appears

---

[15] *New Light on the Evidence for Swift's Marriage* : Publications of the Modern Language Association of America, vol. xlii, pp. 157-161.

[16] Mrs. Brent, whose first name is evidently unknown, even to Elrington Ball, died in 1735, leaving a will dated the 27th July, 1732. Her place as Swift's " Walpole " was thereafter taken by her daughter, Mrs. Ann Ridgeway.

in the great bulk of the marginal corrections to the book—the hand-writing that is now generally accepted as being that of the Rev. John Lyon.

Edmond Malone, who at one time owned this copy of Hawkesworth, wrote a note in it to the effect that he thought these marginal comments were by Mrs. Whiteway's son, the surgeon who performed the autopsy after the Dean's death. But Monck Mason has added to this, the following note, which is very convincing as an identification of the commentator :

> Mr. Malone is mistaken in his gueſs relative to the author of these Notes ; they were written by the Rev. John Lyon, sometime Curate of St. Bride's, and after, a praeb : of St. patrick's. he was the Compiler of the Novum Registrum in Christ's Church. . . . as I have read many thousand pages of his writing, I can not be mistaken & could bear testimony of his hand writing in a Court of Justice. W. Monck Maſon.

As far as I am aware these marginals and additions have never been fully edited and published, although they are frequently referred to by the biographers. In one of the additional volumes of the Hawkesworth edition, published in 1779, a selection of them appears ; but as they are not printed accurately, and as in the case of the Note on the Marriage there is a fraudulent (but interesting) addition from an unknown source, which is not to be found in the original, it is advisable to print the entire comment here, as a sober and illuminating viewpoint on the problem of the marriage from a contemporary source.

As Mr. Maxwell Gold has expressed the opinion that—although written in Lyon's hand—it is not his own composition, but an expression of some-body else's opinion, it is here reproduced together with its corrections and deletions, so that the reader can form his own judgment as to whether the writer is expressing his own views, or is merely copying out a paper that has already been written by somebody else. There is, admittedly, one repetition of words that gives the document the appearance of something that is being copied out. And there is a curious endorsement at the head of the first sheet that appears to be ' TB '. But the mass of other alterations and interlineations is hardly likely to be found in a piece of writing that is not the composition of the actual scribe, or intended as an expression of his own opinion.

In one or two places where it is difficult to make out what is written,

I have left a blank; and it might also be mentioned that there is an indecipherable gloss, surrounded by a circle, opposite the second line of the poem.

TB   Of the Report about Dr. Swift's Marriage

Notwithstanding Dr. Delany's Sentiments of Swift's marriage, & notwithstanding all that Ld Orrery & others have said about it, there is no authority for it but a Hearsay ſtory, & that very ill founded. It is certain, that y Dean told one of his Friends whom he advised to marry; " that he never wished to marry at y time that he ought to " have entered into that State, for he counted upon it as y happyest " condition, especially towards the Decline of Life when a faithful " & tender Friend is most wanted." While he was talking to this Effect, his Friend exprefsed his wishes to have seen him marryed. The Dean asked, " Why ? " " Because " replyed the other, " I shd have had y pleasure of seeing your offspring. All y world wd have been pleased to have seen y Iſsue of such a Genius ". The Dean smiled, & denyed his being marryed in y same manner as before, and said, " he never saw y woman he wished to be marryed to "—And indeed it is certain, that all his Friends as well as y Publick in general, wd rejoyce at that Event, because it is highly probable they wd have seen the Children of this wonderfull Man, as he had a sound constitution strengthened by Temperence and Exercise.

The same Gent : who was intimate with Mrs. Dingley for ten Years before she dyed in 1743 took occasion to tell her, that such a Story was whispered of her Friend Mrs. Johnson's marriage with y Dean ; but she only laughed at it, as an idle Tale founded on suspicion.

Again, Mrs. Brent, with whom the Dean's mother used to lodge in Dublin in the Queen's time, & who was his own Housekeeper
after he settled in Dublin in 1714, & who for her many ∧ qualitys in that station was much confided in, never did believe there was a marriage between those Persons notwithstanding all that Love and fondneſs that subsisted between them. ~~that subsisted between them.~~ She thought it was all Platonick Love. And she often told her daughter Ridgeway so ; who succeeded her in y same office of Housekeeper.

She said that Mrs. Johnson never came alone to the Deanery ; that
together
Mrs. Dingley and she came ∧ always ; & that she never slept in that
y Dean was there
House ∧ only in y time of his sicknefs to attend him, and see
~~and then Mrs. Dingley slept with her.~~
him well taken care of As he writes in 1720

> " When on my sickly Couch I lay,
> " Impatient both of Night & day,
> " Lamenting in unmanly Strains,
> " Call'd ev'ry Pow'r to ease my Pains.
> " Then Stella ran to my relief,
> " With cheerfull face, & inward Grief.
> " And though by Heaven's severe decrees,
> " She suffers hourly more than me,
> " No cruel Master could require
> " From Slaves employ'd for daily Hire
> " What Stella by her Friendship warm'd,
> " With Vigour & delight perform'd ".

And during this course of her generous attendance Mrs. Dingley &
together
she slept ∧ & as soon as he recovered, they returned to their Lodgings
slept   or an . . . pleasant
on Ormond Quay. These Ladys ~~lived~~ two other Times at y Deanery ∧
House, and near his garden called Naboth's vineyard
and that was for those months in 1726 and 1727 which he spent in
chanced
England—It ~~happened~~ that she was taken ill at y Deanery, while he
was in London, & it added much to his Afflictions that it happened
at y Deanery for fear of Defamation, in case of her dying at his Houfe,
whether he was at home or abroad. See his Reflexions to this purpose,
in a Lettr to Mr. Worral in 1726—

Had he been married to her, he cd not have lived in a state of
separation from her, he loved her so pafsionately. For he admired
her upon every Acct that can make a woman amiable or valuable as
a Companion for Life. Is it pofsible to think that an affecte Husband
could first have written, & then have used, those several Prayers (lately

published from his own Hand) by a dying wife ; with whom he never cohabited, & whose mouth must have been filled with Reproaches for denying her all conjugal Rites for a number of years, nay from y very period 1716 that is pretended to be y time of y marriage ?

Wd he have suffered his wife to make a Will, signed Esther Johnson, & to devise £1500 away from him ; of wch 1000£ is enjoyed by y Chaplain of Steevens Hospital for y sick, & accept of a Gold watch only as y Testimony of her Regard for him ? If he cd direct or rather command her to leave her Fortune as he pleased, it is probable that he have directed y application towards y future support of Lunaticks wch was y species of Charity he thought most worthy y attention of

y Publick —Is it not probable that two Gents still living ∧ & who of Honour and Fortune who knew ym both most intimately

are her Execs wd have known of a marriage, if there was one—and yet they always did, and do, positively declare they never had cause to suspect they were marryed, altho' they were in y company of both

some ∧ times. They saw proofs enough of y warmest Friendship ; a thousand & any Love but conubial Love.

If she made him a present of a Book, you may read in y Title page these words, & he distinguished every book she gave him :

"Esther Johnson's Gift
to Jonathan Swift 1719 ".

In his Accn of her in a Page written on y night she died, and 2 or 3 days after—where he speaks of her as " y truest, most virtuous & valuable Friend that he was ever blefsed with ". He was ill y day after her death, & cd not write. But next night he says, " This is y night of y Funeral, wch my sicknefs will not suffer me to attend."— If he had attended he must, in point of Duty as Dean, have read the funeral service ; as she was buryed in his own Cathedral.

Wd he deny his marriage to a woman of good Fortune at that time, when he says, " She had a gracefulness somewhat more than human in every motion, word & action."

An excellent summary of most of the arguments both for and against the marriage is to be found in Maxwell Gold's book *Swift's Marriage to Stella* which has been referred to several times already. Apart from the fact that, like all advocates of the marriage, Mr. Gold is determinedly myopic to the fact that Stella herself should be listed at the head of those who state that she was not married, Gold's estimate of the position is both scholarly and honest, and his valuable references are an immense help to any further study of the subject. It is only where he proceeds to assess the relative value of the authorities, that we find the inevitable tendency to run down those who are on the wrong side, and to accept those who are not, as if each was an independent witness to the wedding.

Gold's treatment of Lyon's opinion is particularly interesting, as an example of the length to which ingenuity can be carried in getting around unacceptable evidence. Gold is much too honest a scholar either to suppress what Lyon says or to deny that it can be read in his own hand-writing. So—as already mentioned—he argues that Lyon cannot be the author, and has merely copied out into his copy of Hawkesworth the faulty observations of somebody else. This is, of course, physically possible. Whether it is likely can be deduced from the text and its amendments.

In marked distinction to Gold, however, is Sir Henry Craik's Appendix IV, entitled *The Marriage of Swift and Stella*, which adopts some of the tricks of mediaeval theology in its effort to establish an article of Faith on a foundation of fact that is only a matter of opinion. According to Sir Henry, Sheridan has " an imperfect recollection of his father's narrative " in so far as he reports the acknowledgment story, but has a perfectly clear recollection of his father on the subject of the marriage. Dr. Lyon was " only Swift's attendant in his later and feebler years," and his opinion is " so vague in its character as to be even on this ground alone valueless." Mrs. Dingley's character and temper were troublesome and " it is not likely that she would be entrusted with the secret at all." Mrs. Ridgeway was an " uneducated drudge," and Monck Mason—that meticulously painstaking retailer of far too many facts about St. Patrick's Cathedral—is guilty not only of " puerility," but is actually conducting a dishonest controversy on the subject of the marriage with " flagrant misrepresenta-tion of evidence by which he imposes upon anyone credulous enough to trust him."

This bad temper and abuse is then followed by Craik's own statement " that Stella used her maiden name in her ordinary signatures and finally in her will," omitting to mention at this stage of his account the important fact that, in an opening sentence of this document, she had added the gratuitous and significant description, " Spinster."

In fact the whole treatment of the subject, under circumstances where we are lucky enough to be able still to see the process at work, throws, again, a vivid light on the way in which controversial history comes to be written.

In contradistinction to these furious flights of fancy that many people tend to indulge in when contemplating events over a hundred years old, here is a contemporary—and apparently a disinterested—outside view of the whole situation, that appeared in a review of the first edition of Orrery's book. From this it will be seen that there is nothing at all new in applying a little healthy scepticism towards what we have been asked to believe about Swift and Stella, and that most of what now can be said, has been said from the earliest days.

This comes from the *Monthly Review* for November, 1751 :

Certainly the dean muſt have had ſome other motive, and a more weighty one, than the ridiculous pride mentioned by lord *Orrery*, for his never living or converſing with his wife as ſuch. And we cannot yet perſuade ourſelves not to afford ſome degree of credit to the report which has been ſo generally believed, that *Swift* was really Sir *William Temple's* ſon, and that *Stella* was alſo Sir *William's* natural daughter. This might be very true, and yet neither the Doctor nor Mrs. *Johnſon* know it before they were married. It has been generally aſſerted, that *Swift* received a letter from *England*, the day after his marriage, the purport of which was, that the writer thereof hoped that it would not come to his hands too late to prevent the conſummation of a match which it was rumoured was intended betwixt Dr. *Swift* and Mrs. *Johnſon*, for that they were both the natural children of one father : and gave the doctor ſufficient reaſon to believe that this information was true.———

But whether the dean ever did receive or credit ſuch information, or not, it may be impoſſible for any one now living to prove or diſprove. However, certain it is, that ſuch reports have prevailed. . . . But will not his lordſhip's ſuppoſition of *Swift's* pride being a probable motive for his owning the daughter of Sir *William Temple* for his wife, appear a little premature, when we recollect that the ſame public rumour that made *her* Sir *William's* daughter, made *him* also Sir *William's* ſon ? Therefore he could never, with decency, have acknow-

ledged Mrs. *Johnson* as his wife, while that rumour continued to retain
any degree of credit ; and if there had been really no foundation for it,
furely it might have been no very hard tafk to have entirely obviated
its force, by producing the neceffary proofs and circumftances of his
birth ; yet we do not find that ever this was done, either by the dean,
or his relations.[17]
Indeed, for the honour of the dean himself, we are fomewhat inclined
to wifh that this fuppofed too near confanguinity between him and
Mrs. *Johnson* may appear to have been really fact ? As then his conduct
towards her may be rationally accounted for, and much more to his
credit, than by fuppofing him capable of treating fo amiable a woman,
(and one too, whom he moft tenderly loved) like a brute, merely to
gratify an inhuman caprice, or a foolifh and vicious pride ; and of
being the caufe of her death by his tyrannical ufage.

But beyond and above the whole tortuous mass of testimony lies a
fundamental question of human behaviour. Whatever kind of eccentric
Swift may have been in his views on marriage—and they have been
elaborated *ad nauseam* by many psychologists—we are entitled to ask what
kind of woman would ever consent to a marriage with a man who said in
effect, " I am only marrying you because you insist ; but the matter must
be kept a secret because you are too mean socially to be acknowledged as
my wife " : or alternatively, " because at 49 I consider myself too old to
bring up children " : or again, " because as Dean of St. Patricks', I am too
poor to keep one joint establishment, and propose instead to maintain
two " ? And even if there was some good reason, apart from these pieces
of nonsense, that induced Stella to marry him on such terms, what woman
would not have resented such insulting conditions for the rest of her life ?

> " For," says Lord Orrery, " . . . The outward honours which fhe
> received, are as frequently beftowed upon a miftrefs, as a wife. She
> was abfolutely virtuous, and yet was obliged to fubmit to all the
> appearances of vice, except in the prefence of thofe few people who
> were witnefses of the cautious manner in which fhe lived with her
> hufband, who fcorned even to be married like any other man."

Orrery does, of course, allege that she sickened and died, " abfolutely

---

[17]*Monthly Review*, November, 1751, pp. 415-417.

deſtroyed by the peculiarity of her fate." But Stella actually survived the enigmatic 1716 by twelve years, and Vanessa by five, during which period she continued to act as hostess of the Deanery, showing no resentment whatever, accepting his support, and bequeathing her property in the manner suggested by Swift. If he was the monster that he is alleged to have been in his treatment of her, she reacted very oddly to this fact in some of the poems that she wrote to Swift on his birthday.

> ST.PATRICK'S Dean, your Country's Pride,
> My early and my only Guide,
> Let me among the reſt attend,
> Your Pupil and your humble Friend,
> To celebrate in Female Strains
> The Day that paid your Mother's Pains ;
> Deſcend to take that Tribute due
> In Gratitude alone to you.
>
> . . .
>
> You taught how I might Youth prolong
> By knowing what was Right and Wrong ;
> How from my Heart to bring Supplies
> Of Luſtre to my fading Eyes ;
>
> . . .
>
> Late dying may you caſt a Shred
> Of your rich Mantle o'er my Head ;
> To bear with Dignity my Sorrow,
> One Day *alone, then die To-morrow*.[18]

Vanessa, on the other hand, whose quandary and resentment are only too understandable, did not behave so serenely. After pleading for recognition for nine years, during which period she was regularly visited by Swift, and assured of his genuine affection in terms that we have already seen, she finally demanded to know the whole truth about the situation, and wrote to Stella herself, hoping to be told whether she was or was not the Dean's wife.

---

[18]This poem, to Swift on his birthday in 1721, is printed by Deane Swift (pp. 86-88). Deane Swift writes that the original was given by JS " to a Lady of his Acquaintance " (presumably Mrs. Whiteway) with the assurance that it was a piece " intirely genuine from the Hands of STELLA, without any Sort of Correction whatsoever."

The only answer that she got was her own letter flung back on her table by the Dean without a word. At this, she tore up her will, and made a new one, bequeathing all her papers to a new pair of Executors—George Berkeley and Robert Marshall, afterwards a Judge of the Common Pleas. She did not specifically enjoin them to publish them, but her intention must have been reasonably plain. Within a month of this lamentable event, she was dead, and Swift set out alone upon a long journey through the south of Ireland, to get away, presumably, from the clacking of City tongues, while Vanessa was laid to rest.

There is no need to explain Vanessa's behaviour. But even if her grave is lost, there is no reason why her character should be lost as well, through the efforts of those of Swift's friends and admirers who wish to save him from the obloquy that he appears to deserve, and who can see no way of doing so except by blaming this unfortunate girl for pursuing a coy married clergyman.

The Ride to Celbridge

The Dean's ride to Celbridge, as a consequence of Vanessa's desperate demand for information, is mentioned in the opening chapter of this book, and is one of the most enigmatic incidents in his life. It has several times been described with a wealth of fanciful detail, and one of the best examples of this is in a short essay in D. L. Kay's pleasant little book, *The Glamour of Dublin*.[19]

The anecdote, itself, has got a very long history. Orrery is the first to refer to it.[20] According to him, Vanessa's letter was not to Stella, but to Swift—

> a very tender epiſtle to CADENUS, inſiſting peremptorily upon as ſerious an anſwer, and an immediate acceptance, or an abſolute refuſal of her, as his wife. His reply was delivered by his own hand. He brought it with him when he made his final viſit at Selbridge : and throwing down the letter upon her table, with great paſſion haſtened back to his horſe, carrying in his countenance the frowns of anger and indignation. . . . She read it with as much reſolution as the preſent cruelty of her fate, and the raging pride of her heart, would permit. She found herſelf entirely diſcarded from his friendſhip and converſa- tion. Her offers were treated with inſolence and diſdain. She met with

---

[19]This pseudonym was that of D. L. Kelleher. The essay is on pp. 103-104 of his book.
[20]*Remarks*, pp. 75-76.

reproaches inſtead of love, and with tyranny inſtead of affection. . . .
She did not ſurvive many days the letter delivered to her by
CADENUS. . . .

Neither Delany nor Deane Swift include this story in the long list of
matters on which they contradict Orrery, and Hawkesworth is the next
to recount it.[21] This he does in terms that merely echo Orrery, but to his
statement that the Dean delivered his reply with his own hand, Dr. Lyon
has written a marginal note that reads as follows :

> This is only tattle & suspicion. For no letter either of her's or his
> appears in y whole correspondence which she did preserve. Had such
> a letter been written by Dean S——t Vanessa would have put it in
> that collection she made of the Dean's Letters and which she desired
> her Executors to publish. The last Letter is 7 August 1722 where he
> says the best Companion for her is a Philosopher which she might
> regard as much as a Sermon that his Love and esteem for her was
> altogether founded on Friendship. It is thought that y Dean's neglect
> of her Tending of Love put her upon cancelling.

Sheridan is the next to describe the incident,[22] from information
presumably coming from his father. According to him it was to Stella
that Vanessa sent " a short note . . . only requesting to know from her
whether she was married to the Dean or not. Mrs. Johnson answered her
in the affirmative, and then enclosed the note she had received from miss
Vanhomrigh to Swift. After which, she immediately went out of town
without seeing him. . . . Exasperated to the highest degree, he gave way
to the first transports of his passion, and immediately rid to Celbridge. He
entered the apartment where the unhappy lady was, mute, but with a
countenance that spoke the highest resentment. She trembling asked him,
would he not sit down ? " No ! "—He then flung a paper on the table,
and immediately returned to his horse. When, on the abatement of her
consternation, she had strength to open the paper, she found it contained
nothing but her own note to Mrs. Johnson."

This is the last account of the incident from a primary source, although
it is difficult to see how the story first got about. It is unlikely that either
Swift or Vanessa told anybody else precisely what took place, unless
indeed, Swift told Stella, from whom some hints may have spread to others.
But from the fact that it ever leaked out at all, and that Stella left town

---

[21]Hawkesworth, vol. I, p. 38.
[22]Sheridan, vol. I, pp. 324-325.

before the Dean set forth, it seems likely that, in this case, Sheridan's version is the more correct one, and that it was to Stella that Vanessa wrote, and not to Swift. Had she written to Swift, merely asking him to marry her there is no reason for such a fury, or for Stella's ever having known about it. According to Orrery[23] Vanessa had " often preſſed him to marry her."

Where Sheridan—and Scott[24] after him—is probably wrong is in stating that Stella ever replied. This assumption is based upon the belief that they were married. If they were not married it is entirely understandable that she would have simply passed the letter on to Swift, and left town in a pet of temper, leaving him to deal with the situation as best he could, which he did by flinging the letter back at the unfortunate sender.

This view is in line with Dr. Lyon's argument that had there been any reply from either Stella or Swift, it would undoubtedly have been included in the correspondence that Vanessa passed on to her Executors. What better proof could she have had of her maltreatment than a letter from either of them, admitting that Swift was a married man? But her own pathetic letter she would never have disclosed, if it was this that was thrown back at her—a point that Lyon overlooks.

From the above it would seem that the ride to Celbridge was an authentic event, that it was inspired by a letter from Vanessa to Stella, and that all she got in reply was her own enquiry pitched onto her table without any further explanation. It was this baffling failure to get any answer whatever that hastened her end, rather than the discovery that the man she hoped to marry was married already.

In justice to Swift it is hard to see what answer he could have given. He was on the horns of a dilemma, where either a Yes or a No might have proved equally fatal. But this, of course, is not the apology that is made for him by his admirers. The most ungallant excuse of all is that evolved by the Rev. Mr. Hay in 1891.[25] According to him Swift probably entered her parlour unannounced and found her in such a condition—presumably from drink—" that, disgusted at the sight, he might indeed turn upon his heel, and without speaking a word, might leave the Abbey, remount his horse, gallop back to his Deanery, and never see her more."

It is Vanessa who always has to pay, to keep Swift right with the world.

[23] *Remarks*, p. 75.
[24] Scott, vol. I, pp. 252-253.
[25] Hay, p. 167.

21

LATTER DAYS

THE death of Vanessa and Swift's simultaneous disappearance into deep Munster for some months, must have caused gossip and much idle speculation around the City, but no discernible ripple disturbed the surface of the strange domestic arrangements of the Deanery during the years that followed.

Whatever Vanessa's intentions may have been, her Executors showed great consideration for Swift in the handling of her papers. A copy of *Cadenus and Vanessa* was admittedly made, and must have passed through other hands from time to time—hands that made further copies. This can hardly be wondered at. But in at least one of these copies the questionable passage beginning, "But what success Vanessa met," was left out, in deference, presumably, to the Dean's reputation. And it was not until 1726 that a printer managed to get hold of the poem and publish it.

In spite of Swift's belief that the printing was inspired by "particular malice"[1] there is no reason to suppose that either of the Executors authorised this publication, and in the absence of any copyright law it was impossible to prevent it, once copies were at large. But, during the Dean's lifetime no printer managed to get access to the more embarrassing correspondence, and we have already seen how Dr. Berkeley would not show it even to Dr. Delany[2]

> as he frequently aſſured me that they contained nothing which would either do honour to her character, or bring the leaſt reflection on CADENUS. His letters contain nothing but civil compliments, excuſes, and apologies, and thanks for little preſents etc. Whereas hers indicated all the warmth and violence, of the ſtrongest Love-paſſion ; but not the leaſt hint of a criminal commerce between them, in the Letters of either.

Although Swift never admired George Berkeley and listed him as "ungrateful," he himself ought to have been grateful to Berkeley, whose influence with his young co-executor, only then recently called to the Bar, was probably considerable in this matter. Not that this is any reason to

---

[1]See his letter of April 19th, 1726, to Knightly Chetwode. *Correspondence*, vol. III, p. 306. Vanessa's will can be read at pp. 186-189 of Freeman's book.
[2]*Observations*, p. 123.

believe that Marshall, either, was maliciously inclined towards Swift. According to Rev. Mr. Carroll[3] he was one of a committee with Lyon and Faulkner who later attempted to promote a national memorial to the Dean. It is generally supposed that Marshall was selected by Vanessa as one of her executors because of his relationship with William Marshall, a clerk to Uncle William Swift, who is said to have had a legal row with the Dean over his uncle's estate. But there is little evidence of this.

So, in spite of the fact that some of the correspondence found its way into Hawkesworth, where it was seen by Dr. Lyon, the Vanessa episode, for a time at any rate, remained, in the eyes of the world, as a lamentable attachment on the part of a silly young woman to a respectably—though secretly—married man. She ought to have known better than to pursue Swift with her unwanted attentions, and she probably got no more than she deserved. And there is little doubt that the situation was greatly eased, to begin with, by the general belief amongst Swift's cronies, and the more casual visitors to the Deanery, that JS and Stella had been married for a number of years. As for the principal parties themselves, they still were careful to make sure that there was no indication that they ever lived together, while at the same time they did nothing to discourage the belief amongst their friends that they were actually man and wife.

Such behaviour is difficult to understand except upon the basis that they wished for the benefits and sanction of the married state which, nevertheless, might get them both into serious trouble if it could be proved by any enemy to exist. If, in fact, they could not marry, or through having married, had exposed themselves to some penalty of the law for so doing, their behaviour would be quite understandable, without any of these far-fetched reasons for secrecy which have been inflicted on us by the biographers.

We have already discussed Swift's difficulty in giving any answer to Vanessa's enquiry. To admit the marriage might have exposed both Stella and himself to this mysterious peril—whatever it was. To deny it would certainly have led to the inevitable question: " Why then, do you not marry me ? " To which there was no answer, except to say that he could not do so without abandoning Stella. And to explain why he could not abandon Stella might also have exposed the secret. As his secret wife, with whom he did not live, for reasons best known to himself, she was at least respectable in the eyes of the town. But had he married another

---

[3] *Succession of Clergy*, p. 26. See also *Correspondence*, vol. III, pp. 463-464.

woman, she would immediately have changed her appearance to that of a cast mistress.

So he told Vanessa nothing : and she died. And Stella was not indignant with him for whatever he did, but remained deeply grateful and his affectionate friend for the remainder of her short life which there is no reason to believe was unhappy.

She was the next of the principal actors in this drama to go—not from grief, as Orrery suggests, but from consumption and asthma, as Sir William Wilde tells us. JS was back in England on his final visit, when she began to sink in the Autumn of 1727. Hastening home in great agitation, he was delayed in Holyhead for over a week, but arrived to find her still alive. Part of the reason for his agitation may, perhaps, be found in a letter to Worrall from London dated September 12th, 1727[4].

> . . . By Dr. Sheridan's frequent letters, I am every post expecting the death of a friend, with whose loss I shall have very little regard for the few years that nature may leave me. I desire to know where my two friends lodge. I gave a caution to Mrs. Brent that it might not be *in domo decani, quoniam hoc minime decet, uti manifestum est : habeo enim malignos, qui sinistre hoc interpretabuntur, si eveniat, quod Deus avertat, ut illic moriatur* . . . if this unfortunate event should happen of the loss of our friend, and I have no probability or hopes to expect better, I will go to France, if my health will permit me, to forget myself, . . .

In other words, if Mrs. Johnson dies—which God forbid—she must not do so in the Deanery, since this would be hardly decent. If she died there, he had malignant enemies who would put a sinister interpretation on such a happening. And no casual eye must know of these fears—hence, the Latin. That he should have been so concerned about such a matter at such a moment of tragedy, is a facet of Swift that is hardest of all to stomach, if the prevailing view is correct, and she was either his secret wife, or a woman whom he had wronged. To think of the death of his most faithful friend in terms of decency or indecency—to be in a state of apprehension, not about her departure, but lest he might be compromised by its taking place in his house, makes JS appear so contemptible that it is surprising that anybody who accepts it at its face value could ever waste their time any longer on such a character. If, however, any implied acknowledgment of the marriage was a matter of peril to both of them, such precautions are at least understandable.

---

[4]*Correspondence*, vol. III, pp. 418-419.

Finally, we have his three prayers for Stella, already referred to in the *Monthly Review*, which have been perserved for us in his Collected Works. Had Swift, himself, been the willing cause of her anomalous position through any of the reasons given—or indeed, for any other reason—one might have expected some hint of personal guilt, some sense of regret, some feeling of contrition to have found its way into these moments when Swift found himself face to face with the Almighty. His God could hardly be unaware of what precisely the position was. But Swift's prayers—strangely enough—are not for his sins, but for Stella's.

> . . . O Merciful Father, Who never afflictest Thy children, but for their own good, and with justice, over which Thy mercy always prevaileth, either to turn them to repentance, or to punish them in the present life, in order to reward them in a better ; take pity, we beseech Thee, upon this Thy poor afflicted servant, languishing so long and so grievously under the weight of Thy hand. Give her strength, O Lord, to support her weakness ; and patience to endure her pains, without repining at Thy correction. Forgive every rash and inconsiderate expression, which her anguish may at any time force from her tongue, while her heart continueth in an entire submission to Thy will . . . Give her a sincere repentance for all her transgressions and omissions . . . Give her a true conception of the vanity, folly and insignificancy of all human things . . . and forgive her all those offences against Thee, which she hath sincerely repented of, or through the frailty of memory hath forgot . . . Forgive the sorrow and weakness of those among us, who sink under the grief and terror of losing so dear and useful a friend. . . .[5]

Is this the prayer of a man who is himself the cause of her afflictions and anguish, or—even more incredibly—has refused to acknowledge her as his wife ? If so, Swift was indeed a monster and a hypocrite of colossal proportions, and not the man whom Stella writes about in her poem that we have already quoted.

She died on the evening of Sunday, the 28th January, 1728, and later on the same night JS began to write the tribute to her memory which is variously known as *Character of Mrs. Johnson*, or *On the Death of Mrs. Johnson*. He continued it on the night of the funeral, " which my sickness will not suffer me to attend," removing himself into another room of the Deanery, so that he could not see the light of the Cathedral, as they laid

---

[5]Temple Scott, vol. III, pp. 313-314.

her in the ground. There is no remorse in this document either, only a
deep admiration and regard that is in complete accord with the sentiments
expressed in the birthday poems—as for example, the famous lines from
that of 1720 :

> Thou *Stella*, wert no longer young,
> When first for thee my Harp I strung ;
> Without one Word of *Cupid's* Darts,
> Of killing Eyes, or bleeding Hearts ;
> With Friendship and Esteem possesst,
> I ne'er admitted Love a Guest.[6]

Combined with these sentiments is a clear determination to place on
record all that he wished to be known or believed about her background,
and the reasons for her coming to Ireland. And in this connection it may
be of interest to note that he makes no reference whatever to Moor Park
or to Temple, saying, merely, that she " lived generally in the country,
with a family where she contracted an intimate friendship with another
lady of more advanced years " ; while Temple's death is referred to as
that of a " person on whom she had some dependence." As in the *Autofrag*,
Swift's circumlocutions are here almost as significant as what he decides
to put in.

About the same time, he did the same service for his own biographers
by writing the *Autofrag*, after which he settled down to face another
seventeen years of life, until death claimed him, too, in the autumn of 1745.

He did not write Stella's Epitaph, although expected by her representatives
to do this for her. All that he had to say about Stella appears to have gone
into his Essay. Nor did he wish to be buried beside her. For himself, he
selected " any dry part " of the Cathedral, preferably close to the statue
of Archbishop Marsh. Not even in the grave were they to be left alone
together. But in his desk was found an envelope endorsed " Only a
woman's hair."

Was he incredibly callous in his attitude towards this woman whom he
is supposed to have loved ? Or was Lyon perfectly right when he wrote
in the pages of Hawkesworth : " They saw proofs enough of y warmest
friendship and any Love but Connubial Love." ?

Mrs. Dingley lived on until 1743, remaining as before under Swift's
financial care, but leaving him nothing in her will, of which Lyon was
the Executor. As for the Dean himself, the last problem of his mortal
life is a medical one.

---

[6] *Swift's Poems*, vol. II, p. 728.

THE AUTOPSY

22

THE DEAN'S DEATH

DR. SWIFT died on the afternoon of the 19th October, 1745—the present anniversary of which is the 30th of that month—at the ripe age of seventy-seven. Alternatively, we are told by Orrery that he passed away peacefully, and by Faulkner, the Publisher, that his end came as a climax to thirty-six hours of painful convulsions, and by Hawkesworth that he died without the least pang.

One might have hoped that death would have put an end to these factual controversies, but such is not to be the case, and the actual manner of his departure is the least of the three problems that are still before us.

To have lived to seventy-seven, and to have had considerable difficulty in dying even at that age, is hardly the sign of a delicate constitution, even when the last four years are spent in a state of senility. Yet from an early age, Swift's indignation on almost all subjects included complaints about his health, and he suffered from recurrent fits of giddiness and nausea that are popularly supposed to have been symptoms of his growing insanity. Clinically, of course, such disturbances are more usually associated with seasickness than with any mental disorder.

Nevertheless, Swift was an oddity, and as he slipped further into his seventies, he grew more and more irritable, more unreasonably violent in his reactions to events around him, and his memory began to fail until, finally, he was quite incapable of looking after his affairs, and from about 1742, lapsed into a state resembling idiocy.

Orrery writes[1]:

> . . . early in the year *forty-two*, the ſmall remains of his underſtanding became entirely confuſed, and the violence of his rage increaſed abſolutely to a degree of madneſs. In this miſerable ſtate he ſeemed to be appointed as the firſt proper inhabitant for his own hoſpital: eſpecially as from an outrageous lunatic, he ſunk afterwards into a quiet, ſpeechleſs idiot; and dragged out the remainder of his life in that helpleſs ſituation.

---

[1] *Remarks*, p. 169.

Delany, on the other hand, who was much closer to these melancholy events than Orrery was, is less ready to fling around the easy generalisation —" lunatic", and gives us[2] a heartbreaking picture of the Dean, well aware of what was happening to him :

> And that he did feel the chaſtiſement, I am fully convinced, from his own bitter complaints to me on that head ; lamenting in manner, that pierced me to the heart, that *he was an idiot* ; that *he was no more a human creature*, &c.

To many of those who are fascinated by Swift, it has been tempting to tie all these loose ends together with his prediction that he would " die first at the top "[3] and assume, not only that he went " off his head ", but that he had anticipated this dénouement throughout the greater part of his life. We might find in these apprehensions a reason for some of his unaccountable behaviour. The fact that this way out, leaves still unexplained the equally peculiar behaviour of Stella, of Abigail, of Godwin, of Sir William, and even of his Archbishop, is a puzzle for another day. Perhaps they were all off their heads too.

Such a remark of Swift's, however, does not have to be interpreted as fear of insanity. It might equally well be an accurate forecast of what exactly did happen to him—he sank into a state of senility, in the course of which his brain died before his body.[4] It would, indeed, have been better for him if he had been constitutionally delicate, and had suffered from some disease that might have killed him before old age performed this service, four or five years too late. But apparently, his was not a fatal disease any more than it was mental.

We have a variety of diagnoses of this complaint from various sources. As will be remembered, he himself attributed it to having eaten a surfeit of fruit at two distant and contradictory ages. Scott adds that it was stone fruit, and Monck Mason—following the precedent set in connection with the Garden of Eden—describes these unnamed inedibles as apples, while suggesting, at the same time, that Swift's distemper was hereditary. What Monck Mason probably has in mind is Epilepsy—no doubt on the evidence of the Dean's references to " fitts ", and also on the similarity of Uncle Godwin's final " lethargy".

[2] *Observations*, p. 151.
[3] Sheridan, vol. I, p. 284 n.
[4] In his *Verses on the Death of Dr. Swift* he gives a whole catalogue of features of his own demise, in the course of which the only insanity that is described is that of others.

We need not, however, lay too much stress on the sincerity of the Dean's own remarks about this over-eating, for he originally produced the story, not to account for the condition of his health, but as a reason for his return to Ireland from Moor Park, and also for his not having remained there.

The Rev. Mr. Stevens, a member of the Chapter of St. Patrick's, was convinced that the Dean was suffering from water on the brain during his latter days, and constantly urged that an operation should be performed to relieve this. Delany tells us that after the death there was, indeed, a good deal of water in the cranium ; but according to the best medical opinion today, this was merely a by-product of senility, and was not the cause of his mental decay.

Here is how Hawkesworth[5] accounts for the Dean's final condition. It is printed together with Lyon's deletion and additions :

> In this ſituation his thoughts ſeem to have been confined to the contemplation of his own miſery which he felt to be great, and which in this world he knew to be hopeleſs ; the ſenſe of his preſent condition was neceſſarily complicated with regret of the paſt, and with reſentment both againſt thoſe by whom he had been baniſhed (who had prevented his preferment in y Queen's time in England) and thoſe who had deſerted him in his exile (to Ireland, as he ſometimes called it). A fixed attention on one object long continued is known to deſtroy the ballance of the mind, and it is not therefore ſtrange that *Swift* should by degrees become the victim of outrageous madneſs (which laſted but a ſhort time and then ended in a mere ſtate of Idiocy as the memory of all things became effaced in his mind for near 3 years before he expired).

In *Hygeia*[6] published in 1807, a Doctor Beddoes argued that Swift's disorder was venereal, and attributed his reluctance to marry to this fact. But this view has been consistently dismissed by later medical authorities, on the evidence of the symptoms that we know.

For example, according to Dr. T. G. Wilson, who will be mentioned at greater length below, deafness caused by syphilis is progressive and not recurrent, as it was with Swift.

---

[5]Hawkesworth, vol. I, p. 56.
[6]*Hygeia*, vol. III, p. 1870.

But it is Scott, following in 1814, who provides the main basis for the widespread belief that the Dean ended his life as a lunatic. In describing a plaster head that is still to be found in Trinity College, and that has been variously referred to as a Bust and as a Death Mask, Scott writes :[7]

> The expression of countenance is most unequivocally maniacal, and one side of the mouth (the left,) horribly contorted downwards, as if convulsed by pain.

But Sir William Wilde, writing in 1849, says :[8]

> . . . on the contrary, the expression is remarkably placid, but there is an evident drag in the left side of the mouth, exhibiting a paralysis of the facial muscles of the right side, which we have reason to believe existed for some years previous to his death. . . .

A photograph of this supposed likeness is here provided, so that the reader can form his own conclusions, between these two opinions. But it should also be pointed out, whatever view we may take of the strange look in the eye (much more noticeable when both eyes are seen from the front), and the sunken lips and the droop in the side of the mouth, that this head in Trinity College, in some respects, is a fabrication as a Death Mask, and consequently is highly misleading as any basis for medical speculation.

To begin with, the eyes are open. If the front portion of the head is to be regarded as a genuine untouched death mask, it must be a unique specimen of its kind. Whoever heard of plaster being placed over the open eyes of a corpse? And if the eyes were given to the cast afterwards, they are not genuine and have no medical significance. The rest of the head is certainly fanciful, and the entire back portion has been added, showing a different texture and a clear line of division.

It will also be noticed that an ear is missing. There is an ear on the right side of the head, which is also a later addition, although it appears to come from a genuine cast of the Dean's right ear. Apparently, they never got round to taking any cast of the left ear, before the body was buried.

Nor—according to Wilde[9]—is the front of the head the original mask,

---

[7]Scott, vol. I, pp. 465-466 n.
[8]Wilde, *The Closing Years*, p. 61.
[9]Wilde, p. 62 n.

THE TRINITY HEAD

but a secondary cast taken from it—and altered, it may be added, in the taking. The original mask, Wilde says, was accidentally destroyed in the Museum of the College, shortly before the writing of his book. This is all very mysterious, as it will shortly be seen that Wilde, himself, was in possession of a genuine death mask of the Dean, at a later stage of his life, which much more closely corresponds to the placid description quoted above, than does the picture that he reproduces in his book. This will be further discussed presently.

Wilde's book gives the best collation to that date of the various stories told of the Dean's death, together with a clinical analysis of his symptoms, and pictures of the skulls of both Swift and Stella, drawn in the course of certain excavations that will shortly be described. In Wilde's opinion :[10]

> . . . up to the year 1742 Swift showed no symptom whatever of mental disease, beyond the ordinary decay of nature.

He then goes on to diagnose the disease " under which he laboured so long " as *cerebral congestion*, which " might . . . be styled by some pathologists ' epileptic vertigo'."

The complaint was further discussed in 1882 by Dr. Bucknill in a periodical called *Brain*. Bucknill[11] was the first to diagnose it as Ménière's Disease—a view that is fully borne out by the most complete and satisfying analysis of the whole situation, which appeared in the *Irish Journal of Medical Science* for June, 1939. In this, an eminent contemporary specialist, Dr. T. G. Wilson, surveys the medical and literary history of the case, and confirms that the answer is Ménière's Disease—a disturbance of the semicircular canals in the ear, which was the cause of Swift's symptoms of giddiness and vertigo, but not the cause of his death—which was simply senility.

Dr. Wilson has also performed the enormous service of clearing up this problem of the death mask, by discovering another—an earlier and true one that must have been taken from the dead man's face before and not after, the post mortem by Dr. Whiteway. This other mask, Wilson describes in *The Journal of the Royal Society of Antiquaries of Ireland*,[12] and a photograph of this illuminating cast is also shown here.

---

[10]Ibid, p. 66.

[11]*Brain*, vol. IV, pp. 493-506.

[12]J.R.S.A.I., vol. lxxxi, part II, pp. 107-114.

It was purchased by Dr. Wilson from the executors of the late Frank Crawley of Dublin, whose father had previously acquired it in 1885 from the elder son of Sir William Wilde. How it came into Sir William's hands in the first place is a mystery. Perhaps the mask that Wilde alleges had been " accidentally destroyed " was actually retained by himself.

The measurements and general appearance of Wilson's mask make it quite certain that it is genuinely Swift, and also that it was taken from his face before the one that was used for the fabrication of the Trinity head. Although it is not clear from the photograph, the marks caused by Whiteway's cutting open of the skull are distinguishable on the head, showing that this cast was made after the post mortem. There are no such marks on Wilson's mask, where, too, the eyes are closed and the distorted effect around the mouth, of which so much is made by Scott, is almost entirely missing. This last important difference, Wilson points out, is not due to any miraculous change in the Dean's expression after death, but to the very simple fact that in the course of the post mortem his dentures were removed, thereby causing the mouth to cave in.

It is clear, therefore, that two casts were taken from the Dean's face— one before the post mortem, and the other afterwards—that the former and better specimen came by some undiscovered route into Wilde's possession, although he never mentions having it, while the other, and inferior specimen, was made use of as a face for a head, fabricated by some person, who never got around to giving it its second ear. No wonder the reopened eyes are maniacal.

After taking some castings of the newly discovered mask (which contains a name—DEL VECCHO—presumably that of the original maker, and a note by Chetwood Crawley) Dr. Wilson presented his treasure to Trinity College, where it is now to be seen. Probably, in so doing, he was returning it to its original home. But of this, only Sir William Wilde would know.

We can see, therefore, how the tradition of the Dean's madness—his supposed maniacal expression, his bulging eyes, and the idea of his mouth distorted with pain—has largely grown out of Scott's conclusions that are based in turn on a secondary death mask, the eyes of which are false, the back of the head an invention, and the tragic contortions of the mouth due to the removal of a set of false teeth.

On this insecure foundation, an elaborate edifice has since been erected, to the effect that all his life through, JS was haunted by the fear of madness, that he would not run the risk of propagating children on that account,

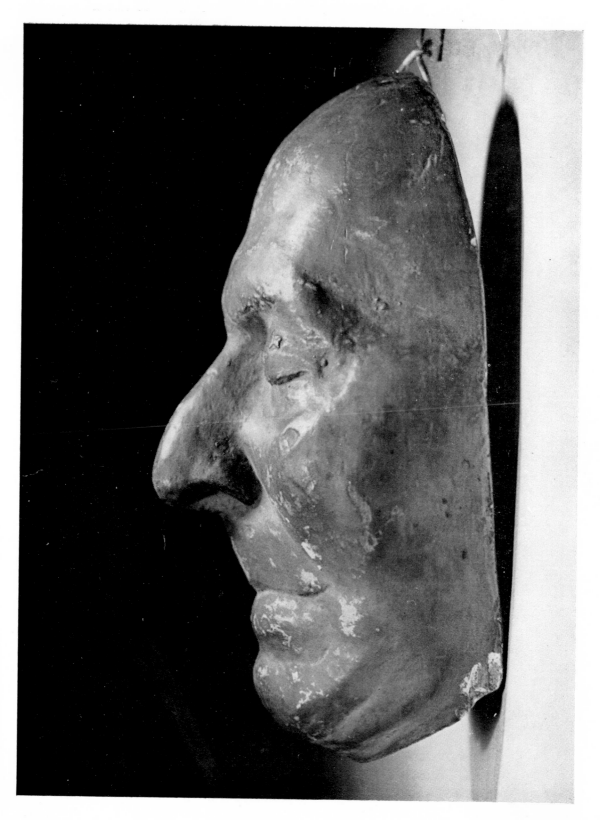

THE TRUE DEATHMASK

and that he actually did die insane. In pursuance of this idea, he is supposed to have married, but refused to admit his marriage—a most extraordinary method of carrying out such a purpose, even if it were true. For one of the most striking expositions of this theory, the reader should refer to W. B. Yeats' play, *The Words Upon the Window Pane*.

But it is not only over his mental condition that these myths have continued to accumulate since the Dean's death. The circumstances and position of his, and of Stella's burial, have also been a source of a controversy, that is only slightly less ghoulish than the fate of his bones. And this must be the subject of yet another chapter.

23

THE BATTLE OF THE GRAVES

A HEAVY black plaque, displaying an equally ponderous epitaph, hangs on the wall above the door of the Vestiaries, close to the only entrance to St. Patrick's Cathedral that is normally open to the public. Although not previously in its present position, it has been available for public inspection for over two hundred years, during which time many writers have given summaries and extracts from its well-known periods, while others have professed to reproduce it line by line, with capitalisation and punctuation complete. But after all that we have been through, the reader will hardly be surprised to learn that—as far as can be ascertained—nobody has yet managed to perform the feat of copying it down correctly and in full.

So in order to avoid adding another mistranscription to the heap, a photograph of this elusive statement is here provided.[1]

As regards the inscription itself, the first mistake in publishing it, is usually to give the degree as ' S.T.P.' Then ' Vindicatorem' is commonly written (and actually improved) as ' Vindicem'. Some writers confine themselves to one or other error, but many of them have both, because of the fact that they are copying a copy of Hawkesworth's original mis-information, rather than looking at the plaque for themselves. A faulty arrangement of the lines is also an unfailing indication that the writer has merely consulted some descendant of Hawkesworth's version.

In 1933, Stephen Gwynn almost succeeded in getting it right, but then fell down on his spelling, while also misdescribing the plaque's position. In 1937, Bertram Newman would have scored a perfect round but for a possible error in one word, and for his capitalisation and punctuation. Leslie Stephen quotes only two lines, in the course of which he manages to get the words in the wrong order, while Dr. Wyse Jackson misstates a tense. It was left to Miss Evelyn Hardy in 1949 to discover the fact that

---

[1]There is an excellent picture by the same photographer, the late Mr. Thomas H. Mason, in John Harvey's *Dublin* (Fig. 112, p. 77) which shows the present arrangement of both Swift's and Stella's memorials, and of Cunningham's well-known bust of the Dean.

Hic depositum est Corpus
IONATHAN SWIFT S.T.D.
Huyus Ecclesiæ Cathedralis
Decani,
Ubi sæva Indignatio
Ulterius
Cor lacerare nequit.
Abi Viator
Et imitare, si poteris,
Strenuum pro virili
Libertatis Vindicatorem.

Obiit 19 Die Mensis Octobris
A.D. 1745. Anno Ætatis 78.

THE EPITAPH

the Dean's first name is apparently spelled IONATHAN, and not JONATHAN (although there still may be some argument as to whether the tail of a ' J ' is not concealed under the inner wooden frame that surrounds the plaque).[2] But then Miss Hardy misplaces her ULTERIUS, and spatters her text with uncanonical commas.

Guide Books to the Cathedral are usually inaccurate only as regards the punctuation. This may be attributed to the fact that writers of Guide Books tend to look at the thing itself, or alternatively at Monck Mason's History of the Cathedral, in which it is reproduced almost correctly, while writers on Swift usually look at previous books on Swift. So now we have at least ten eminent authorities in the field, all bearing witness to errors in observable fact which, fortunately, in this case are of no consequence whatever, except on the issue as to whether the Dean was good at his Latin. Orrery[3] described the Latin as " ſcarce intelligible " ; but as the wording was probably intended to be idiomatic as well as enigmatic, these criticisms are, on the whole, unjust.

Here is deposited the corpse of a Doctor of Sacred Theology, Dean of this Cathedral Church, where the heart is unable any further to be lacerated by savage indignation. And you, a traveller to some unspecified destination, are to go away, and to imitate, if you are able, a strenuous vindicator of liberty, to the utmost of something not stated, but presumably of your ability. He died on the 19th day of the month of October in the year of our Lord, 1745, in the year of his age 78.

The poet, Yeats, who like myself was unencumbered with too much interest in classical niceties, translated it freely as follows :

> Swift has sailed into his rest ;
> Savage indignation there
> Cannot lacerate his breast.
> Imitate him, if you dare,
> World-besotted traveller ; he
> Served human liberty.

This is good, imaginative verse and does not hesitate to use poetic licence in leaping some of the hurdles. Yeats adds, as part of his own contribution, that the passer-by is world besotted, and he pays no attention at all

---

[2] A recent Beadle of the Cathedral, Mr. W. Evans, was kind enough to mount a ladder to examine the letter closely, and he assured me that it is an I.

[3] *Remarks*, p. 168.

to that troublesome word, *Virili*. As in the original, Whose liberty to do What ? is not disclosed, any more than the reason for the savage indignation that this storm-tossed parson can only escape in the grave.

Below and to one side, a more graceful and chatty piece of marble states untruly, but with a charming plethora of capitals :

Underneath lie
interred the mortal Remains
of Mrs. HESTER JOHNSON better
known to the World by the Name of STELLA,
under which ſhe is celebrated in the Writings of
Dr. JONATHAN SWIFT Dean of this Cathedral.
She was a Perſon of Extraordinary Endowments and Accompliſhments in Body, Mind and Behaviour ; juſtly admired and reſpected, by all who
knew her, on account of her many eminent vir-
tues, as well as for her great natural and
acquired Perfections.

It concludes with some details of the date of her death, and with several lines of not-quite-disinterested praise for the clause in her will that endows a Chaplain. At which point we may legitimately move on into the central portion of the Nave, where we come upon two brass plates let into the tiled floor, side by side, at the foot of the pillar opposite the door. The larger of these bears the inscription :

SWIFT.
Decan : 1713.
Obt. 19 Oct : 1745.
Aet : 78.

The other, which is somewhat smaller, professes, in frank competition with the announcement on the wall, to mark the burial place of the lady, which we see at once must be a matter of some dispute. Indeed, these doubts will be even stronger if we happen to have visited the Cathedral between 1924 and 1935, when Stella's brass was to be found not where it now is, but about ten feet away to the west, opposite the end of a neighbouring buttress. Further enquiries from those who remember the arrangements earlier still, will unearth the information that this peripatetic plate has been on the move throughout its existence, and has only, at the moment, returned to where it was in the first place.

The fact is that a succession of Deans, holding different opinions on the relationship of these two people, has made a business of altering the position of the plates in conformity with this or that view. As the record stands today, practically all the biographers who refer to the matter at all follow Dean Bernard in stating categorically that Swift and Stella were buried together, and ignore Dean Lawlor's documented arguments that they were not. It is reasonably certain that, with the exception of a few small items of Swift's anatomy that were stolen in 1882 and were last heard of in the United States, the two skulls with the greater part of Swift's bones now lie under the position indicated by the plates. The real question is, whether they were always there?

By some complicated process of thought, the problem of whether they were interred together has come to be regarded as having a bearing upon the issue of their supposed marriage. If you believe that they were never man and wife, you are supposed also to believe that their original graves were dug at a respectable distance. The social reasons for such fuss in the case of corpses is not at all clear, but feeling has been intense in the matter. And it has produced an even stronger reaction against the available evidence in the breasts of those who feel that as they *should* have been buried together, they consequently were.

Lecky, Churton Collins and Van Doren all state that they were buried together. The late Archbishop Bernard states categorically (*St. Patrick's Cathedral, Dublin*, p. 64) that " She is buried two or three feet to the west of the spot where Swift lies". But a later Dean called Lawlor[4] with somewhat less weight, but considerably more evidence, has written at some length to prove that they were not. The history of this free-for-all has never been fully set down, so I shall now describe it from the start.

First of all, the Cathedral books appear to contradict both the plates and the epitaphs. Of Stella we read :—

Jan 30th. (1727, *inserted*) Hester (*corrected to* Esther) Johnson interred in the Great Ifle near the first (Pillar *interlined*) upon the Entrance (of the Church *interlined*) to the South Side of the West gate.

This correction of Stella's first name is of interest, especially after we

---

[4]"The Graves of Swift and Stella." *English Historical Review*, vol. 33, pp. 89-93.

have noticed its form on her Memorial described above. Elrington Ball,[5] quoting Dr. S. Lane-Poole, says that she was " baptised as Hester", and in the use of this expression he is followed by Maxwell Gold ;[6] while Professor Homer Woodbridge goes a step further and tells us : " Her name was Hester, but she chose to call herself Esther"—another example of his scholarly respect for anything written down. But baptism is not an orthographical sacrament. What they all mean, of course, is that some Parish Clerk spelt her name in this way in the Richmond Parish Register. The fact that she invariably spelt her name as Esther—in so far as we have seen her signature—should decide this vexed matter finally, notwithstanding any views to the contrary of the Richmond Parish Clerk or the unknown composer of the Epitaph.

Of the Dean, we read :—

> The Revd. Docr. Jonathan Swift Late Dean of St. Patrick's Deceased Oct. the 19th 1745 ; And was Interred the 22nd. of the same, at the 2nd. pillar from the West Gate in the South Side of the great Isle. He was Installed Dean of this Cathedral the 13th. day of June 1713.

Stella's entry is signed by Jon. Worrall, the Dean's Vicar, and seems to be written in his own hand, corrections and all. The page on which Swift's entry appears is signed at the bottom by Jon. Worrall, but the entry itself is by another hand. If the facts as stated in both entries are correct, it means that they were not buried under the Epitaphs, nor beside the same column, nor is Swift's plate in the right place. The only thing right is the present position of Stella's plate.

But No, say the upholders of the common grave. In describing Stella's burial, Worrall has ignored the pillar that forms the end of the Baptistry buttress, and he counts the first entirely separate pillar as number one, while Swift's unknown scribe counts it as number two. They were buried in the same place. However, if we examine an 18th century floor plan of the Cathedral[7] we will find that at the time of both burials there was no buttress on the south side of the Baptistry, and the disputed Column No. 1 was separate and unattached—a proud and undeniable column, like its twin on the opposite side of the Nave. If Worrall did not number

---

[5]*Correspondence*, vol. I, p. xxvi.
[6]Gold, p. 3 n.
[7]Bernard's *St. Patrick's, Dublin*, p. 61.

it, he must have made an unaccountable mistake, and how can we believe that he could have overlooked such an error, when he took the trouble to make four other corrections, of much less importance, in his entry? So, they were buried apart.

However, when we turn to William Monck Mason's authoritative but unreadable history of the Cathedral to check on what he has to say, we find[8] that the Dean is stated to have been:

> interred, agreeable to his own directions . . . at the foot of the 2nd. column from the west gate, on the south side of the nave of his cathedral.

while on another page,[9] Stella is also described as buried:

> on the south side of the nave of St. Patrick's cathedral at the foot of the second column from the west entrance.

So that not only were they buried in the same spot, but this state of affairs was brought about by the Dean's specific direction—a magnificent victory for the advocates of the wedding. He loved this woman, and having refused to acknowledge their marriage during her lifetime, remorse and better sentiments supervened, and his only desire in old age was to lie at last beside his best and dearest friend.

But before we join in the cheering, let us take one quick look at what Swift's directions actually were. In a letter to his cousin, Mrs. Whiteway,[10] dated March 26th, 1737, he asks

> to have my body brought to town, and deposited in any dry part of St. Patrick's Cathedral.

Not only is this a dry request, but it is also a well-nigh impossible one, as the building was encompassed by an underground river, the Poddle, which regularly flooded it out. Worse is to come when we turn to his will. Here, his express instruction is to be buried, not, as we had hoped, by the side of his friend, but

> next to the monument of primate Narcissus Marsh,

---

[8]Monck Mason, p. 411.

[9]Ibid., p. 368.

[10]This letter appears in Swift's *Works* edited by Scott, vol. I, cxxviii-cxxix. For some reason it is not to be found in the *Correspondence* edited by Elrington Ball. Both the letter and the will were stated by Scott to be in the Prerogative Office, Henrietta St., Dublin. There is now no such office.

one of the few prelates of the Church of Ireland of whom he consistently approved. And as for Stella's grave, it remained unmarked for twenty years after her death, although as Rev. Mr. Lyon says in his marginal notes to page 48 of Hawkesworth, she " left money for a monument which through negligence was never erected. The Executors indeed waited for an inscription which he (Swift) promised to write". But although he was careful to provide for his own Epitaph, he never troubled to compose any public tribute to her. The inscription that is on the wall today was composed and erected after his death.

This is very tiresome of Swift, not only because of his lack of gallantry, but also because, in asking to be buried next to a monument, he introduces an entirely new area and several more columns. This monument to Marsh, which at one time stood in the Churchyard, and now is in a corner of the South Transept, stood at the time of Swift's death between the fourth and fifth columns on the south of the Nave.[11] And Monck Mason, having already told us that the Dean is interred at the foot of Column No. 2, now proceeds to move up the Church to Columns 4 and 5, where he tells us :[12]

> Next adjoining to the monument of Primate Marsh, is that of Dean Swift, described in another part of this volume; and fixed in the column, next to this last, is a marble slab, consecrated to the memory of Mrs. Esther Johnson, which likewise has been described elsewhere.

This would seem to contradict his previous description of Swift's epitaph as being then attached to Column 2, and it causes endless confusion over Stella, whose plaque has been stated on page 368 to mark " the place of her sepulture." What is the meaning of " next to this last " ? A picture appearing in *Walker's Hibernian Magazine* of June, 1802, shows Swift's plaque and bust attached to a pillar, but no sign of anything connected with Stella.[13]

So we are now well on our way to having them buried each separately

---

[11]Monck Mason, p. lix.

[12]Ibid.

[13]The fact that this picture shows a window behind the column is of no significance in trying to determine which column it is. The entire north and south aisles were completely rebuilt during the period from 1863 to 1865, and in the course of this reconstruction the bust and both memorials were taken from wherever they were, and placed in their present positions (Bernard's *St. Patrick's*, p. 63).

in two different places, or alternatively interred together in the one place, while their memorials were erected in two places elsewhere.

Finally we have Richard Garnett and Thomas Seccombe, in a somewhat misinformed article on Swift in the celebrated 11th Edition of the *Encyclopaedia Britannica*,[14] going so far as to tell us that they were not only buried in the same grave, but actually in the same coffin—a tricky piece of undertaking, one would imagine, remembering that they died over seventeen years apart.

This extraordinary piece of information is probably due to a misreading of a statement of Sir Henry Craik[15] about a contemporary opening of the grave. How what is probably Stella's skull eventually got into Swift's coffin will shortly appear. It was not there originally.

On the balance of the evidence that we now have it would seem most likely that Stella was buried at the foot of the pillar that now forms the eastern end of the buttress wall of the old Baptistry at the west end of the Cathedral, where her grave remained unmarked until some years after the death of the Dean. Then an inscription was composed by some person now unknown, and inscribed on a plaque which was attached to this same pillar.

He was buried about ten feet away from Stella's grave, at the foot of the next pillar under the spot at present marked by the brass plate in the pavement, and his plaque was originally placed on this pillar, together with Faulkner's bust.

But this is not the end. In the year 1835, the floor was opened in the course of some reconstruction of the Cathedral, and a number of coffins were exposed to view. The British Association was then meeting in Dublin, and considerable interest was expressed when the news got around that one of these coffins had a legible plate bearing the name of Swift. The Association washes its hands of the nasty performance that followed, and places all the blame upon a group of Phrenologists that was also in the city. It is clear, however, that in the crowd that hastened to St. Patrick's there were more than experts on bumps, although these may have headed the stampede.

At any rate, when two of these boxes were opened, they were found to contain respectively the undisturbed bones of a man and a woman,

---

[14]*Encyclopaedia Britannica*, vol. 26, p. 230.
[15]Craik, p. 405 n.

which were then enthusiastically disturbed, dried, measured and passed around Dublin.

Dr. J. Houston, writing in the *Phrenological Journal and Miscellany*,[16] states that Swift's coffin was " transversely in from the pillar supporting his tablet, and as close as it could be placed "—whatever that means. It was surrounded by wet mud and largely filled with water. (So much for " a dry place".) " Side by side" lay another unmarked coffin which, on the word of the sexton, Maguire, he took to be that of Stella. Maguire, in his turn, alleged that he had his information about the burial places from Swift's rascally servant Brennan who, incidentally, died when Maguire was still only fourteen years old.[17]

It is difficult to make out from what Houston writes whether " side by side " means that the two coffins were really close together, or whether a large section of the floor was open, and that they were merely in the same general area, because at a later stage of his statement he goes on to say that Stella's remains lay " in the same relation to the pillar bearing the tablet to her memory as that of the Dean", and this would seem to suggest a separate column and separate graves in so far as it suggests anything at all.

Sir William Wilde takes up the next part of the tale in his book, *The Closing Years of Dean Swift's Life*, and reproduces drawings of the two skulls, a1d reports amusingly on the findings of the Phrenologists :[18]

> The University, where Swift had so often toiled, again beheld him, but in another phase ; the Cathedral which heard his preaching,— the Chapter House which echoed his sarcasm,—the Deanery which resounded with his sparkling wit, and where he gossiped with Sheridan and Delany,—the lanes and alleys which knew his charity,—the squares and streets where the people shouted his name in the days of his un-exampled popularity—the mansions where he was the honoured and much-sought guest,—perhaps the very rooms he had often visited,— were again occupied by the dust of Swift !

The Phrenologists, however, were somewhat disappointed. A Mr.

---

[16]*Phrenological Journal*, vol. IX, pp. 604 ff.
[17]Lawlor, p. 92.
[18]Wilde, p. 53.

Hamilton, who alleges in a letter to Sir William Wilde that he had both skulls in his possession in September, 1835, writes of the male remains :

> On looking at Swift's skull, the first thing that struck me was the extreme lowness of the forehead, those parts which the phrenologists have marked out as the *organs of wit, causality, and comparison, being scarcely developed at all* ; but the head rose gradually, and was high from benevolence backwards. The portion of the occipital bone assigned to the animal propensities, philo-progenitiveness and amativeness, etc., appeared excessive.[19]

Mr. Hamilton also furnished Wilde with drawings of the skulls, on which Sir William observed that that of the man resembled " in a most extraordinary manner, those skulls of the so-called Celtic aborigines of North-Western Europe, . . . which were found in the early tumuli of this people throughout Ireland." With the lady, however, he was gravely delighted.

> . . . this skull is a perfect model of symmetry and beauty. Its outline is one of the most graceful we have ever seen ; the teeth, which, for their whiteness and regularity, were, in life, the theme of general admiration, were, perhaps, the most perfect ever witnessed in a skull.[20]

Whether or not this paean of medical enthusiasm was lavished on the actual remains of Swift and Stella, or whether the Poddle mud, in league with the Dean, has played a ghoulish prank upon the pundits by disgorging some relic of the Firbolg, is a matter which the reader must decide for himself. But if a decision must be made by this writer—it seems reasonably certain that the bones were authentic in the case of Swift, and it is possible, though not at all certain, that the other skull was that of Mrs. Johnson. But the balance of probability still seems to be ponderously on the side of Dean Lawlor that the relics, genuine or not, were not taken from a common grave, and that the Dean and his lady—wherever they are now— began the Life-to-Come under separate pillars.

The rest of the story is quite well authenticated, but is no less striking. When the unpilfered remains were eventually returned to the Cathedral, it was left to a sexton, Maguire, to put them decently back to rest. And

---

[19]This passage is here quoted as in Wilde, pp. 55-56.
[20]Ibid., p. 121.

Maguire—doubtless for the same sentimental reasons that make us all feel slightly disappointed in the above conclusions—took it upon himself to place both skulls in Swift's coffin—a fact unknown to Wilde. Maguire had written a memorandum when the bones were first removed, and now he added a rider about their return. And he placed this paper in a bottle which was put between the severed portions of Swift's skull. According to a transcription that was made much later, his memorandum runs as follows :

Aug. the 3rd. 1838

Doctor Swift grave opened This day by the British Association who Got Permission from the Dean. They were holding there Meeting in Dublin. The Scull of Swift was in two as it now appears having been opened after his Death to examine the Braine.

Stella's Scull was taken out of the adgoing Grave and is now Deposited with Swift.

William Maguire Sexton. 13 August 1835.

The floor was then closed up.

Dean Lawlor[21] states on the doubtful authority of this Sexton, Maguire, that the skulls were actually returned to the Cathedral for reinterment on the 13th August, 1835, in which case Hamilton cannot have had them in his possession as late as September. But Lawlor's article omits a further detail related by Wilde,[22] that at least one portion of Swift's remains was stolen by a bystander, and was believed to have been taken to the United States. Wilde, on the other hand, says that " the skull of Stella was returned to its former and, we hope, its *last* resting place, at the same time as that of Swift ". So he evidently does not know of its final destination, as determined by Maguire.

Maguire's memorandum is printed by Dean Lawlor[23] from a copy made by a later Sexton, John Lambert, and although there is no reason to believe that Maguire was any more literate than Lambert, many of the stylistic features of the document are probably faults in the copying. For example, there is an obvious error in the transcribing of the opening

---

[21]Lawlor, p. 92.
[22]Wilde, p. 53.
[23]Lawlor, p. 93.

date, which should be 1835. I have not located the original of this copy
or of Lambert's additional note, reproduced below, but Lawlor appears
to have been meticulously careful in reproducing the illiteracy of both
memoranda, which adds greatly to their poignancy, as the last well-
intentioned apostrophe of the Yahoos to the human remains of Swift.

The identity of Swift's skull is well confirmed by the reference in
Maguire's note to the fact that it had been opened after death. This we
know was done by Mrs. Whiteway's son, Surgeon John Whiteway,
" to ascertain the cause of his insanity", as Brennan is reported to have
told Maguire.[24]

In 1882 the floor was opened again for the purpose of more permanent
repair, and the coffin containing the two skulls was seen once more by
people who have talked to others who are still alive. Thus there is now no
question about its present position. Although the wood was in an advanced
stage of decay, and there was no sign of any coffin plate, the presence of
the bottle containing Maguire's memorandum identifies the remains as
those that were desecrated in 1835. No mention is made of Stella's coffin,
which fact adds weight to our surmise that they were never literally
" side by side ".

Once again the same strange procedure seems to have been followed,
and another sexton, John Lambert, was left to perform the most important
part of the final obsequies on Swift. He took a copy of Maguire's paper,
and left us another memorandum of his own which runs as follows :

> In Swift Scull was found the Bottle containing the paper. It was
> Sealed with red wax and had the arms of the Maguire famley impresed
> on it. it was inside Swift Scull, it had been in to part. I have seen
> Dean Swift grav opened and the two Sculls of Swift and Stella, and
> the remains of what was left of Swift. The Coffin was cleaned of the
> Mud and water that was in it And a box Made by a Carpenter who was
> working at the time in the Cathedral. And the two Sculls, and the
> remains of Swift put in the box. And from two to three feet of Concrete
> put over it. I suppose Never to be opened Any More until the Great Day.

[24]Wilde, p. 52. Actually no weight whatever should be attached to the report of
" many particulars concerning the Dean " (Wilde's expression on p. 62) that Brennan
is supposed to have communicated to Maguire. Maguire was not Brennan's immediate
successor as Beadle or Sexton, as Wilde's text implies, and they can hardly have known
each other, except as an old man, incapacitated by age and infirmity, and a child hardly
in its 'teens. Lambert was still alive in 1918, when Lawlor wrote his article for the
English Historical Review.

At the same time i did ask the Verger Mr. Cornegie to get a Nother
Bottle while the Grave was opened and to write on a paper what took
place at the time and put it in the Box with Swift. but he took to
long to Make up his Mind and the grave was closed it May be for ever.
I would have put a bottle and Paper in with the remains of Swift.
Something about what took place at the time. but he the Verger
would not Consent.

JOHN LAMBERT,
Assistant Sexton.   1 Sept. 1882.

It was at the time of this concreting of the floor that Swift's brass was
laid down below what is now the first distinct pillar. Dr. Lawlor says that
both brasses date from this time, but one of his successors, the late Dean
D. F. R. Wilson, assured me that this is not the case. There was no plate
for Stella, he said, in the early years of this century, when he was a Clerical
Vicar and Succentor. In fact it was he who suggested to the then Dean
Bernard that this was a pity, and that something ought to be done about
it. According to Dean Wilson, Bernard agreed that the omission ought
to be rectified. So he directed that a brass for Stella should be placed in
the position indicated by Wilson, next to Swift's. It need hardly be added
that Dean Wilson was a staunch believer in the marriage.

Not so, however, was Dr. Lawlor, who was then Curate of Bray, a
Professor of Ecclesiastical History, and Precentor of the Cathedral. Taking
the view that the Cathedral Books meant what they said, he moved
Stella's brass to a position below the buttress, about ten feet away, as
soon as he became Dean in 1924. This so infuriated Mr. Wilson, then
Rector of Donnybrook, that he seems to have determined to restore the
status quo in the only unanswerable manner—by becoming Dean himself,
which he duly did in 1935. Almost his first official act was to move the
plate back again.

Dean Wilson retired in 1950, and it remains to be seen whether the
present occupant of the Deanery is deeply concerned about the issue.
But there is little doubt that somewhere in the lower ranks of the Church
of Ireland another clergyman is at present working his way towards the
office of Dean of St. Patrick's in order to be in a position to shift the
brass again. At least I hope so, as it would be an indication of a continued
and healthy interest in Swift. And, between ourselves, I think that the
newcomer will be right.

24

TOWARDS A CONCLUSION

So far, the present writer has attempted little more than to clean up the record—to point out the inconsistencies and to correct mistakes and mis-statements, while drawing only such conclusions as appear to be inevitable.

My opening statement to the effect that there was much of this to be done, must now seem reasonably justified; also my secondary charge that our difficulties in making sense of the story are not entirely due to honest mistakes on the part of the reporters. Including the Dean himself, at least seven of our informants have turned out to be mendacious in some of the things that they have said.[1] As was further predicted, the majority of these are clergymen—two of them Bishops, in which list I am not including either Evans,[2] Bishop of Meath, or St. George Ashe, Bishop of Clogher.

If the results are irritating and confusing, this regrettable state of affairs is not made any better by ignoring the parts of the data that happen to give us pain. There is obviously some answer to the puzzle—some missing piece or pieces which, if found, could clear up all that is unbelievable. Even if we have made up our minds that Swift and Stella were married, this does not really help us, for it is not the marriage but the secrecy that is our major problem. It is quite possible that both Delany and the anonymous writer in the *Monthly Review* are right when they take the line that it was not until immediately after the wedding that any impediment was discovered. It is clear that there was some impediment, and whether they knew about it and consequently did not wed, or did not know about it until after they had done so, is irrelevant to the main question as to what the impediment was.

---

[1] Jonathan Swift, Dr. Berkeley, Dr. Bernard, Rev. Mr. Carroll, John Forster, Sir Henry Craik and Dr. Sheridan.

[2] Evans, though bitterly hostile to Swift, is maliciously but accurately repeating to Archbishop Wake what he has heard, and is not a liar in this respect. Ashe can only be suspected of lying if we believe both Dr. Berkeley and Berkeley's widow and grandson. And Dr. Berkeley is already on the list.

The obvious answer—that it was an impediment of consanguinity—so happily explains all of their conduct that it is surprising that no writer after C. M. P., with the possible exception of the Rev. Mr. Hay, has ever pursued this solution any further, once they have been satisfied that Swift and Stella were not brother and sister. For there are other degrees of consanguinity besides this that are mentioned in the Book of Common Prayer, and are also prohibited by the secular law of England and Ireland.

The fact that this seems to have occurred to nobody is a fascinating example of the way in which the best cloak for truth is an unsustainable half-truth. In satisfying ourselves that there was no brother-sister relationship, everybody, without exception, has forgotten that it is not this particular connection that is the issue, but consanguinity as a whole. Exhausted by our investigation of Sir William Temple, we have omitted to look for anybody else, once that suspect has been triumphantly found Not Guilty, Mr. Hay alone—and wrongly—dissenting.

So let us pause for a page or two to survey the clues that we already have, that point to the kind of person Swift's real father must have been. For he obviously had some father, and it was not an individual who was dead ten or more months before he was born.

First of all, this mystery man must have been in Dublin in the last days of February or the early March of 1667. If he had a house in the County, outside the city limits, so much the better. He was a person with English connections, and of reasonable wealth, in a position to make a small life settlement on Abigail Swift, out of English funds. As it is probable that he already had obligations, in recognition of which he found her a husband, it is also likely that he was originally responsible for the presence of this Englishwoman in Dublin. This means that he probably had something to do with Leicestershire. He was also a person of some influence, able to induce or frighten those who knew about the situation into hushing it up, and in particular, he must have been in a position to persuade Godwin Swift reluctantly to accept this by-blow into his household, and to pose as the child's benefactor during the time of his education at Kilkenny and in Trinity.

From the fact that he could so influence Godwin, we may perhaps further assume that he was also a lawyer, and in the upper layers of that profession. And from the fact that Jonathan the elder looks like having been rewarded with the job of Steward of King's Inns for marrying this much older woman, it might also be expected that he was a Bencher with such a job in his gift. He was probably still alive in the early 70's, otherwise why would the child be brought back to Dublin from Whitehaven, after the Mother had already gone back to Leicester? But it is unlikely that he was still alive in 1690, when young Swift returned to Dublin in Southwell's train, and found that he could get no more assistance in that country.

But even though the original subject of our search was then dead, it is fairly clear that there were other members of the same connection who —presumably for family reasons—continued to assist the young man, whose interest it was to keep the matter quiet, and to provide jobs, annuities and even a small dowry for Jane Swift—persons who might also be expected to be in the secret, and whose mouths could be kept shut in this way. In short, he was probably a man of maturity and a family, a fact that put marriage with this woman of low social position out of the question, but who did for her, in 1664, precisely what Sir William Temple did for another woman about sixteen years later—he settled her in respectability with a husband and a name. Indeed he was probably another Temple, since it was the Temples who continued to look after JS, and were the initial impetus behind his career. And it is exactly here that the whole question of consanguinity bobs up again.

For when we look back at the pages of the Black Book of King's Inns to see whether there are in fact any candidates that answer the description outlined above, we see at once amongst the signatures something of great interest. So please let us do so again, before continuing with any solution.

Two John Temples repeatedly sign the pages, some of which have already been reproduced in facsimile, and one of them actually signs the very minutes that record Jonathan Swift the elder's appointment as Steward. This one is Sir John Temple, Master of the Rolls for Ireland, a man of sixty-four at that date, who had been a widower since 1638, a lifelong friend and associate of Robert Sidney, Earl of Leicester, and the father of Sir William Temple—

whose Father—says the *Autofrag*—had been a great Friend to the Family.

This is the same man whose career has already been partially outlined in connection with Sir William's marriage, and whom we have also met in the imaginary conversation attributed to Abigail by Deane Swift, when first despatching her son to Sheen :

...his Father, Sir JOHN TEMPLE, had a Regatd and Friendſhip for your Father and for your Uncles until his laſt Hour.

The other John, who throughout the Minutes writes his name as " Jo Temple," is Sir John's son and Sir William's brother, the Solicitor General (later Attorney General), and for a time, temporary Speaker of the Irish House of Commons, described by Lady Giffard as one of the best lawyers in Ireland, and of whom Archbishop Sheldon is supposed to have said : " He has the curse of the Gospels. All men speak well of him ". One of his sons (John) also subsequently lived at Moor Park, and had a long-standing hostility towards Swift, and another son (Henry) was the first Viscount Palmerston.

Both of these Temples fill all the requirements outlined above, with this difference, that while the father died in 1677, the son was still alive in 1690, and if the Attorney General had been the father of JS, the latter would have been first cousin to Stella, and there would have been no prohibited consanguinity. But if the Master of the Rolls were the father, then Swift and Stella would have been Uncle and Niece.

Our next and final task, therefore, is to review the background and movements of the Master of the Rolls to see how it fits in with what we may now reasonably suspect.

The Temple Family

Elrington Ball in his *History of the County of Dublin*[3] says :—

> In writing of the branch of the Temple family to which the Prime Minister (Lord Palmerston) belonged, it has been remarked that it was little allied with the higher nobility, but frequently with the leading families of the commercial class, and that its members, who remained thoroughly English in spite of their connection with Ireland, enjoyed nearly uninterrupted intellectual distinction for three centuries with a pervading likeness of character in their practicability as statesmen or lawyers, in their fondness for literature, in which they were sometimes famous, and their success as men of the world without loss of higher attributes.

This encomium, which comes through Ball from Gough Nichols, the editor of *The Herald and Genealogist*, was not written with Swift in mind, but is of peculiar interest if he was in fact a product of this family, and if

---

[3]Elrington Ball's *County Dublin*, part IV, p. 94.

there is anything in heredity. It is a family that occupies no less than thirty-seven pages of the Dictionary of National Biography. The Swifts, on the other hand, have provided the world with no other figures of either literary or notable public significance throughout their three and a half centuries of recorded genealogy. It may also be added that the Irish connection of the Temples at the time of JS's birth was about fifty years longer than that of the Swifts.

Lodge's *Peerage of Ireland*[4] describes the Temples as being descended from Leuric or Leofric, Earl of Chester in 716. The line of descent from such a date is, of course, mythical, but it claims to include : Leofric of Leicester, the cruel husband of the celebrated Lady Godiva ; Edwyn— who first assumed the family name by taking it from the Manor of Temple in the same county ; Richard Temple of Bosworth, who was deprived of his property by Henry VII because of his adherence to the loyalist side in the battle close to his home ; and Richard's cousin, William of Whitney, Oxfordshire, the great-great grandfather of William Temple, born in 1553 —who was the first of the family to go to Ireland.

This last William was a Fellow of King's College, Cambridge, and Master of the Free School, Lincoln. He also began three generations of close association between his family and the Sidneys of Leicester. He himself was Secretary to Sir Philip Sidney, from 1581 until the latter's death in 1586 when Governor of Flushing. Indeed, Sir Philip is said to have died in his arms at the Battle of Zutphen—an incident that is the subject of a well-known picture by Lancelot Speed.

Incidentally, many of Sidney's Sonnets are addressed to the love of his life, Penelope Devereux, whom he apostrophised under the name of Stella.

Robert Devereux, Elizabeth's Essex, later brought Temple to Ireland as his secretary on his disastrous expedition of 1599. William remained behind after his master's return to trial and execution, probably in order to avoid participation in Essex's downfall, and the hostility of the Cecils. Here, he became fourth Provost of Trinity College in 1609, and was a Master in Chancery from the following year. He sat in the Irish Parliament as Member for Dublin University from 1613 till 1615, was knighted in May, 1622, died in January, 1627, having written four Latin treatises, and was buried in the Chapel of the College, under the Provost's seat.

In 1591 William Temple married Martha Harrison, by whom he had

---

[4]Lodge, vol. V.

two sons and three daughters :—John, with whom we are now concerned, and the Rev. Thomas, Fellow of Trinity College, Cambridge, Preacher to the Long Parliament, and later Incumbent of Battersea. This Dame Martha Temple, as she was called, spent her widowhood in Ireland. According to the Funeral Entries in the Genealogical Office, she died intestate in 1653.

Her sister, Mary Harrison, was the wife of Dr. John Hammond of Chertsey, Physician to Henry, Prince of Wales, who was presented by Lord Leicester to the living of Penshurst in Kent in 1633, and was the link with both the Hammond and the Dingley connections. This Mary's daughter, Mary, married our John Temple, and died in her mother's home at Penshurst Rectory, where the grandchildren Martha and Henry Temple were born and brought up.

The complicated relationship of the Hammonds, Temples, Dingleys and Berkeleys of Stratton is best shown on the accompanying genealogical tree.

The son John was born in Dublin in 1600, and attended his father's College, where he apparently had a good academic record :—Scholar and B.A. in 1617, Fellow in 1618, and M.A. in 1620[5]. This same year he was admitted to Lincoln's Inn in London, and commenced his career at Court and at the Bar, with the blessing and support of Robert Sidney, Earl of Leicester, in whose particular friendship and confidence he remained for the whole of his earlier life—according to his daughter Martha Giffard's monograph.

In the same year as the death of his father the Provost, he married his cousin Mary Hammond, and next year on the 25th April, 1628[6], his eldest son William was born in Blackfriars, but like his brothers and sisters, was brought up principally at Penshurst, where the playmates of these Temple children were the children of the Earl of Leicester.

Temple returned temporarily to Ireland in 1636, apparently for the first time for some years, to see to his property there. And on the 5th September, 1638, his wife died at Penshurst, eight days after having given birth to the twins, Henry and Martha (Giffard). In 1639 he went north with the King's expedition against the Scots, and in the January of the following year he was appointed Master of the Rolls for Ireland, and was knighted.

---

[5] *Alumni Dublinenses.*
[6] See Moore Smith, *Temple. Early Essays*, p. 191 n., for the correction of this date.

This was shortly before the time of the appointment of Leicester as Lord Lieutenant. But although Temple duly went back to take up his new duties in Dublin, Leicester, on the other hand, had not made the crossing by the time of the outbreak of the sanguinary Irish Rebellion in October, 1641, and he never actually functioned in Ireland as the King's Deputy.

During the early part of this long-drawn-out rebellion, Temple was extremely active in the defence of the Anglo-Irish, and in Carte's Biography of Ormond we get an account of the distinction he won by his successful revictualling of Dublin Castle[7]. But next year, the Civil War broke out in England, and the struggle in Ireland became three-sided —Crown, Parliament and Rebels. The Cessation—or armistice—between Ormond, on behalf of the Crown, and the Irish rebels, was violently opposed by Temple, with the result that in August 1643 he was imprisoned by Ormond, and a list of charges was formulated against him that can be read in Carte.[8]

However, in the following year there was an exchange of prisoners between Crown and Parliament, and Temple was sent back to England, where he sat in the Long Parliament as member for Chichester from 1646 until Pride's Purge in 1648, when he was " secluded " by Cromwell.

The next part of his history has already been described in the Chapter dealing with the marriage negotiations of his son William, from which it will be seen that, in the spirit of the time, Sir John's sentiments and loyalties were neither wholly Cavalier nor wholly Roundhead, but moved with the fluctuating tides of political development. And the fact that, at each stage, he was largely in sympathy with typical prevailing opinion, contributed much to the growth of his fortune. It is probably unfair to regard him as a timeserving politician who always supported the winning side. In a better sense, his sentiments were those of Protestant Parliamentary England, and were characteristic of the changing sentiments of his age.

He was a King's man, until the King betrayed his office by making peace with the Catholic Irish at the expense of the Protestant planters. Imprisoned by Ormond, he was then exchanged, and became a member of the Long Parliament, without, however, becoming a Cromwell man. But even here, he was not so much at odds with the Commonwealth as

---

[7]Carte's *Ormond*, vol. I, p. 171.
[8]Ibid, vol. II, pp. 503-506 and vol. V, pp. 518-520.

to prevent his employment by Cromwell in Ireland as a Commissioner for Forfeited Estates in which office one may be certain that his own property was adequately assured. But like England as a whole, he approved of the Restoration, and in 1659/60, was a member of the Council of State that promoted the return of the King. To begin with, he had some natural fears that his earlier employment by the Commonwealth might be frowned upon by the new King. But he survived this peril. And so his family not only rode out every tempest, but actually managed to put each successive wind to a good purpose. Yet it must be remembered in fairness to Sir John, that in the middle part of his career he was not a particularly wealthy man, and that he ran himself into debt in the late forties through keeping his son William at College.

Diarmid Coffey,[9] in his book *O'Neill and Ormond*, described him as " a notorious adventurer in Irish lands, and was himself completely ruined by the Rebellion ". A further note somewhat inconsistently accuses him of having made large sums out of confiscated lands, and of having made some illegitimate profit out of the maladministration of a mill at Kilmainham. But, on the whole, these strictures may perhaps be taken as reflecting the natural resentment of the dispossessed Irish against one who was smart enough to outwit successive confiscations himself. And Temple's book on the Rebellion of 1641, though one-sided in its sentiments, could hardly be expected to be anything else, published, as it was, before the troubles that it describes were over. It makes great play, of course, with lists of atrocities, and it supports and justifies confiscation. But it is the work of a man of literary ability, and is still a standard partisan account of the period.

His daughter Martha tries to convince us that, from the date of his escape from Ireland until the Restoration, he " lived privately " in London. But this, of course, is said in order to cover up his activities during this period in the employment of Cromwell.

Philip Sidney, Lord Lisle, the son of his friend Leicester, was appointed Lord Lieutenant by the Parliament in April, 1647, following the final defeat of the King. And, from 1653 onwards, Sir John, as Estates Commissioner, was frequently back and forward from Ireland, in which country he was joined by his son and daughter, William and Martha. Indeed the former spent much of his early married life in Dublin with his father.

---

[9]Coffey, p. 42.

Sir John was restored to his office of Master of the Rolls by the Parliament, and in 1657 was Treasurer of King's Inns.[10] According to the Hearth Money Roll for 1658,[11] Sir John and his two sons John and Henry were then living in a house on " Damaske Street ". There is also a map in the possession of the Dublin Corporation, which shows that his City home was on a holding between Dame Street and the river, surrounding the position of the present Temple Lane. This is in what became in 1665 the restored Parish of St. Andrew, which, however, had no Parish Church or registers till the 70's. It may also be of significance to note that from 1666 till 1695, his son John, the Solicitor General—now a married man[12]—lived in Palmerston House on the main turnpike to Galway, which house was not in the City, but in the County.

Now it will be remembered that in 1653 Sir John's mother, Dame Martha Temple, died in Ireland. This was at the beginning of Sir John's constant traffic to and from Dublin, and it is not beyond the bounds of probability that soon after this lamentable event deprived him of his sole remaining parent, he acquired the services of a young woman to aid his sister, Martha, in the running of his several establishments—and in particular this house in Dame Street. And in due course—I suggest—this woman came to perform some of the other functions of these so-called Housekeepers—if a euphemism may be forgiven that is not unknown, even today.

The rest is speculation, for there is no direct evidence that this is how Abigail Erick first came to Dublin. Nor do we know when she came. All that one can say is that it is not only possible, but understandable, that Sir John—a man still at the robust age of fifty-three, with no wife to give him comfort—should acquire a sprightly and intelligent young woman in her middle twenties to perform these services. And if so, it is not at all unlikely that he would find such a person at or near his friend and patron's home at Leicester—a place that he must frequently have visited at precisely this period of his life. Furthermore it is difficult to believe that when Abigail sent her son to Sheen in 1689, she did not already know the man to whom she was recommending him. It is equally difficult to see when she could possibly have met Sir William, if not during his residence with his father in Ireland, prior to 1664.

---

[10]*Black Book.*

[11]In the Royal Irish Academy—where it is misdescribed as a Census Return.

[12]Attorney General from 1690.

The other Temple in whom we are interested—John, the Solicitor General—married a Dublin woman, Jane Yarner, in August 1663, and was happily begetting ten legitimate children during the next decade and a half. So, although it is not impossible, it is unlikely that he would have further secret domestic complications during the same period. It might be that, soon after this marriage of the younger John, a husband was found for an earlier dependant. But it is even more likely that the father, on reaching the age of sixty-four, saw fit to perform this civilized act for a woman of thirty-four who had been his responsibility for some years past. And who would be better suited to provide her with a name than this young man of respectable parentage, with no home of his own, who had been hanging around the Inns for some years past, picking up odd jobs —the younger ne'er-do-well brother of the rising Counsellor Godwin Swift, whose career in a new country could be made or marred by people in precisely the position of the Master of the Rolls ?

It was an estimable arrangement, if a somewhat delicate one. The marriage was performed in private by special licence. The bride was provided with a small dowry secured in English funds. And immediately the first vacancy in the Stewardship of the Inns occurred, the bridegroom was given the job, and the next day, admitted as an Attorney, to add further substance to his position.

The marriage in its course produced a dull and unattractive daughter, Jane—" rather beyond what is called the agreeable ", as Deane Swift[13] discreetly says of her. But it did not prosper, and perhaps fortunately, it was brought to an end in the last days of 1666 by the death of the husband.

It is tempting to speculate in what pungent dramas may have surrounded and even caused, the premature end of Jonathan Swift the elder, and the return of Abigail from an unhappy household to her old protector[14]. But none of this is necessary to our purpose. Assuming that the man died from an Itch, as stated, or from any other natural cause, there would be nothing unnatural or unexpected in the temporary revival of an old relationship, while some new arrangement was being worked out for Abigail. And if an unexpected consequence of this upheaval should have

---

[13]*Essay*, p. 107.

[14]At the date of the conception of JS, Sir John Temple was 66 years of age—or possibly 67. Godwin Swift was almost exactly the same age when his son, John Swift, was conceived.

been another pregnancy, how fortunate it is for English Literature that the Dean of St. Patrick's should have been the result. If in fact he was born " *in comitatu Dublinensis* ", it was probably in the privacy of the son, John's, house at Palmerston, where few would know of it, and the Master of the Rolls would not suffer the embarrassment of any such event occurring in Dame Street.

It is after this, of course, that the child was shipped abroad, until its mother was safely resettled in her old home in Leicester. But the Temples —as always—were conscientious about the future of their offspring, whether legitimate or not. So after a year or two, in which it might be hoped that tongues would quieten down, the services of Uncle Godwin were invoked. The child was brought back and placed in his household, where for the next six or seven years, it grew up under the eye of Godwin's good and influential friend—the Master of the Rolls.

He died in 1677 and was buried beside his father in the College, leaving a will that has never been published, and that was finally destroyed in the Record Office. All that we know of its contents are some Genealogical Extracts abstracted by Betham.[15] But my suggestion is that, whether by will or otherwise, Sir John provided for the education of his secret child, and that his wishes were duly carried out, probably by his son John, through the channel, and under the cloak of Godwin Swift.

No open scandal ever embarrassed the Temple family name, and it was as much to the interest of Sir John's legitimate children—Sir William, Sir John the younger, and Lady Giffard—to prevent this happening, as it had been to the older man to provide for his youngest son. And because these obligations were properly carried out, no voice from the older generation of the Swift family was ever raised in disavowal of the child. What gossip there may have been was soon engulfed in the upheavals of the Williamite War, in the flight to England of a large part of the Protestant population, and in the resettlement that followed the Battle of the Boyne.

Even so, we know that there was such gossip, and that from the start there were those who whispered that JS was really a Temple. But after the Revolution, old Sir John was largely forgotten. He was half a Cromwellian anyway—and it was to Sir William, the patron and friend of

---

[15]These are to be found in vol. 67, pp. 106-107 of the Phillips MSS. in the reconstituted Dublin Record Office.

the young man in his twenties, that these stories of an unofficial paternity were mistakenly attached. The truth was lost in the half-truth—the most effective way of concealment. But Swift, himself, could never be sure. To his last day there was always the possibility that somewhere in Ireland some impoverished relative, some little Attorney's clerk with a long memory, some venomous political enemy, might turn up with a tale which, if proved, could ruin him.

This does not imply a mere hankering for respectability. When we come to consider the implications of the situation with regard to his relations with Stella, we will see at once, that Swift was not just a man who objected to being called a bastard. He was actually in danger from the criminal law.

This is what is behind his extraordinary shiftiness about the year and place of his birth, and why he lies unblushingly about his mother's relationship to Dorothy Osborne, and about the nature of Stella's claims upon the Temples. This is why he invents absurd stories about having been stolen away by his nurse, and sent back to Ireland in a bandbox, and confuses the dates of his first return to Dublin from Moor Park with a poorly thought-out fable about having been upset by a surfeit of fruit.

In this connection, I am suggesting that it was the Solicitor General who paid for Swift's education at Kilkenny and in Trinity. There is actually no evidence of this, except that of propinquity and probability. But it is borne out by the fact that when Swift turned up at Sheen to pay his addresses to Sir William Temple, the first reaction of the latter was to ship him back to Ireland where he belonged, at the earliest available opportunity.

But in Dublin, I suggest, his brother John wanted no more of the boy. He had paid for his schooling at his father's behest, and if anything further was to be done for JS, it was now the turn of other members of the family. So back to Moor Park went Swift, to be given his first employment there, with obvious reluctance.

A humiliation of this kind would adequately account for Swift's curious myopia towards this particular trip, when computing the number of his journeys between the two countries, and the fact that he never mentions anything connected with the tremendous events of the Williamite War, either in his works or his correspondence, after two early sycophantic Odes to King William, in spite of the fact that these upheavals must have made a considerable impact on some of his most impressionable years.

It also accounts for the distinct hostility of the next generation of the Temples towards JS, with the exception of Sir William, who in due course found his presence useful and his vigorous intelligence an asset in a secretary. The second Sir John returned to England in 1695, where he died at East Sheen in March, 1705, and as far as we know, Swift saw no more of him. But his son, John of Moor Park, was always an enemy of Swift, as was also Lady Giffard, although neither of them ever opened a mouth about the real basis of any objection.

As for Swift's own reactions to those who probably knew his secret, these are equally understandable, and will be dealt with in our next, and final, chapter.

25

THE DILEMMA

In Hawkesworth's account of the Dean,[1] we find an illuminating example of Swift's reaction towards the threat of blackmail. The matter arose as a result of the Government's proclamation, offering a reward for information on the authorship of *The Drapier's Letters*.

This proclamation gave the dean a remarkable opportunity to illuſtrate his character. It happened that his butler, whom he had employed as his amanuenſis, and who alone was truſted with the ſecret, went out in the afternoon of the day of the proclamation, without leave, and ſtaid abroad the whole night and part of the next day. There was great reaſon to ſuſpect that he had made an information, and, having received his reward, would never return. The man, however, came home in the evening, and the dean was adviſed by his friends to take no notice of his fault, leſt he ſhould be provoked to a breach of truſt, from the dread of which his return had juſt delivered them. But the dean rejecting this counſel with the utmoſt diſdain, and, commanding the man into his preſence, ordered him immediately to ſtrip off his livery and leave the houſe. You villain, ſaid he, I know I am in your power, and for that very reaſon I will the leſs bear with your inſolence or neglect.

The man, in very ſubmiſſive terms, confeſſed that he had been drinking all night, and intreated to be forgiven, but *Swift* was inexorable. . . . During all the time of danger, *Swift* obſtinately refuſed to contribute one farthing towards his ſupport, nor could he be perſuaded to ſee his face; but when the time limited in the proclamation was expired, he was permitted to return to his ſervice.

From this violence in his reaction to the sense of being in anybody's power, we may deduce how Swift might be expected to behave towards those who knew the secret of his birth. Let us speculate, therefore, as to who would be likely to know and see how the Dean did behave towards each of these.

First of all we have his vehement hatred of his Uncle Godwin, who to all outward appearances was his greatest benefactor, but who probably treated the child and young man with some disdain. Even when Godwin was in the grave, Swift pursued his memory with the deepest venom, and in so doing, laid himself open to a charge of fantastic ingratitude. "He gave me the education of a dog", is a statement that is patently untrue, if Godwin was, in fact his benefactor. That he was treated like a dog is possible, but not as regards his education, which was better than that provided for any of Godwin's own children, with the exception of the eldest son.

We have noted, too, the Dean's lack of interest in the other Swifts, and how he avoided the family like the plague during his later life in Ireland, with the exception of one or two of the younger females, who obviously knew nothing of the truth. He states the family background in a somewhat sketchy way in the *Autofrag*, while making enormous claims for his mother, and he does not even trouble to ascertain which of his uncles actually came to Ireland, or which of them left male issue. The only uncle whom he can stomach is William, who was kind to his mother at the time of the Steward's demise, and who provided a home for his sister.

As for Jane, who was probably in the secret, he made her marriage to Fenton into an excuse for never seeing her again, encouraging her departure to England at a time when he was beginning to come to public notoriety, and paying her a pension for the rest of her life on condition that she stayed away from Ireland. And it is interesting to note, too, that, over in England, it was Lady Giffard who took Jane into her employment in exactly the same way as she gave a home and a job to her brother's mistress. Her household was a nest of women with dangerous secrets concerning the Temples. Yet Swift always disliked Lady Giffard, just as he reciprocated the hostility of John Temple of Moor Park, and of Henry, first Viscount Palmerston, the sons of the Attorney General. It will also be realised that a family of the Temples' distinction must be even more nervous at the prospect of its bastards claiming a relationship than the bastards are about being exposed by them.

Hence the barbed politeness of Swift's correspondence with this half-sister and two half-nephews.

As for the Attorney General himself, we know nothing of the Dean's attitude towards him, save that he is never mentioned, and that he died before the development of the situation became acute. Alone of the Temples, Sir William was Swift's friend. After some initial uncertainty, Sir William never patronised him openly, and reciprocally, each needed the services of the other. For had not Sir William a secret of his own, in which the younger man participated? So, towards Sir William, JS did show a becoming gratitude.

To continue, it is probable that his Archbishop knew, having forced him to disclose the reasons behind his equivocal behaviour towards a lady who was popularly supposed to be his wife. It would be perfectly right for King to make such enquiries of the Dean of his principal Cathedral, and it would be like what we know of this highminded cleric to keep his mouth shut after having been given the answer.

> " You have just seen the most unhappy man on earth,"—he said to Dr. Delany—" but on the subject of his wretchedness you must never ask a question."

Yet Swift hated King, too, while at the same time never daring to treat him with anything but calculated respect.

Delany and the Archbishop

Scott places this meeting with Delany immediately after the date of Swift's supposed marriage, and goes on to say that

> Delany's inference from this circumstance was a suspicion that Swift, after his union with Stella, had discovered that there was too near a consanguinity between them to admit to their living together, and that he had been then stating the circumstance to the Archbishop.[2]

However, as Scott believes in the marriage, and does not believe in any such consanguinity, he dismisses this explanation as highly improbable. How could such a relationship have been " a secret to both parties, during their intimacy of so many years, and yet should all at once have become known to them upon their marriage . . ."? What Scott ignores is the much simpler explanation that they did know, and that consequently there was no marriage.

---

[2]Scott, vol. I, p. 239 n.

Then there is Dingley. The Dean never hated her, nor had he any occasion to do so. Maybe she only knew the truth about Stella. But whether or not she suspected that all was not well with Swift also, she was always his dependant, and one of his household, and received his pension till her death. There was no need to be alarmed about dear Dingley.

As for Stella, and the consequences of a mutual attachment that was involuntary, as much as intentional—this must be the subject of our final analysis. It is sufficient to conclude by saying that nobody else need ever have known, and that none of the above would be likely to speak.

In the early stages of the investigation of any historical conundrum, one tends to find that each additional piece of information only makes confusion worse, and provides yet another problem that has to be waved aside by complicated explanations. While this state of affairs continues, one may fairly assume that one is wrong in some basic assumption, or that the only fact that matters has not yet come to light.

But if one works grimly on, allowing the data to pile up without reaching any dogmatic conclusions about its meaning, there sometimes comes a point at which each new piece of information is found to fall neatly into some sort of pattern that seems to have created itself. When this stage is reached, one may say, without any undue risk of wishful thinking, that one has probably got hold of the truth.

There are many more minor aspects of this tangled history that it would be tedious to enumerate. It is probably sufficient to say at this stage of our battle with the facts, that they no longer surprise us as they come to light, and that each of them now fits into a coherent picture. What the sum total amounts to is that—as with Sir William and Stella—Sir John Temple the elder could physically, geographically and in common-sense have been Jonathan Swift's father. And while it can never be proved that he was, there is a colossal mass of inconsistencies, of lies, and of unbelievable behaviour on the part of at least half a dozen people in Swift's orbit, that cannot be accounted for if he was not.

Stella's Uncle

Now, what if JS was Stella's uncle?

To begin with, it would be understandable for Sir William, on his deathbed, to have entrusted the future of his only surviving child to the half-brother for whom he had done so much.

It is possible that Stella did not at first fully understand the reason for this, and may have expected Jonathan to marry her. If so, the Tisdall episode would have brought this matter to a head, as doubtless it was intended to do, and then Swift would have had to explain to her why it could never be. We have no reason to believe that JS stood in the way of her marriage to Tisdall, or imposed impossible conditions, apart from Deane Swift's assurance that he has read such things in letters that have never come to light. It is certainly quite out of line with the not-unreasonable letter to Tisdall that we do have. It may well be that Swift despised this future Vicar of Belfast, and could not bear to see his ward throwing herself away on one whom he considered to be a numskull. But to believe that he was against her marrying anybody is a standpoint that is not supported by any evidence.

The outcome that I suggest is that Stella, unaware of any blood relationship between herself and her friend, had by the age of twenty-three allowed herself to get into such an emotional condition about Swift that she did not want to marry anybody else, and, knowing that a marriage to another man would inevitably mean her separation from her tutor, she told him that, if she could not marry him, or remain as his companion if married to another, she would rather remain single for the rest of her life.

What could be more fatally flattering to a man of Swift's temperament? —to be told by a woman like Stella that she would rather remain his friend and companion than become a married woman! After years of humiliation, he accepted this compliment as food for his soul, and for a time, this very odd solution probably worked well enough for both of them. It was all right for their mutual friends to believe, either that they were married already, or that they intended to be married some day, when their fortunes had improved. All that was necessary was to be certain that it could never be said that they were living together.

This was not prudery on Swift's part. It was due to his fear that if they did otherwise, they would for ever afterwards be in the power of anybody who knew the truth. And they could never be certain that some hostile person who did know the truth was not waiting to catch them, with the frightful accusation of incest. To have lived together as man and wife, whether legally married or not, was not merely a canon law offence. It was a crime; and this is why they adopted this attitude of exceptional prudery—never to be found together except in the presence of a third party—who could be a witness against this possible charge of incest.

In the light of this peril—justifiable or not—his fears that she might die in the Deanery are far from disgusting, and can claim a reasonable excuse.

But such a peculiar relationship, satisfactory as it may have been for a time, was ultimately fatal for JS, not because he was sexually abnormal, as so many recent psychologists have tried to show, but because he was perfectly normal. His earlier life gives every evidence of a natural intention to marry at some date in the future. The disaster happened, when this desire came to its ordinary fruition—with Vanessa.

For, consider his appalling position then. He could not marry her without abandoning Stella. And even if Stella were to agree to this—which possibly she did, on terms—he could not break up his association with a supposed wife without denying the marriage, and disclosing the truth. In the absence of the truth, Stella would then have become a cast mistress, and this is a role that resolute young woman would never have accepted.

Marry her if you must—one can hear her say. But if you do, you must tell the world what lies between us two. Tell the world—scandalise his mother's name—and make a bastard of his best friend? Maybe he should have done so, but he didn't. And who can blame him?

Yet the excruciating fact remained—that he wanted marriage, and there was no legal impediment. Yet he could not marry, and he could not tell. He could not stay away from Celbridge, and what he wrote in French to that unfortunate woman was the truth—nobody adored and worshipped her more than her friend Cadenus. But more than friend he could not be, in spite of the fact that there was no impediment. And so, driven frantic by doubts and despair, she vanished at last into her unknown grave under the pavement of St. Andrew's Church—a victim, if ever there was one, not of cruelty, or of envy, or of hatred, but of love.

In his old age, after both women were gone, and he was left alone in the world, tormented by the memory of what love had done to him and to them, it hardly is surprising that Swift should have written some of the most dastardly attacks on this supposedly tender emotion, that have ever been penned by man. Nothing that the Christian Fathers have said against the sex relationship can equal the savage hatred with which Swift treats it. And can one doubt why, after what it did to him?

Some say that his trouble was Scatology. Others insist that it all may be explained by some inborn sexual perversion. But it does not have to be so.

History, by itself, can account for what the Dean had got against human love, and for the savage indignation that was lacerating his heart.

And so he did no wrong to Stella, and that is why, in spite of her knowledge of the existence of this other woman, she never showed any resentment, and never appeared to expect anything more from life than what she got. He could look his God in the face over his treatment of Esther Johnson, and pray for forgiveness of her sins without such a prayer being an act of blasphemy. The one whom he did wrong was Vanessa. But he wronged her, not as the monster that he seems to be, but through his need for her as a woman—through his inability to be cruel without hatred. When cruelty was the only thing that could have saved her, he should have been cruel. In short, she was wronged through the demonic pity that was the keystone of his character.

We might never have known that there was anything more in his life than an odd perverted distaste for human contact—an abnormality that prevented him from acknowledging and consummating his marriage—had it not been for Vanessa's exposure of his correspondence with her. As a phenomenon of this type, he is of interest to psychologists and alienists to an even greater degree than is Shaw, who discloses some of the same symptoms. But, to the present writer at any rate, Swift is of far greater importance than any psychological museum piece. He was a perfectly normal man, of colossal proportions, motivated by two of the most universal, the most lovable, and most dangerous of all human emotions —Pride and Pity. And thanks to Vanessa we now know too much about him, and yet not enough.

If he was an aberration of hypocrisy and cruelty, if he was a freak whose savage indignation was merely an expression of jealousy and baffled conceit, it is incumbent upon us to remember this fact when studying his works today. But if there was a reasonable cause for his distemper, we surely owe it to his memory to show that he was not—in the verdict of the 19th century—" the apostate politician, the ribald priest, the perjured lover, the heart burning with hatred against the whole human race". (The expression is Macaulay's.) Yet on the basis of the accepted record even the most friendly of the biographies give ample evidence to support such a conclusion.

Those who are averse to any further investigation of his origins are content that he should remain so, and I have no patience whatever with that brand of suburban gentility that can look with greater equanimity on the imaginary spectacle of his wantonly driving two women into the grave, than on any suggestion that he was illegitimate.

In the last analysis, the best verdict on whether or not this man was a monster comes from the several sensitive and intelligent women who admired him, and who found his friendship worth having. And in the forefront of these, is the proud woman who preferred his friendship to married life, secure from scandal. So it is perhaps appropriate to allow her farewell to be our last word on the Dean of St. Patrick's:

> Late dying may you caſt a Shred
> Of your rich Mantle o'er my Head;
> To bear with Dignity my Sorrow,
> One Day *alone, then die To-morrow*

APPENDIX

Iт is only proper to conclude with a summary of the more impressive objections that have been levelled against my original paper, so that both sides of the argument to date may be placed before the reader. After having had my say in the body of the book, I undertake to refrain from making any further comment on any of these, however tempting this may be.

With the exception of those of Sir Harold Williams, all these criticisms are directed at my proposed solution of the problem, and little or no attempt is made to counter my principal attack, which is on the scandalous unreliability of the existing record. For example, in a radio discussion with me about ten years ago, Mr. Frank O'Connor admitted freely that the Steward of King's Inns could not have been the father of the Dean, and confined his arguments to the contention that whoever the father was, he was not Sir John Temple. In a lively article in the Dublin *Sunday Independent* for the 21st October, 1945, he substantiates this point by quoting the letter of Swift's cousin and college-mate, Tom, written in 1706, in which he asks " whether Jonathan be married ? Or whether he has been able to resist the charms of both these gentlewomen that marched quite from Moorpark to Dublin . . . with full resolution to engage him ? "

" Tom Swift ", O'Connor continues, " who had lived in Moorpark, would not have been likely to write in that tone if his cousin were really Stella's uncle ! "

Mr. Middleton Murry, who gives the impression that he did not come across my pamphlet until the substantial part of his recent book was finished, disposes of any possible Temple connection in his Appendix I, where he writes that my argument " depends, very largely, on the assumption that the connection between Jonathan Swift and Sir William Temple was peculiar to himself and otherwise inexplicable". But, in fact, Jonathan's cousin, Thomas, acted as Temple's secretary during the Kilroot interlude. " Plainly, therefore, there was nothing peculiar to Jonathan in the Temple connection. Once this is admitted, Mr. Johnston's theory falls to the ground."

Nor was Miss Rose Macaulay satisfied, and said so in a article in *Time and Tide* in October, 1945. When challenged by Mr. Andrew Wilson to give some reasons for her hostility, she replied with four, in the issue of the same paper dated the 8th November :—

(1) Sir John Temple was 67 when Swift was born.

(2) So far as she knew, there was no contemporary gossip.

(3) Swift was such a snob, that had it been true he would have boasted about it. And,

(4) Uncle Godwin would never have paid for the education of Sir John's bastard.

In the first chapter of his delightful little book on Stella, Mr. Herbert Davis makes a good humoured attack on me, and twits me in the most friendly manner on having spent more time on reading the biographies than on studying Swift's works—on which task I would have been much better employed. On the subject of the Dean's paternity his argument seems to be that the Dean would have been a liar and a hypocrite to have written in such affectionate terms about his mother had he known her to have been Sir John's mistress. " I have lost the last barrier between myself and death " is a sentence that could never have been written in sincerity by any man who knew such a secret about his mother.

Miss Evelyn Hardy dismisses the whole matter as strained and far-fetched, and Mr. John Hayward in an interesting letter to Mr. Maurice James Craig—in which he says, " If you want to make use of any of these cursory remarks please do "—puts forth some of the really basic objections in a very frank and understandable manner.

" O dear ! it's all rather a bore, to tell ye truth, this theorizing about Swift's relations with the Ladies on insufficient evidence. . . . I still think that Swift's relations with Stella and Vanessa are most plausibly explained psychologically and somewhat along the lines that I follow in my 'Anne-Victoria' paper. . . . I don't trust Johnston's judgment in this matter. . . . There is in fact no proof that Stella was Temple's daughter. Johnston's theory collapses without this presumption. . . . The penultimate paragraph is silly and ignorant and inaccurate."

It is Sir Harold Williams who, alone, takes off the gloves in defence of authority-in-general by quoting, not as might perhaps have been expected a list of items on which I, and not Forster, can be shown to be mistaken, but a list of authorities from Orrery to Quintana who agree with himself. In a long letter which appears in the *Times Literary Supplement* for the 29th November, 1941, headed *Swift's Secret*, Sir Harold states that I am quite unjustified in my " wholesale dismissal, with the single exception of the late Dr. Elrington Ball, of scholars who have interested themselves in Swift, asserting their want of ' original investigations ' and failure even so much as to visit Dublin."

The grounds upon which he demurs at what are described as my " misrepresentations " are that from his personal knowledge of Dr. Ball —a fine and modest scholar—he is certain that Ball would have demurred too. And furthermore that, " with the exception of Monck Mason, Wilde and Elrington Ball, Ireland has contributed comparatively little to original research upon Swift and his writings." He objects to my description of Vanessa as an " Ingénue ", and repeats his conviction that Stella was not Sir William's daughter, for the reasons already described ; namely, that "the truth is far otherwise", and that there is no authority for any such proposition except Dr. Delany, Emil Pons, and this person of dubious credit who writes in the *Gentleman's Magazine*.

Ignoring the Black Book, he insists that the Steward died in the month of April, because Ball " usually had authority for his dates". And finally he tells us that it is impossible to believe that Swift " whose outstanding characteristic was an ardent sincerity, carried about with him through his life the knowledge that his mother had been a cast-off mistress . . . and that despite all this, he professed love and respect for her, and when opportunity served, stayed with her in Leicestershire."

In spite of these very serious adverse comments, I notice with some interest that my proposition regarding the Dean's paternity has been adopted in the new one-volume edition of the *Cambridge History of English Literature*[1], although no reference to the source is indicated.

---

[1] *The Concise Cambridge History of English Literature*, p. 465 in the 1945 edition.

BIBLIOGRAPHY

The following bibliography deals only with the various items and editions cited in the course of this work, and does not include some important and authoritative contributions to the study of Swift to which it has not seemed necessary to direct the reader's attention, in relation to the matters under review. For an excellent selective bibliography down to the summer of 1952, the reader should see the appendix to Ricardo Quintana's book, *The Mind and Art of Jonathan Swift*, published by the Oxford University Press in 1953. The standard bibliography is that of Dr. H. Teerink, published in The Hague in 1937, which appears to be very exhaustive, but has been the object of some criticism.

1. *WORKS*

(a) *Collected Editions.*

The Works of Jonathan Swift, D.D., edited by John Hawkesworth. London, 1755. Volume I contains a *Life of Dr. Swift* by Hawkesworth, a copy of which in the Victoria and Albert Museum has been annotated by Lyon and Malone. See Supplementary Volume XIII published by Nichols in 1779 for some of Lyon's notes. Referred to throughout under the abbreviated title of "Hawkesworth."

The Works of the Rev. Jonathan Swift, D.D., arranged by Thomas Sheridan, A.M. A new edition in nineteen volumes was corrected and revised by John Nichols, F.S.A. London, 1808. Volume I contains *Life of Doctor Swift* written by Sheridan in 1784. It also contains Dr. Barrett's *Essay on the Earlier Part of the Life of Swift*, published separately by the same publishers in the same year. Referred to throughout as "Sheridan."

The Works of Jonathan Swift, D.D., edited by Walter Scott, Esq. Edinburgh, 1814. Volume I contains *Memoirs of Jonathan Swift, D.D.*, by Scott. Referred to as "Scott."

The Prose Works of Jonathan Swift, D.D., edited by Temple Scott. London, George Bell and Sons, 1905. Volume I contains a Biographical Introduction by W. E. H. Lecky, M.P. Volume XII consists of a bibliography and index. Referred to as "Temple Scott."

The Correspondence of Jonathan Swift, D.D., edited by F. Elrington Ball. London, G. Bell and Sons, Ltd., 1910. Volume I contains an Introduction by The Very Rev. J. H. Bernard, D.D., then Dean of St. Patrick's. Referred to as "Correspondence."

The Poems of Jonathan Swift, edited by Harold Williams. Oxford at the Clarendon Press, 1937. Volume I contains a Bibliographical Summary by the editor.

225

The Prose Works of Jonathan Swift, edited by Herbert Davis. Oxford, Shakespeare Head Press, published by Basil Blackwell, 1939. This edition is not yet complete.

(b) *Separate Items.*

A Tale of a Tub, edited by A. C. Guthkelch and D. Nichol Smith. Oxford at the Clarendon Press, 1920.

Vanessa and her Correspondence with Jonathan Swift, edited by A. Martin Freeman. London, Selwyn & Blount, 1921.

Gulliver's Travels by Jonathan Swift, D.D. The text of the First Edition, edited by Harold Williams. London, First Edition Club, 1926. A forged Volume III was published in London in 1727.

Unpublished Letters of Dean Swift, edited by George Birkbeck Hill. London, 1899.

The Letters of Jonathan Swift to Charles Ford, edited by David Nichol Smith. Oxford at the Clarendon Press, 1935.

The Drapier's Letters to the People of Ireland, edited by Herbert Davis. Oxford at the Clarendon Press, 1935.

Swift. Journal to Stella, edited by Harold Williams. Oxford at the Clarendon Press, 1948.

2. *MS. AND OTHER UNPRINTED SOURCES.*

Autobiographical Fragment, written in Swift's own hand. The original document is in the Library of Trinity College, Dublin. I have been unable to trace the actual copy made by Bishop Cobbe. Abbreviated throughout as *Autofrag.*

Betham's Genealogical Abstracts. Prerogative Wills. Phillips MSS. Vol. 67, pp. 106–7. Amongst these abstracts, which are to be found in the present Record Office, Dublin, is a summary of the genealogical information contained in the Will of Sir John Temple, Master of the Rolls, dated 4th July, 1676. The Will itself perished in the old Record Office in 1922. Further Abstracts by Betham are in the Genealogical Office, Dublin Castle.

The Black Book of King's Inns. This MS. volume is in the Library of the Inns.

Carroll, Rev. W. G. Extracts from and Notes on the St. Bride's Parish Books. Library of Trinity College.

Dublin Corporation 17th Century Map showing the position of Sir John Temple's holding between Damask Street and the river. Dublin City Hall.

Fisher MSS. Genealogical Office, Dublin Castle.

Forster Collection. Victoria and Albert Museum, London. This valuable collection of Forster's papers contains (*inter alia*) letters to him about his *Life of Swift*, including one from O'Hanlon, Under-Treasurer of King's Inns.

Funeral Entry lodged by William Swift in connection with the death of his brother, Godwin. Genealogical Office, Dublin Castle.

Guinness, H. S. Copy of a memorandum giving the result of his search of the St. Andrew's Parish books (now destroyed) for information concerning the Vanhomrighs. In this writer's possession.

Hailes, H. S. MS. letter bound up with the original Vanessa correspondence in the British Museum. Add. MSS. 40254f10.

Hearth Money Rolls. There are some plain copies of these in the present Record Office. They have been partially printed in the Deputy Keeper's Reports.

Lodge MSS. There is a copy in the present Record Office.

Lyon, Rev. John. For his original marginal notes and addenda to his copy of Hawkesworth's *Life of Swift*, see the copy in the Victoria and Albert Museum. Dated by Nichols as " about July 1765."

Malone, Edmund. He has added MS. notes to Lyon's copy of Hawkesworth mentioned above.

Orrery, The Earl of. For his marginal notes and addenda to his own copies of his *Remarks* see the two volumes in the Houghton Library of Harvard University. Some of these are in his own hand ; others are apparently written by a secretary. These additions also include a copy of his mother's comments on his book.

Poll Tax Roll. Royal Irish Academy.

Protestant Refugees, List of. Trinity College Library.

Rental of Landgable Values. Record Office, Dublin. A copy of this is printed in the Deputy Keeper's Report, No. 57.

St. Patrick's Cathedral Registers. St. Patrick's Cathedral.

Southwell Papers. Library of Trinity College.

Stearne's MSS. Extracts from the Dublin Parish Registers. Library of Trinity College.

Trinity College Entry Lists. Senior Lecturer's Book. Translated and printed in *Alumni Dublinenses*.

3. BIOGRAPHICAL MATERIAL & CRITICISM

Acworth, Bernard. Swift. 1947.

Alumni Dublinenses. *See* Burtchaell.

Alumni Oxonienses.

Anon. Swiftiana. 1804. Teerink attributes this work to Richard Phillips etc.

Ball, F. Elrington. History of County Dublin. Part IV. 1906.

   ,,   ,,   Notes to *The Correspondence of Jonathan Swift*. 1910.

   ,,   ,,   *Swift's Verse*. 1929.

Barrett, Rev. John. An Essay on the Earlier Part of the Life of Swift. 1808.

Berkeley, George Monck. Literary Relics. 1789. Abbreviated throughout as "Relics."

Bernard. Rev. John H. The Cathedral Church of St. Patrick. 1903.

   ,,   ,,   *The Relations between Swift and Stella*, p. 85 et seq. in the Index Volume of the Temple Scott Edition of the "Works."

Burke, Bernard. Landed Gentry of Ireland.

Burtchaell, D. and Sadleir, T. U. Alumni Dublinenses 1593-1846. 1924.

Calendar of Ancient Records of Dublin. Edited by J. T. Gilbert.

Canterbury Marriage Allegations. Printed in the Harleian Society Publications.

Carroll, Rev. W. G. Note on Dean Swift's Birthplace included in Succession of Clergy in the Parishes of S. Bride, S. Michael le Pole, and S. Stephen, Dublin, 1884.

Carte, Thomas. The Life of James, Duke of Ormond. Oxford. 1851.

Cecil, Lord David. Two Quiet Lives. New York, 1947.

Coffey, Diarmid. O'Neill and Ormond. 1914.

Collins, John Churton. Jonathan Swift. 1893.

Craig, Maurice James (Editor). The Legacy of Swift. 1948.

Craik, Henry. The Life of Jonathan Swift. 1882.

Courtenay, Thomas P. Introduction to Temple's Correspondence. 1836.

Davis, Herbert. Stella. A Gentlewoman of the Eighteenth Century. 1942.

Delany, Patrick. Observations Upon Lord Orrery's Remarks on the Life and Writings of Dr. Jonathan Swift. 1754. Abbreviated as " Observations ".

Delany, Patrick. A Letter to Dean Swift Esq. 1755.

Deputy Keeper's Reports (on the Irish Records).

Dictionary of National Biography. London, 1885—

Dilworth, W. H. The Life of Dr. Jonathan Swift. 1758.

Duhigg, Bartholomew Thomas. History of the King's Inns. 1806.

Encyclopaedia Britannica. See Garnett.

Flach, Jacques. Jonathan Swift Son Action Politique en Irlande. Paris. 1886. A Lecture.

Forster, John. Life of Jonathan Swift, Vol I. (the only volume published). 1875.

Garnett, Richard and Seccombe, Thomas. Article on Swift in Vol. 26 of the eleventh edition of the *Encyclopaedia Britannica*. 1911.

Giffard, Lady Martha. Life of Sir William Temple " by a particular friend ". Published in Moore Smith's edition of Temple's Essays. 1930.

Gold, Maxwell. Swift's Marriage to Stella. 1935.

Goodwin, Frank. Jonathan Swift. Giant in Chains. New York, 1940.

Gray's Inn, The Pension Book of, edited by Reginald J. Fletcher, London 1901-10. 2 Vols.

Greenacre, Phyllis, M.D. Swift and Carroll. A Psychological Study. New York, 1955.

Gwynn, Stephen. The Life and Friendships of Dean Swift. 1933.

Hamilton, Gustavus Everard. An Account of the Honourable Society of King's Inns, Dublin. 1915.

Hardy, Evelyn. The Conjured Spirit of Swift. 1949.

Harleian Society Publications. See Canterbury Marriage Allegations.

Harvey, John. Dublin. 1949.

Hawkesworth, John. The Life of the Revd. Jonathan Swift, in Vol. I of the Hawkesworth (London) edition of the " Works ". 1755.

Hay, Rev. James. Swift. The Mystery of his Life and Love. 1891.

Hearsey, Marguerite. " New Light on the Evidence for Swift's Marriage." In Vol. XLII. of the Publications of the Modern Language Association of America. 1927.

Hill, George Birkbeck. Introduction to Unpublished Letters of Dean Swift. 1899.

Hone, Joseph M. and Rossi, Mario M. Swift, or the Egoist. 1934.

Horne, Colin J. Swift on his Age. London, 1953.

Hughes, Rev. S. C. The Church of S. John the Evangelist, Dublin. 1889.
,,   ,,   The Church of S. Werburgh, Dublin. 1889.
Hygeia : or Essays Moral and Medical, by Thomas Beddoes. Vol. III. 1803.
Jackson, Rev. R. Wyse. Jonathan Swift, Dean and Pastor. 1939.
,,   ,,   Swift and his Circle. 1945.
Jeffrey, Francis. Review of Scott's edition of the " Works ", in the *Edinburgh Review*, Vol.XXVII. 1816. *See* Vol. I, p. 158 et seq. of the 1844 reprint of Jeffrey's Reviews.
Johnson, Samuel. Swift. In Vol. II of the Dublin edition of " The Lives of the English Poets ". 1779.
Johnston, Denis. " The Mysterious Origin of Dean Swift." In Vol. III. No. 4. *Dublin Historical Record*. 1941.
,,   ,,   Introduction to " The Golden Cuckoo ". 1954.
Kay (Kelleher), D. L. The Glamour of Dublin. 1918.
Kendall, Paul Murray. Richard III. 1955.
King, Richard Ashe. Swift in Ireland. 1895.
Lane-Poole, Stanley. "The Alleged Marriage of Swift and Stella." In the *Fortnightly Review*, Vol. 87. 1918.
Lecky, W. E. H. " Swift " in Leaders of Public Opinion in Ireland. 1861. Reprinted in Vol. I of the Temple Scott edition of the " Works ".
Leeper, Rev. Alexander. Historical Handbook of St. Patrick's Cathedral, Dublin. 1891.
Leslie, Shane. The Script of Jonathan Swift and other essays. 1935.
,,   ,,   The Skull of Swift. 1928.
Lodge's Peerage of Ireland. Dublin, 1789
Longe, Julia G. Martha Lady Giffard. Her Life and Correspondence. 1911.
Luttrell, Narcissus. " A Brief Historical Relation of State Affairs." Luttrell's contemporary diary was published in 1857 under this title.
Macaulay, Thomas Babington. Essay in the *Edinburgh Review* for October, 1838, reviewing Courtenay's " Sir William Temple."
Malcolmson, Robert. The Carlow Parliamentary Roll. 1872.
Marburg, Clara. Sir William Temple. A 17th Century Libertin. 1932.
Mason, G. Monck. The History and Antiquities of the Collegiate and Cathedral Church of St. Patrick near Dublin. 1820.
Mercurius Rusticus.
Moriarty, G. P. Dean Swift and his Writings. 1893.
Murry, John Middleton. Jonathan Swift. 1954.
Newman, Bertram. Jonathan Swift. 1937.
Nichols, John. Editorial additions to the Supplementary Volume of Hawkesworth, 1779.
,,   ,,   Editorial footnotes to the Nichols edition, 1801.
,,   ,,   Literary Anecdotes of the Eighteenth Century. 1812.
Ordnance Survey of Ireland. Edition of 1839.
Orrery, John Earl of. Remarks on the Life and Writings of Dr. Jonathan Swift. 1752. The third edition, corrected. Abbreviated throughout as " Remarks ".
Parish Register Society of Dublin, Publications of the.
Parish Registers of the County of Surrey.
Parry, Sir Edward. Letters of Dorothy Osborne. 1888.

Pilkington, Letitia (*sic*). Memoirs. 1748–1754.

Pons, Emil. Swift. Les Années de Jeunesse et 'Le Conte du Tonneau.' Strasbourg. 1925.

Porter, Classon. Swift in Kilroot. In " Ulster Biographical Sketches," reprinted from *The Northern Whig*.

Quintana, Ricardo. The Mind and Art of Jonathan Swift. 1953 (2nd edn.).

Richardson, Samuel. Works. 1883.

Sampson, George. *The Concise Cambridge History of English Literature*. 1945 reprint.

Saussure, Cesar de. A Foreign View of England in the Reigns of George I and George II. Translated by Mme. Van Muyden. 1902.

Scott, Sir Walter. Memoirs of Jonathan Swift, included in Vol. I. of Scott's edition of the " Works ". 1814.

Sheridan, Thomas. The Life of the Rev. Dr. Jonathan Swift, 1784. Reprinted in Vol. I of the Nichol's edition of the " Works."

Smith, G. C. Moore. The Letters of Dorothy Osborne. Oxford, 1928.
    ,,   ,,   The Early Essays and Romances of Sir William Temple, Bart.
                              Oxford, 1930.

Smith, Sophie Shilleto, Dean Swift. 1910.

Spence, Rev. Joseph. Anecdotes. 1820.

Stephen, Leslie. Swift. In " English Men of Letters " Series. 1889 Edition.

Swift, Deane. An Essay upon the Life, Writings and Character of Dr. Jonathan Swift. London and Dublin. Reprinted in 1755. Abbreviated throughout as " Essay ".

Taylor, W. D. Jonathan Swift. A Critical Essay. 1933.

Teerink, Dr. H. A Bibliography of the Writings in Prose and Verse of Jonathan Swift, D.D. 1937.

Temple, The Works of Sir William. London, 1757. Vol. I.

Thackeray, William Makepeace. The English Humorists of the Eighteenth Century. 1858.

Van Doren, Carl. Swift. 1931.

Walker, Dr. John. The Sufferings of the Clergy. 1714.

Walpole, Horace. Letter of 20th June, 1766, to George Montagu. In Walpole's Letters, edited by Mrs. Paget Toynbee. Vol. III publ. 1903.

Warton, Joseph. Essay on Pope. 3rd Edition, 1764.

Wheeler, Henry A. and Craig, Maurice James. The Dublin City Churches of the Church of Ireland. 1948.

Wilde, Sir William R. The Closing Years of Dean Swift's Life. 1849.

Wilson, Dr. Thomas G. See *The Irish Journal of Medical Science* and *The Journal of the Royal Society of Antiquaries of Ireland*.

Wood's Peerage of Scotland.

Woodbridge, Homer E. " Sir William Temple, The Man and his Work." New York, 1940.

Yeats, W. B. " Swift's Epitaph ". A Poem. 1933.
    ,,   ,,   " The Words Upon the Window Pane ". A Play. 1934.

4. PERIODICALS

Brain. Vol. IV. " Dean Swift's Disease " by Dr. J. C. Bucknill.

Dublin Historical Record. See Denis Johnston.

Edinburgh Review. See Francis Jeffrey and T. B. Macaulay.

English Historical Review. Vol. 33. " The Graves of Swift and Stella¹" by the Rev. Hugh Jackson Lawlor. 1918.

Faulkner's Dublin Journal. 22nd October, 1745.

Fortnightly Review. Vol. 87. *See* Stanley Lane-Poole.

Gentleman's and London Magazine. Nov. 1757. Article signed C.M.P.G.N.S.T.N.S.

Herald and Genealogist, The. Edited by J. Gough Nichols. " The Family of Temple " in Vol. III.

Irish Builder, The. For 1895 and 1896 (April).

Irish Journal of Medical Science. June, 1939. " Swift's Deafness and his Last Illness ", by T. G. Wilson.

Irish Memorials Association, Journal of the. See Parish Register Society, whose publications it incorporates.

Modern Language Association of America. *See* Marguerite Hearsey.

Miscellania Genealogica et Heraldica. Vol. I. 2nd Series.

Monthly Review. November, 1751.

Phrenological Journal and Miscellany. Vol. IX. Article by J. Houston.

Royal Society of Antiquaries of Ireland, Journal of the. Vol. LXXXI. Part 2. " A Hitherto Undescribed Death-Mask of Dean Swift¹" by T. G. Wilson. 1951.

The Tatler. No. 188. 1786.

Transactions of the Leicestershire Architectural and Archaeological Society. Vol. VI. " On Dean Swift's Mother¹" by the Rev. W. G. Dimock Fletcher.

University of Buffalo Studies, Vol. XVI. No. 4. February, 1941. Jonathan Swift and Women, by Joseph Manch.

Walker's Dublin Directories.

Walker's *Hibernian Magazine.* June, 1802.

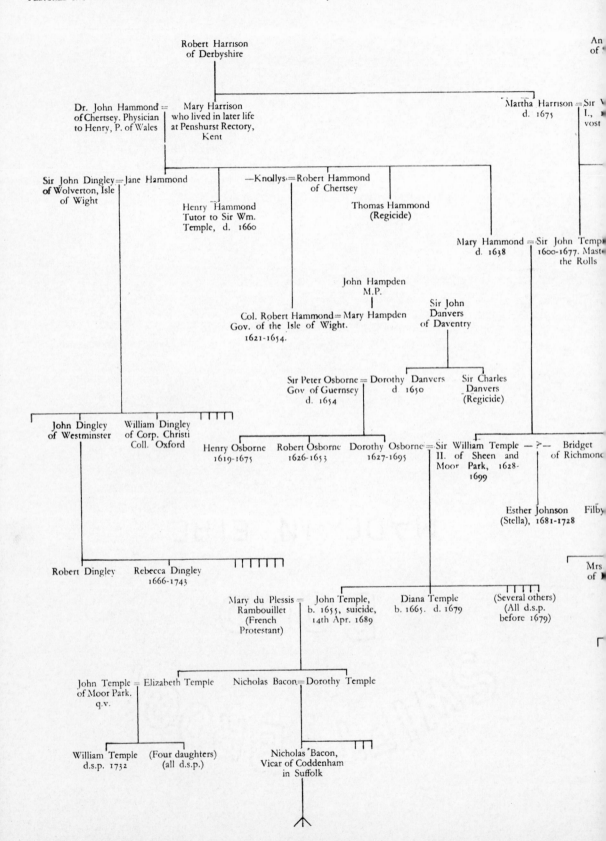

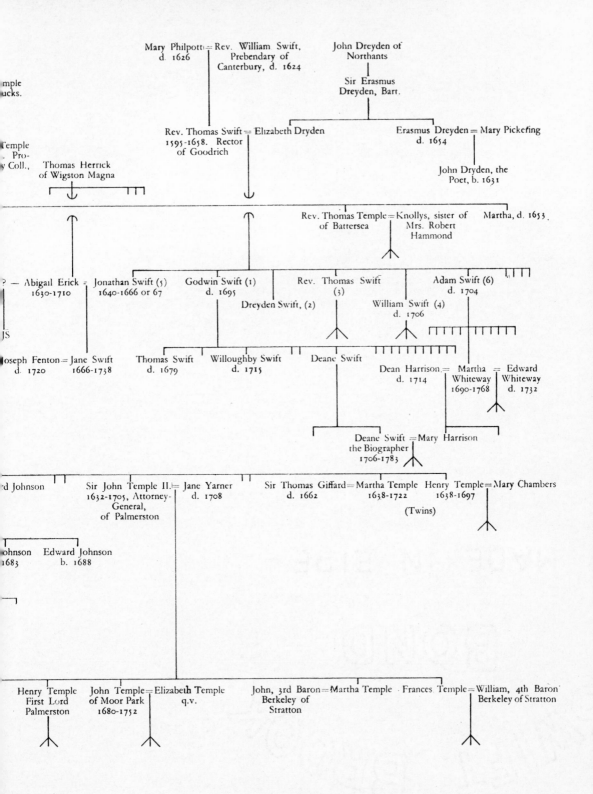

Mary Philpott = Rev. William Swift,
d. 1626   Prebendary of
Canterbury, d. 1624

John Dreyden of
Northants

Sir Erasmus
Dreyden, Bart.

mple
ucks.

Rev. Thomas Swift = Elizabeth Dryden
1595-1658. Rector
of Goodrich

Erasmus Dreyden = Mary Pickefing
d. 1654

John Dryden, the
Poet, b. 1631

Temple
. Pro-
y Coll.,

Thomas Herrick
of Wigston Magna

Rev. Thomas Temple = Knollys, sister of   Martha, d. 1653
of Battersea   Mrs. Robert
Hammond

? — Abigail Erick = Jonathan Swift (5)
1630-1710   1640-1666 or 67

Godwin Swift (1)
d. 1695

Rev. Thomas Swift
(3)

Adam Swift (6)
d. 1704

Dreyden Swift, (2)

William Swift (4)
d. 1706

JS

Joseph Fenton = Jane Swift
d. 1720   1666-1738

Thomas Swift
d. 1679

Willoughby Swift
d. 1715

Deane Swift

Dean Harrison = Martha = Edward
d. 1714   Whiteway   Whiteway
1690-1768   d. 1732

Deane Swift = Mary Harrison
the Biographer
1706-1783

rd Johnson

Sir John Temple II. = Jane Yarner
1632-1705, Attorney-   d. 1708
General,
of Palmerston

Sir Thomas Giffard = Martha Temple
d. 1662   1638-1722

Henry Temple = Mary Chambers
1638-1697

(Twins)

ohnson   Edward Johnson
1683   b. 1688

Henry Temple
First Lord
Palmerston

John Temple = Elizabeth Temple
of Moor Park   q.v.
1680-1752

John, 3rd Baron = Martha Temple
Berkeley of
Stratton

Frances Temple = William, 4th Baron
Berkeley of Stratton

[Sir John Temple's own statement about his
marriage and other family matters was
found at Broadlands by Professor J. A. Rice
shortly before 1930, and is printed in Moore
Smith's " Temple Early Essays," at p. 191.]

INDEX

Ackworth, Bernard, 96.

Anne, Queen, 98, 103, 134, 138, 149.

Ashe, St. George. Tutor at T.C.D. and Bishop of Clogher, 59, 151, 152, 158, 161, 201.

Asparagus, 119.

"Autobiographical Fragment," 8, 10, 13, 14, 28, 31, 36, 46, 53, 54, 58, 66, 67, 74, 75, 78, 116, 117, 122, 148, 178, 203, 215.
   Copied by Bishop Cobbe, 11.
   Makes no mention of Stella, 11, 97.

Baldwin, Dr. Richard. Provost of Trinity College, 77.

Ball, Francis Elrington, 24, 30, 33, 35, 43, 45, 82, 83, 115, 123, 124, 131, 134, 139, 142, 143, 147, 162, 192, 193, 204, 224.

Bandbox Anecdote, 61, 67.

Banim, The Brothers, 73.

Barrett, Rev. John. Vice Provost of T.C.D., 22, 75, 76, 79.
   Forster's attack on him, 75, 76.

Beddoes, Dr. Thomas, 183.

Berkeley—
   Ann (Foster). Wife of the Bishop of Cloyne, 161, 201.
   Lady Betty (afterwards Lady Germain), 113.
   Charles, 2nd Earl of. One of the Lords Justices, 14, 123, 130.
   Countess of. His wife, 130.
   John, 2nd, Baron of Stratton. Husband of Jane Temple, 130.
   George, Bishop of Cloyne. The philosopher, 16, 130, 150, 161, 171, 174, 201.
   George, Prebendary of Canterbury. Son of the Bishop of Cloyne, 16.
   George Monck, 16, 19, 20, 90, 104, 123, 124, 126, 130, 152, 156, 158, 161, 162, 201.
   William, 4th Baron of Stratton. Husband of Frances Temple, 130.

Bernard, John H. Archbishop of Dublin, 152, 153, 191, 194, 200, 201.

Berwick, Rev. Mr. of Esher, 21.

Betham's Genealogical Extracts, 28, 42, 43, 211.

Bible. Age at which JS could read any verse of the, 66, 67.

Bickerstaff, Isaac, 7.

Birthday Poems, 170, 178.

Birthplace, Swift's, 58–65.
   Craik's view, 63.
   Forster's view, 62, 63.
   Johnson's view, 61.

"Black Book of King's Inns," 8, 33, 34, 45, 47–57, 203, 224.

"Bon Mots de Stella," 137.

Boyle. See the Earl of Orrery.

Boyle, Hamilton, 16.

Boyne, Battle of the, 116, 140, 211.

Bradshaigh, Lady, 118.

Brasses in the Cathedral floor, 190, 195, 200.

Breda, Treaty of, 89.

Brennan, Richard, 20, 80, 196, 199.

Brent, Mrs, 162, 176.

Bride Street, 38, 41, 63, 64.

Bridstow, 28.

British Association, 195, 198.

Bromeston (or Burnstone), Dorothy. See Swift, Dorothy.

Browne, George. Archbishop of Dublin, 141.
   John, of the Neale, 125.

Brussels, 89.

Bucknill, Dr. J. C., 185.

Bull Alley, 38, 41, 43, 58, 59, 63.

Bush, Arthur, 130.

Butler. See Ormond.

Butler, Lady Elizabeth, daughter of Thomas, 10th Earl of Ormond. See Baroness Dingwall.

C.M.P.G.N.S.T.N.S., 19, 90, 91, 93, 94, 95, 100, 102, 104, 106, 107, 108, 109, 110, 112, 202, 224.

"Cadenus and Vanessa," 20, 137, 144, 174.

Calendar, correction of, 7, 49.

Caltrop, 31.

Capel, Henry, 1st Baron. Lord Justice, 121.

Carlingford, Baron. "Cavaliero Swift," 27.

Carnegie, Richard M, verger of St. Patrick's, 200.

Carrickfergus, 116.
Carroll, Rev. W. G., 23, 38, 41, 58, 63, 64, 175, 201.
Castle Steps, 63.
Cecils, The, 205.
Celbridge, 3, 145, 146, 149, 150, 171, 172, 173, 219.
Cessation, The, 207.
Chancery Lane, 63, 64.
"Character of Mrs. Johnson," 82, 91, 130, 131, 177.
Charles I, 32, 36, 87, 88.
Charles II, 32, 41.
Chester, Leofric (or Leuric), Earl of, 205.
Clarendon, Edward Hyde, Earl of, 28.
Cobbe, Charles, Bishop of Kildare, 11.
    Charles, of "Newbridge," Donabate, 12.
    T.L., of "Newbridge," Donabate, 12.
"Coffee," drinking of, 144, 148.
    Horace Walpole's interpretation, 148.
Coffey, Diarmid, 208.
Collins, J. Churton, 22, 86, 124, 161, 191.
Congreve, William, 73.
Corbet, Rev. Francis. One of Stella's executors, 162.
Cottrell, Margery, wife of Adam Swift, 43.
Craik, Sir Henry, 22, 63, 68, 76, 122, 133, 135, 195, 201.
Crawley, Chetwood, 186.
    Frank, 186.
Cromwell, Henry, 88.
    Oliver, 88, 207, 208.
Crowe, Thomas, steward of King's Inns, 51.
Crowe Thomas, porter of King's Inns, 51.
Cunningham, maker of bust of Swift, 188.

Damask (Dame) Street, 209, 211.
Danvers, Sir Charles. Regicide, 88.
Davis, Herbert, 23, 223.
Dawson, Joshua, 143.
Deane, Hannah. See Swift, Hannah.
    Admiral Richard. Regicide, 36, 88.
Death masks, 8, 184, 185.
Delany, Mrs. Mary (Mrs. Pendarves), 5.
    Dr. Patrick, later Dean of Down, 17, 60, 77, 93, 102, 108, 127, 151, 174, 196, 201, 204.

    on Swift's degree, 75.
    on the scene with Dr. Whittingham, 74.
    on the Archbishop King episode, 3, 5, 216.
    on Swift's final condition, 182, 183.
    on the reasons for secrecy, 159.
De Sausseur, César, 148.
Devereux, Penelope ("Stella"), 205.
    Robert. See Earl of Essex.
Dilworth, W. H., 11, 151.
Dingley, Sir John of Ventnor, 87, 130.
    Rebecca, 20, 93, 95, 114, 129, 130, 131, 132, 162, 178, 217.
        Craik's views on Rebecca, 167.
Dingwall, Richard Preston, Baron, 32.
    Baroness, Elizabeth Preston née Butler, 32.
Dobbs, Dean, 125.
Dobbs, Richard of Castle Dobbs, Co. Antrim, 124.
"Don Carlos." See Charles Ford.
"Drapier's Letters, The," 125, 214.
Dryden, Elizabeth, 27.
    Rev. Jonathan, 28.
    William, the poet, 27.
Dublin University. See Trinity College.
Duhigg, Bartholomew Thomas, 34, 48, 49, 67.
Dunbrew, 35.
Dunlavin, prebend of, 131.
Dunstable, 144.

Elizabeth I, Queen, 205.
Epitaphs—
    Stella's, 178, 190, 194.
    Swift's, 188, 189.
    Hawkesworth's version, 188.
Erick the Forester, 30, 45, 58.
Erick, Abigail. See Swift, Abigail (for her family, see Herrick).
Essex, Robert Devereux, Earl of, 205.
Evans, John, Bishop of Meath, 92, 108, 151, 154, 155, 201.
Examiner, The, 134.

Farnham, 79, 80, 92, 100, 110, 130.
Faulkner, George, publisher, 58, 103, 119, 175, 181.
Fenton, Jane, 39, 42, 98, 100, 108, 113, 120, 203, 210, 215.

Fenton Joseph, 100.
   Delany's views, 100.
   Craik's views, 100.
   Elrington Ball's views, 100.
Filby, Anne, Stella's sister, 90, 91, 108.
   "Mrs." of Farnham, 91.
   her husband, brother to Anne's
     husband, 100.
"Finnegans Wake," 5.
First Fruits, 138.
Fisher Mss., 53.
Fleetwood, Lieut. Gen. Charles, Lord
   Deputy, 88.
Ford, Charles, 150.
Forster, John, 12, 22, 33, 44, 49, 68, 86,
   122, 133, 201, 224.
Freeman, A. Martin, 21, 149.
Fruit, a surfeit of, 116, 117, 128, 212.

Gentleman's Magazine, The, 19, 90, 91, 93,
   95, 104, 105, 107, 108, 109, 110.
George I, 148.
Giffard, Lady Martha, née Temple, 80,
   82, 86, 87, 88, 95, 100, 101, 102, 107,
   113, 118, 128, 129, 153, 204, 206,
   208, 211, 213, 215.
Gilbert, John, 140.
Gilliver, Lawton, publisher, 7.
"Glassheel." See Charles Ford.
Godiva, Lady, 205.
Gold, Maxwell, 17, 23, 110.
   on the resemblance of the portraits,
     102.
   on Stella's parents, 106.
   on the marriage, 153, 161, 166, 167.
   on John Lyon, 163.
   on the Archbishop King episode, 5.
"Golden Cuckoo, The," ix.
Goodrich in Herefordshire, 27, 28, 29, 31.
Gray's Inn, 13, 33, 34, 35.
Guernsey, 87.
"Gulliver's Travels," 4, 134.
   Forged 3rd volume, 7.
Gwynn, Stephen, 86, 188.

Hailes, D., 21.
Hall, Susannah. See Swift, Susannah.
Hamilton, Gustavus, 48, 49.
   Phineas, 197, 198.
   Richard, 80, 81.
Hammond, John, of Chertsey, 206.
   Mrs. John, née Harrison, 206.

Mary. See Temple, Mary, Lady Temple
   II, wife of Sir John Temple I.
Col. Robert, Governor of the Isle of
   Wight, 87.
Thomas, 88.
Hamon (Hammond) Lane, 40.
Hampden, John, 88.
   Mary, 88.
Hardy, Evelyn. Success with the epitaph,
   188, 189, 223.
Harley, Robert, Earl of Oxford, 125, 134,
   138.
Harrison, Martha. See Temple, Martha,
   Lady Temple I, wife of the Provost.
Mary. See Mrs. John Hammond of
   Chertsey.
Rev. Theophilus, Mrs. Whiteway's first
   husband, 98.
Hart Hall (Hertford College), Oxford,
   118.
Hartstonge, Matthew Wild: his copy of
   Abigail's Memorial, 34.
Hawkesworth, John, 18, 20, 28, 34, 61,
   67, 78, 95, 127, 132, 133, 162, 194,
   214.
   on the marriage, 151.
   on the final condition of JS, 183.
   on Celbridge, 4.
Hay, Rev. John, 96, 202.
   his comment on the Celbridge incident,
     173.
Hearn, Mrs. Stella's niece, 90, 104, 160.
Hearsey, Marguerite, 162.
Henry VII, 205.
Henry, Prince of Wales, 206.
Hereford, parliamentary committee of, 28.
Herrick, Thomas, butcher of Wigston
   Magna, 45.
   his other children, 45.
Hoey's Court, 37, 42, 44, 58, 59, 63, 64,
   65.
Holyhead, 79.
Hone, Joseph, 23, 64, 96.
Hopper, Martha. See Swift, Martha.
Howard, Henrietta, later Countess of
   Suffolk, 116.
Hughes, Rev. S. C., 39, 42, 141.
Hyde, Edward. See Earl of Clarendon.

Jackson, Mrs., occupying 7 Hoey's Court,
   62.

Jackson Rev. R. Wyse, Dean of Cashel, 8, 23, 188.
James I, 32.
James II, 78, 81, 140.
Jeffrey, Francis Lord, 22, 124.
Johnson—
    Anne. See Ann Filby.
    Bridget, 90, 95, 101, 106, 111, 112.
        Craik on, 92, 106.
        Forster on, 106.
        Longe on, 106.
    Edward the elder, merchant, 93, 103, 111, 112.
        Forster on, 92, 106.
        Craik on, 92, 106.
    Edward the younger, 90, 91, 94, 108.
    Esther (Stella), 4, 91, 94, 95, 96, 97, 146, 151–173, 175–178, 190–200, 217–221.
        her first meeting with JS, 82, 83.
        her supposed child by JS, 20.
        her death, 177.
        her epitaph, 178, 190.
        Thackeray on, 137.
        Davis on, 23, 223.
        Williams on, 107, 153.
        Woodbridge on, 192.
    Dr. Samuel—
        his comment on the birthplace, 19, 61.
        his comment on the marriage, 152.
Johnston, Mr. Justice, Treasurer of King's Inns, ix.
Jones, Betty, 80, 128.
"Journal to Stella," 138, 142, 143, 144.
Joyce, James, 5, 6.

Kendall, Rev. John, vicar of Thornton, 45.
Kennett, White, Bishop of Peterborough, 138.
Kildrohod. See Celbridge.
Kilkenny College, 59, 73, 202, 212.
Kilroot, 19, 121–128, 131, 133, 222.
King, Frances. See Swift, Frances.
    Rev. William, Archbishop of Dublin, 3, 122, 182, 216.
King's Inns, 30, 34, 37, 38, 44, 47–57.

Lambert, John, assistant sexton at St. Patrick's, 198, 199, 200.
Laracor, 12, 123, 130, 132, 133, 134.

Lawlor, Rev. Henry Jackson, Dean of St. Patrick's, 191, 198, 199.
Le Broquey, Sibyl, 148.
Lecky, W. E. H., 191.
Leicester, 27, 45, 62, 121, 133, 203, 211.
Leicester, Earls of—
    Leofric, 205.
    Robert, 203, 206, 207, 208.
Leland, Dr. Thomas, 119.
Leslie—
    Sir Shane, 8, 23, 96.
    Miss, of Glaslough, 21.
Lincoln's Inn, 206.
Lisle, Philip Sidney, Lord Lisle, of Sheen, 208.
Lloyd, Dr. Owen, 75, 77.
Long, Miss Anne, 140.
Longe, Julia, 86, 95, 111, 113.
Loughboy (Bow Lane), 40.
Luttrell, Narcissus, diarist, 140.
Lyon, Dr. John, 18, 20, 39, 46, 61, 67, 75, 119, 132, 133, 163, 167, 194.
    his search of the registers, 11, 68.
    on the supposed wedding, 162, 172, 173.
    on the ride to Celbridge, 4.
    on the final condition of JS, 183.
    Gold's comment on Lyon, 167.

Macaulay, Thomas Babington, Lord, 22, 85, 220.
MacNeill, J. G. Swift, 18.
Madden, Dr. 152, 153.
Maguire, William, sexton at St. Patrick's, 196, 197, 198, 199.
Malone, Edmund, 19, 105, 125, 163.
Marburg, Clara, 85.
Marley Abbey, Celbridge, 3, 150.
Marriage, the supposed, 151–173.
    Craik's views, 167.
    Mrs. Whiteway's views, 161.
    Lyon's views, 163, 164, 165, 166, 167.
    Gold's views, 166, 167.
    Dingley's views, 162, 164.
    Scott's views, 152.
    The *Monthly Review*, 168.
Marsh, Narcissus, Archbishop of Dublin, 131, 178, 193, 194.
Marshall, Robert, one of Vanessa's executors, 21, 171, 175.
    William, William Swift's clerk, 175.

Mary, Queen, 82, 85, 86, 113.
Mason, Thomas H., 188.
    William Monck, 22, 42, 62, 163, 167, 189, 194, 224.
    married a Winder, 127.
    on Swift's illness, 182.
    on his burial, 193.
Mayne, Mrs. of Farnham, 93, 100, 101, 102, 113.
Meade, Eleanor. See Swift, Eleanor.
Ménière's Disease, 185.
Monthly Review, The, 111, 132, 168, 177, 201.
Moor Park, 13, 79, 80, 82, 83, 89, 90, 98, 101, 113, 117, 119, 127, 128, 129, 131, 133, 178, 183, 212, 222.
Moreton, William, Bishop of Kildare, 122.
Moriarty, Gerald P., 96.
Morrison, Alfred, 21.
Mose Ralph, steward at Moor Park, 92, 100, 101, 102, 106, 114.
Mundt, 127.
Münster, Bishop of, 89.
Murry, J. Middleton, 23, 222.

Newman, Bertram, 5, 139, 150, 188.
Newry, 36, 43.
Nichols, Gough, editor, 204.
    John, publisher, 18, 19, 54, 76, 91, 124, 131, 139.
Nurse, Swift's anonymous, 66, 67.

O'Hanlon, John B., Under-Treasurer of King's Inns, 49.
Old Dublin Society, ix.
On the Death of Mrs. Johnson." See" "Character of Mrs. Johnson."
Orders, Swift's taking of Holy, 119, 121.
Ormond—
    Pierce Butler, 8th Earl of, 73.
    Thomas Butler, 10th Earl of, 32.
    James Butler, 12th Earl and 1st Duke of, 32, 73.
    Elizabeth Butler, née Preston, 1st Duchess of, 32.
    "Old Marchioness of," 29, 32.
Orrery, John Boyle, 5th Earl of, 16, 17, 27, 54, 60, 119, 127, 154, 168, 224.
    on Abigail, 30.
    on Swift's degree, 77, 118.
    on Stella's father, 97.
    on the ride to Celbridge, 4.
    on rumours regarding Temple, 84.
    on the Vanhomrighs, 149.
    on Vanessa, 171.
    on the reasons for secrecy, 159.
    on Swift's supposed lunacy, 181.
    on his death, 181.
    on the epitaph, 189.
Orrery, Elizabeth Boyle, née Cecil, Countess of, his mother, 145.
Osborne—
    Dorothy. See Temple, Dorothy, Lady Temple III.
    Henry, her brother, 88.
    Sir Peter, her father, royalist Governor of Guernsey, 87.
    Richard, 87.
    Robert, 87.
Oxford, Robert Harley, Earl of. See Harley, Robert.

Pall Mall, 82, 113, 127.
Palmerston, village and house, 3, 209, 211.
Palmerston—
    Henry Temple, 1st Viscount, 215.
    Henry John Temple, 3rd Viscount and Prime Minister, 204.
Parish Records of Dublin, 37.
Peel, Sir Robert, 21.
Penshurst rectory, 206.
Perkins, Anne, 80.
Perry, James, 43.
Phillips, Richard, 19.
Philpott, Mary, 27, 28.
Phrenologists, a corps of, 195, 196.
Pilkington, Mrs. Laetitia, 14, 15, 44, 54, 59, 74, 84, 151.
    on the Whitehaven incident, 66, 67, 68.
    Stephen, 55, 56.
"Pindaric Odes," 83.
Poddle river, 193, 197.
Pons, Emil, 23, 64, 83, 86, 96, 107, 110, 224.
Pooley, Mary, 42.
Pope, Alexander, 27, 60, 61, 139.
Popish Plot, 111.
Prayers for Stella, Swift's, 133, 177.

Preston—
    Lady Elizabeth. See 1st Duchess of Or-
        mond.
    Sir Richard. See Baron Dingwall.
Pride's Purge, 88, 207.
Prior, Matthew, 21.
Psychology, 6, 23, 220.

Raglan Castle, 28.
Record Office, Irish, 38.
Richard III, King, x.
Richardson, Samuel, 117, 118.
Richmond, 36, 79, 92, 111, 192.
Ridar, Mr., headmaster of Kilkenny Col-
    lege, 59.
Ridgeway, Mrs. Anne, Swift's house-
    keeper, and daughter of Mrs. Brent,
    162, 167.
Rochfort, John, one of Stella's executors,
    162.
Rossi, Mario, 23, 64, 96.

Sadleir, Thomas U., xii, 24.
St. Andrew's Day, 7, 14, 53, 68.
St. Andrew's parish, 3, 37–9, 41, 141
    209, 219.
St. Bride's parish, 13, 23, 37, 41, 43, 59,
    63, 64, 65.
    Books in the library of T.C.D., 38.
St. John's parish, 38, 41.
St. Michan's parish, 35, 37–44, 52.
St. Malo, 87.
St. Patrick's Cathedral, 37, 131, 134, 139,
    189–200.
    The deanery, 15, 98, 150, 196, 219.
St. Werburgh's parish, 37–9, 42, 44, 58,
    59, 63, 64, 79, 141.
Salter, Dr. Samuel, Master of Charter-
    house, 126.
Sawbridge, Dr. Thomas, Dean of Ferns,
    125.
Schonberg, Frederick Herman, Marshal
    the Duke of, 140.
Scott, Sir Walter, 22, 28, 34, 35, 61, 119,
    182, 216.
    on Stella, 105.
    on her education, 106, 129.
    on her supposed father, 105.
    on the supposed wedding, 161.
    on Swift's supposed lunacy, 184.
    on the Archbishop King episode, 5.

on Swift's career at T.C.D., 75.
on Celbridge, 4.
Sea crossings, Swift's, 79, 133–4.
Shaw, George Bernard, 23, 220.
Sheen, 13, 79, 80, 81, 82, 83, 90, 98, 111,
    203, 209, 212.
Sheldon, Gilbert, Archbishop of Canter-
    bury, 204.
Sheridan, Thomas, Senior, 19, 152, 155,
    156, 161, 167, 196.
    Thomas, Junior, 19, 61, 66, 102, 103,
        104, 122, 135, 152, 156, 157, 167.
    on the ride to Celbridge, 4, 172.
    on Stella's legacy, 94.
Sican, Mrs. E., 156, 162.
Sidney, Sir Philip, 205.
    Philip of Sheen. See Lord Lisle.
Sidney, family. See Earls of Leicester.
Smith—
    Clement, 91.
    G. C. Moore, 87, 111, 206.
    Sophie Shilleto, 85, 96.
        her description of Vanessa, 145,
            146.
Southwell, Sir Robert, 115, 117, 121, 133,
    203.
"Speciali Gratiae," 75, 118.
Speed, Lancelot, 205.
Spence's "Anecdotes," 54, 61, 62.
Stearne, John, Bishop of Meath, 39.
Steevens Hospital, 166.
Stella. See Esther Johnson.
Stephen, Sir Leslie, 22, 108, 188.
Stevens, Rev. Mr., 183.
Stone, Hester. See Mrs. Vanhomrigh.
    John, 140.
Stuart, Lady Louisa, 5.
Swift—
    Abigail, née Erick, 30, 40, 58, 63, 67,
        69, 202, 209, 210, 215.
        her ancestry, 82.
        her reunion with her son, 79.
        her letter of introduction to Temple,
            79, 81.
        her petition to the Benchers, 69, 70,
            71.
    Abraham, 36.
    Adam, uncle, 11, 13, 36, 37, 43, 44, 78,
        98.
    Adam, cousin, 43.

Swift Arthur, Major, of Swiftsheath, 18.
"Cavaliero." See Baron Carlingford.
Deane, the elder, 121.
Deane, the younger, biographer, 5, 7, 11, 17, 18, 28, 36, 53, 60, 78, 84, 99, 117, 218.
    Forster's attack, 62.
    description of Tisdall, 135.
    description of Vanessa, 146.
    on the reasons for the secrecy, 160.
    Orrery's informant, 98.
    JS's offer to Jane Fenton, 101.
Dorothy, née Bromeston (or Burnstone), wife of William, 41.
Dryden, 13, 34.
Elinor, née Meade, wife of Godwin, 15.
Elizabeth, née Dreyden, wife of the Rev. Thomas of Goodrich, 27.
Elizabeth, née Wheeler, wife of Godwin, 32.
Ernest Godwin, police magistrate, 18.
Frances, née King, wife of William, 41.
Godwin, uncle, 7, 13, 15, 29, 31, 36, 39, 40, 41, 42, 43, 44, 58, 61–65, 73, 74, 99, 116, 129, 182, 202, 210, 211, 215, 223.
    his children, 40, 42, 73, 74.
    his insanity, 42, 78, 79.
Hannah, née Deane, wife of Godwin, 7, 36, 42.
Jane. See Jane Fenton.
John, 210.
Jonathan the elder, supposed father, 29, 33, 36, 37, 39, 40, 44, 50, 52, 53, 69–72, 137, 202, 210.
    his death, 54, 68, 72.
Katherine, née Webster, wife of Godwin, 35.
Martha, née Hopper, wife of Adam, 36, 44.
Mary, née Philpott, wife of the Rev. William, 27, 28.
Meade, 74.
Michael, 74.
Philip, 41.
Susannah, née Hall, wife of William, 35, 41, 44.
Theophilus, 74, 161.
Rev. Thomas, the elder, of Goodrich, grandfather, 27, 28, 31, 34.
Rev. Thomas, the younger, of St. Edmund's, Lombard St., uncle, 13, 34, 35.
Thomas 3, of Gray's Inn, son of Godwin, cousin, 42.
Rev. Thomas 4, rector of Puttenham, son of Thomas 2, cousin and classmate of JS at T.C.D., 73, 130, 131, 222.
    his flight from Trinity, 79.
William, uncle, 33, 34, 35, 36, 37, 38, 39, 40, 43, 44, 74, 75, 119.
    escapes to England, 78.
    assists Abigail, 69–71, 215.
    files funeral entry for his brother Godwin, 13.
William (Billy), son of William, cousin, 35, 41.
Willoughby, son of Godwin, cousin, 119.
Swiftsheath, 18, 35.

Taine, Hippolyte, 76.
"Tale of a Tub, A," 122, 138, 139.
Taylor, W. D., 96.
Teerink, Dr. H., 10.
Temple—
    Diana, 86, 111.
    Dorothy (Osborne), Lady Temple III, wife of Sir William II of Moor Park, 81, 82, 85–89, 106, 110, 212.
    Edwyn, 205.
    Henry, twin brother of Lady Giffard, 206, 208.
    Henry. See Viscount Palmerston.
    James, 88.
    Jane (Yarner), Lady Temple IV, wife of Sir John II, Attorney General, 210.
    Sir John I, Master of the Rolls, 81, 88, 89, 203, 204, 206–9, 217, 222, 223.
    Sir John II, Attorney General, his son, 204, 208, 210, 211, 213, 215.
    John, son of Sir William II, 80, 81, 111.
    John (Jack), of Moor Park, son of Sir John II, 204, 213, 215.
    Martha (Harrison), Lady Temple I, wife of Sir William I, the provost, 205, 206, 209.
    Martha, daughter of Sir John I. See Lady Giffard.

Temple Mary (Hammond), Lady Temple II, wife of Sir John I, Master of the Rolls, 40, 206.
  Peter, 88.
  Colonel Sir Peter, 88.
  Richard of Bosworth, 205.
  Rev. Thomas of Battersea, brother of Sir John I, 206.
  William of Whitney, 205.
  Sir William I, provost of Trinity, 205.
  Sir William II, of Moor Park, 13, 79, 81, 84–9, 110–13, 115–21, 126–31, 202, 203, 206, 208, 211, 216, 217.
Temple Lane, 209.
Thackeray, William Makepeace, 22, 96, 137
Tipperary, Palatine County, 29, 33.
Tisdall, Rev. William, Dean of Belfast, 133, 134, 135, 136, 158, 218.
Triennial Bill, 14, 119.
Trim, 132.
Trinity College, Dublin University–
  Admission lists, 14, 35, 40, 206.
  Record of JS at, 74, 75, 76.
Tripos, 76.
Turnstile Alley, 150.
Twickenham, 134.
Tyrconnell, Richard Talbot, Earl of, Lord Deputy, 80.

Van Doren, Carl, 23, 64, 86, 139, 119.
Vanhomrigh, 37.
  Bartholomew, the elder, Lord Mayor of Dublin, 140.
  Bartholomew, the younger, his son, 142.
  Esther (Vanessa), his daughter, 142, 143, 144, 145, 146, 147, 148, 149, 150, 170–76, 219, 220.
    no mention by Mrs. Pilkington, 15.
    Delany's view, 145.
    Orrery's view, 4, 144, 145.
    Monck Berkeley's view, 20, 146.
    Sophie Smith's view, 145, 146.
    her burial, 171.
    at Celbridge, 3, 171.
  Ginkel, 142, 149.
  Hester (Stone), Vanessa's mother, 140, 143, 144, 149.
  Mary (Moll), her sister, 142, 150.
Varina. See Jane Waring.

Wake, William, Archbishop of Canterbury, 92, 151, 201.

Wale, Isobel, 47, 55.
  Thomas, her husband, steward of King's Inns, 47, 49, 51, 54, 71.
Walpole, Horace, 148, 162.
Ward, Dean, 155.
Waring, Jane (Varina), 122, 123, 124, 125, 128, 131.
  Richard, 122.
  Westenra, 122.
  William, 122.
Webster, Catherine. See Swift, Catherine.
Wharton, Thomas, Earl of, 77, 125, 126.
Wheeler, Elizabeth. See Swift, Elizabeth.
Whitehaven, 66–72, 89, 133, 203.
  Sheridan's account, 66.
  Mrs. Pilkington's account, 66, 67.
  Duhigg's reference, 67.
Whittingham, Rev. Charles, archdeacon of Dublin, 74.
Whiteway, Edward, 98.
  Surgeon John, 185, 186, 199.
  Mrs. Martha, his mother, 11, 17, 43, 82, 98, 102, 103, 106, 109, 161, 170, 193.
  Mary, her daughter, wife of Deane Swift, 7.
Whitworth, Charles, Earl of, 21.
Wight, Isle of, 87, 130.
Wilde, Sir William, 22, 62, 176, 184, 185, 186, 196, 197, 198, 199, 224.
William, the Conqueror, 30.
William III, King, 14, 38, 78, 80, 115, 116, 119, 212.
Williams, Sir Harold, 83, 95, 107, 149, 153, 222, 223.
Wilson, Claude Henry, 19.
  Rev. David F. R., Dean of St. Patrick's, 200.
  Dr. Thomas G., xii, 183, 185, 186.
Winder, Rev. John, 19, 125, 126, 127.
Woodbridge, Professor H. E., 86, 96, 107, 110, 112, 192.
Worrall, Rev. John, Swift's Vicar in St. Patrick's, 80, 165, 176, 192.

Yarner, Jane. See Temple, Jane, Lady Temple IV.
Yeats, W. B., 128, 129, 187.
  His verse on the Epitaph, 189.

Zutphen, Battle of, 205.